WITHDRAWN

THE CLASSICAL FACADE
A Nonclassical Reading of Goethe's Classicism

THE CLASSICAL FACADE

A Nonclassical Reading of Goethe's Classicism

Kenneth D. Weisinger

THE PENNSYLVANIA STATE
UNIVERSITY PRESS
University Park and London

This book is dedicated to
the memory of my father,
whose encouragement and common
sense were always there

Library of Congress Cataloging-in-Publication Data

Weisinger, Kenneth D.
  The classical facade.
  Bibliography: p.
  Includes index.
  1. Goethe, Johann Wolfgang von, 1749–1832—
Criticism and interpretation. 2. Classicism.
I. Title.
PT2177.W4 1988   831'.6   87-18957
ISBN 0-271-00616-1

Contents

88 - 6958

Acknowledgments

A BOVE all, I am indebted to the University of California at Berkeley for the time, the scholarly resources, the financial support and collegial encouragement which all helped bring this book to its present form. In particular, I am grateful to the Berkeley Humanities Research Fund for a grant which enabled me to complete most of the research for the book within a year. And to the many colleagues who have read all or parts of my work and given advice and help, I wish to give my sincerest thanks. To name a few: Thomas Rosenmeyer, Andrew Jaszi, Gerd Hillen, Daniel Wilson, and Joseph Duggan. Thanks are due too to the many students who over the past five years have shown remarkable patience while listening to my ideas and who have often taught me a great deal about the literary works in question.

Finally, I wish to mention two friends who have played a significant role in bringing this project to completion. The first of these is Professor Richard Yee, whose invitation to give a series of lectures in his Humanities course at Holy Names College provided the original impetus to examine *Faust* within a wider historical-intellectual context. Critical discussions with Professor Yee and the reading he gave my manuscript were invaluable to the clarification of my thought, as were similar discussions with Professor Neil Flax, whose own work on Goethe set standards for excitement I can never hope to match.

I wish to thank Frederick Ungar Publishing Company for permission to quote passages from the fine translation of *Iphigenia in Tauris* by Charles E. Passage. Passages from the Roman Elegies are cited from the translations of F. D. Luke, which were published first by Chatto and Windus and then in a revised version by Libris Press. I am grateful to both publishers for permission to use this material.

Introduction

*And why are we moderns so preoccupied, why so
driven to challenges we can neither live up to nor accomplish!*

          —Goethe, *The Italian Journey*

THREE years after the death of Goethe, Heine wrote of him, "one
could study Greek art in his works as if in the works of an
ancient."[1] To many of his contemporaries, Goethe seemed the very
embodiment of classical ideals, for by 1832 he had so completely
impressed the image of himself as the "Olympian," the patriarchical
literary Jupiter, upon the course of the arts in Germany that his very
name had become synonymous with all that was recognized as best
in the classical Hellenic world as it had been presented to the Germans by Winckelmann and by subsequent generations of classical
scholars and critics. Not only had Goethe created masterworks of
classical perfection according to the aesthetic which had emerged
from the contemporary German preoccupation with the ancient
world, he had himself helped to formulate that aesthetic with his
own energetic efforts in the fields of art history and classical scholarship. So, when Goethe spoke as a classicist, either as artist or as
critic, an entire generation, in fact an entire century of readers accepted his voice as authoritative and believed with Heine that his
works could be accepted as normative surrogates of the original
ancient products. Goethe's literary works, especially the "classical"
works, were for Heine cool, self-contained monuments of art:
". . . they ornament our beloved homeland as beautiful statues ornament a garden, but they *are* statues."[2] If there is hesitation here in
his admiration for Goethe, it is because Heine sees these monu-

ments as *too* classical, too far removed from the political and social realities of the historical epoch which gave birth to them, and too far removed from the historical realities of Heine's own time. Goethe's works were for Heine distant and detached, but they *were* classical.

Under the persuasive influence of the Olympian pose which Goethe cultivated so convincingly throughout the latter half of his life, a reader as perceptive as Heine could be moved to include even works as unclassical and as unstatuesque as *Faust* and *Werther* as integral elements of a completed oeuvre which, taken in its totality, conformed to a classical aesthetic, an aesthetic which demanded of any artistic work that it maintain standards of harmony, balance, and consistency:

> Goethe's greatest achievement is the perfection *in everything which he presents;* there are no sections which are strong while others are weak, no part which is finished out while others are only sketched in; there are no embarrassments here, none of the usual filler, no predilection for mere detail.[3]

To gather all the works of Goethe under this undeniably broad conception of classicism is a bold extension of the concept to its furthest possible limit, but by the early nineteenth century the image of Goethe as *the* classical artist was so universally accepted that such a categorization not only could be made but is perfectly understandable within the historical context.

Now, a century and a half after the death of Goethe, readers are no longer under the spell of the Olympian image of the poet and are less compelled to read the ideals and standards of the older poet into the works of his youth. Contemporary readers are less inclined to see in the autobiographical writings Goethe left as a record of his self the gradual and majestic unfolding of a consistent and unified personality, and they are less willing to accept the interpretative light thrown by the older poet onto his earlier works. Today, the nineteenth-century project of working toward an understanding of the man and his works beneath the benign shelter of a harmoniously evolving unity of personality is not one that inspires much critical effort. In general, those works of the poet which seem to invite such an understanding and which have played a significant role in the creation of the image of Goethe as the serene Olympian—that is, the so-called classical works—are by no means the literature most eagerly read today. If these works are read at all outside the walls of the German *Gymnasium*, they are read by readers who are far more interested in finding in them an antipode to the darkly unclassical *Faust*. It is, in fact, this very artistic schizophrenia which appears to exist between *Faust* and such consciously classical artifacts as *Iphigenia in Tauris* or *Hermann and Dorothea* that is much more likely to attract contemporary literary critics, for it may well be that it is the disunity of personality revealed here that can account for the extraordinary productivity of the poet. Contemporary readers are far more likely to seek out indicative signs of that artistic division within the literary works, as well as within the autobiographical writings themselves, as evidence against the poet's imposition of a ponderous teleological unity onto the ambiguous and heterogenous elements of his own life.

In the search for such revealing evidence, certain images of the poet are especially compelling as indicative of the bifurcation of creative direction. One of the most famous and most poignant of these is the image of Goethe sitting in the sunny gardens of the classical Villa Borghese in Rome working not on one of his classical works but on the most darkly Gothic scene of his *Faust*, the Witch's Kitchen. This is an image that runs counter to that of the poet in Italy as painted by Tischbein, a Goethe resting serenely in the Roman Campagna, surrounded by the remains of a classical culture. And it runs counter to the Goethe searching for the "Urpflanze," the primal plant that represented to the poet biological proof of the morphological unity behind all phenomena. The picture that has come down to us of Goethe sitting in the Roman garden creating a scene of murky northern hocus-pocus is not the image of a Goethe striving for clarity and light, but of a man actually enjoying the discrepancy between aspects of his own personality. Since this image has become a stock element in any report of the genesis of *Faust I*, the source of the image is important to ascertain because, like so many of the autobiographical fragments which have become parts of our picture of Goethe, this little episode conceals as much as it reveals. First to be noted is that the story originates with the old Goethe himself; Goethe and Eckermann are looking at a map of Rome:

> Then Goethe showed me on this map of Rome the most remarkable buildings and squares. "This," he said, "is the Farnese Garden." "Was it not there," I asked, "where you wrote the Witch's Kitchen scene of *Faust*?" "No," he said, "that was in the Borghese Garden."[4]

In the records of the Italian journey, Goethe mentions only that he worked on several of the scenes from *Faust* while in Rome; what they were and where the writing actually took place can only be guessed at from the actual documents of the period. We can never know the historical truth of the anecdote, but what we have instead is an equally valuable insight into the older poet. We have in this image an emblem of symbolic content, one created by Goethe himself, perhaps even created as a conscious countercurrent to the other image of himself the old poet was simultaneously constructing; and so, at the very time Goethe was most concerned with projecting onto his personality a teleological trajectory that would eventually culminate in the formation of a "classical" poet, he was also leaving for posterity the fragments of an opposing anticlassical personality, creating an alternative image which would at times subvert and obscure the other.

It is tempting to ask whether the rift in the classical facade which Goethe leaves behind in this image and in other similar anecdotes was a conscious act of rebellion against his own dominant will or an involuntary eruption of a part of the personality suppressed and submerged by the energetic and pervasive will to classical form. Probably we will never know for certain which is the truth, if in fact the two can be separated so decisively. The image of Goethe in the Villa Borghese imagining the witches of Germanic fairy tales or of *Macbeth* is an appealing one since it is rare; far more frequent from the later period of Goethe's life are the autobiographical reflections of a younger Goethe attempting to raise himself out of the narrowness and provinciality of German culture to the greater universality of classical learning and art. In fact, Goethe's drive to place a firm classical facade over the past events of his life was so rigorous as to seem at times to be titanic in the sense of that word as we know it from the Sturm und Drang. If we examine, for example, a passage from the *Italian Journey*, we can observe this drive as it seeks to reconstitute the poet's actual experience of the past and to set it firmly into a framework carefully worked out by the older man. The book of Goethe's travels in Italy was published in 1816 and appears to be the journal kept by the poet as he traveled for the first time to the seat of classical culture. The journey itself began in 1786, and the book, published thirty years later, is in fact a highly edited, reconstructed version of the notes Goethe kept while traveling. It is very difficult to cull fiction from truth in the *Italian Journey* because Goethe burned most of the documents on which it is based, and even at the time he kept the original journals, there is a strong likelihood that he was already consciously casting the events of the journey into a literary frame. Just as many of the letters Goethe wrote around the time he was writing *Werther* look suspiciously like exercises for the novel, so too the original journal of the Italian journey may already be conscious preliminary sketches for a literary reworking. We may surmise from the original documents which were not destroyed that in general the facts are as Goethe reports them in the *Journey;* nevertheless, in his extensive revisions of the original notes, Goethe has definitely created for his earlier self a literarily constructed persona, one that is consistently portrayed as a young man thirsting for classical culture. Here is the description of his first encounter with a Roman building:

> I left my coachman at Madonna del Angelo . . . and began the climb to Assisi against a stiff wind, for I had longed to go on foot through this world which was for me so lonely. On my left I passed with aversion the monstrous mass of churches, piled one on top of the other like a Babylon, where Saint Francis lies at rest. . . . Then I asked a handsome youth the way to the Santa Maria della Minerva, and he accompanied me up into the town. . . . Finally, we reached what is properly called the old town, and look! the noblest work stood before my eyes—the first complete monument of the ancient world which I had ever seen.[6]

The traveler then describes the building, sets it over against its representation in Palladio and concludes that the real sensation of the temple cannot be compared with the secondhand literary experience even when that comes through as trusted a guide as Palladio. The traveler is already aware as he reports this first experience of classical architecture that it will be an experience of immense importance to his own development, for he comments, "What will develop in me through my having seen this work is inexpressible in words, but will bear eternal fruit."[7] Goethe is at pains to show that the teleological meaning of the experience was already apparent, if only in an embryonic way, to the young man in his travels.

The literary components of this autobiographical report are numerous and evident. The poet leaves his carriage in the town at the foot of the climb into Assisi so that he may go alone and on foot, although there is a stiff wind blowing, to the temple of Minerva at the top of the hill. The poet thus becomes, not just a tourist, but a pilgrim, deliberately abandoning the comforts of travel in the pursuit of a spiritual goal, and the harsh conditions of the pilgrimage here remind us strongly of the frightening and hostile world through which the young poet of the Sturm und Drang must battle to attain the arms of his beloved. The elements and even the vocabulary seem to be taken from "Welcome and Farewell," a poem which dates from 1771:

> Already in a cloak of mist the oak
> Stood there, a towering giant . . .
> Thc wind . . .
> Whistled frighteningly round my ear. . . .
> The night created a thousand monsters. . . .[8]

Like the lover in the poem, the lover of antiquity must face a stormy wind, monsters, and towering giants, but in the description of the Italian experience, it is no longer nature which supplies the poet with his frightening opposition, but rather the architectural works of the postclassical age. The notebooks for this section of the journey survive, and in the description of the events of this day there is no negative attitude expressed toward the Franciscan basilica: "I passed on my left the Gran Convento and the honored and sanctified Calvary, I did not see the burial place of Saint Francis."[9] If anything, the notebooks seem to treat the Christian elements of Assisi with great respect. It is only a later Goethe who will allow his drive to create for his former self the image of a young man resolute to find the classical world beneath the accumulated layers of subsequent centuries to lead him to describe the Franciscan complex as "monstrous" and as "towering Babylonian structures." In the notebooks, there is no "aversion" to the medieval aspects of Assisi.

The addition of obvious Sturm und Drang imagery to give dramatic weight to the young man's drive to cut through to the classical temple of Minerva and to ignore the architecture and the frescoes of the Franciscan churches (in fact, later plans for a second trip list the Giottos in Assisi as a "must-see") gives the entire passage a symbolic tone; like the poet of Horace's *Odes* (III, 30), who is led by the Muse to the heights of the Capitoline as a *poeta vates*, Goethe is led to the heights of this little town, a climb which, like the Horatian model, is intended to represent an artistic transformation. Once we recognize the allegorical nature of the passage, it seems natural to interpret the pretty young boy who guides the poet up the path to the heights as a kind of *psychopompos* from classical mythology. The poet is led by a spirit of beauty out of the violence and aesthetic misproportion of an earlier intellectual phase and into the broader vision of classical harmony and balance, represented here by the temple of Minerva at the top of the hill. Once the acropolis is attained and the temple is in view, the strong wind seems to have subsided and we hear no more of the Christian parts of the town (which were then and still are the major reason most pilgrims come to Assisi). Now having been brought to the heights of the town, the poet himself becomes the guide as he directs our gaze in the same direction as his own—"And look, the most praiseworthy work stood before my eyes . . ." In the original notebook, this sentence reads simply, ". . . and see, the lovely, holy work stood there."[10] The later addition calls attention not simply to the building but to Goethe *looking at the building* and so focuses our attention on the shift which is taking place in the character of the poet. What we are directed to see is not so much the classical world, but rather Goethe as the admirer and interpreter of that world. The *Italian Journey* is intended as a guidebook, not to Italy, but to Goethe himself, and the image Goethe wills in that book has persisted. Ernst Beutler summarizes generations of critics and readers when he writes, "it was in Italy that Goethe overcame his titanism."[11] But in truth no such complete change ever took place; vestiges of titanism remained integral parts of Goethe's personality to the end, and the conversion to classicism must be seen, at least partially, as a literary construct. It was an important element in the creation of the classical interpretation Goethe wished to impose on his life, and a better symbolic representation of this triumph than the description of the day in Assisi would be difficult to imagine.

Later in the evening of that same day in Assisi, Goethe reports that he encountered a group of soldiers as he was walking around the town and that they questioned the poet as to his business there. When he tells them that he has not come to see the Franciscan churches, but rather to admire the temple of Minerva, they are taken aback. The soldiers, he reports, took it poorly that he held the saint in such low esteem, and let it be known that they suspected him of smuggling contraband.[12] Of course, Goethe soon convinces the soldiers that he is no such criminal, but their suspicions and the hint of arrest are details Goethe includes in this symbolic first encounter with the classical world because they give further support to the image he is casting for himself as the developing apostle of classicism. Like the true martyr of a new religion, Goethe even gives his tormentors a little lecture, trying to persuade them that the temple of Minerva is a "model building."[13] One can see that, in one sense, there is a truth in the soldiers' accusations, for Goethe is in fact smuggling back into the territory of the enemy a new belief, a new aesthetic, and a new attitude toward the world. Into one of the holiest of Christian shrines, Goethe is reviving a kind of paganism. The Goethe who encounters the soldiers is no longer the Goethe who began the journey, for this passage is the symbolic depiction of a conversion, the emergence of the classical Goethe out of the artist of the Sturm und Drang, and the world as he now depicts it rises to meet the new man. As he leaves Assisi, the temple looks on him with love and comfort, and he takes one last look at the "sad basilica of Saint Francis." There is now no more talk of loneliness or of wind, of misproportion in nature or in the works of man. Goethe is now in a landscape transformed by his own transformation:

> The way to Foligno was one of the most beautiful and most charming walks I have ever taken; four full hours walking beside a mountain, to my right a richly cultivated valley.[14]

The *Italian Journey* is a magnificent piece of editorship. In discussing his method of redaction, Goethe wrote to his friend Zelter that he had been careful to change as little as possible from the original documents and only expunged the "insignificant details of the day" and the many repetitions.[15] But a brief examination of the passage above and the changes that were made in the original notebooks convinces us that Goethe's own description of his "editorship" is somewhat disingenuous. Much more detail is added in than he would have us believe, and it is not clear what we are to understand by the "insignificant details of the day" which have been erased. It often seems that what is insignificant to the Goethe of 1814–15 is what does not cohere with the image of himself that he wants to project in this work. Finally, much of the material for the later parts of the *Italian Journey* was destroyed by Goethe himself so that the only record we have for much of the period is this later, highly edited (and, judging by the passage we have examined, one can assume also highly reconstructed) image of the past. That Goethe wanted future readers to take this conflation of art and history as a true representation of the artist's travels is evident in the original title of the work: *From My Life: Part Two.* Part One of the autobiographical writings was *Poetry and Truth,* published at the time Goethe was working on what later would be called the *Italian Journey.*

The will to create a classical facade for his own personality was so strong that even as skeptical a reader as Heine accepted the image as the true Goethe and for over a century critics were reluctant to look beneath the mask; readers and critics alike were inclined to let Goethe's own image of himself stand as a reassuring monument to the strength and health of the classical perspective. This picture of Goethe as the light-seeking, clear-thinking figure of a late Enlightenment was particularly strong in the critical works written around 1949, the bicentennial of the poet's birthdate, a period which saw German scholars rallying behind this image of their greatest poet as a much-needed counterexample to the years of Nazi culture just past and to the cult of vicious irrationality which characterized the time. The darker side of Goethe's personality, the part of the man that could despair of any real progress in life and that retained the almost nihilistic aspects of the Sturm und Drang titanism, was too frequently subordinated to the happier Olympian aspect the poet himself had cultivated in his later years. Goethe knew that his autobiographical writings would have their intended effect; he knew how he was perceived in his own time and how later generations would see him. But he also knew the one-sidedness of this preferred image of himself:

> People have always praised me as one particularly favored by good fortune; and I neither wish to complain nor to find fault with the course of my life. But in truth it has been nothing but hard work and struggle, and I can say that in my seventy-five years I have not known four weeks of real pleasure. It has been the eternal rolling of the stone which had to be started from the beginning again and again.[16]

The frustration Goethe felt and the sense of futility, symbolized by the stone of Sisyphus alluded to above, is often expressed in a bleak vision of nature which stands just at the periphery of his more optimistic moods. It is a vision of nature as an indifferent, grinding force which chews up life only to spit it out again. This is a vision which appears again and again in his conversations and can be found as a kind of ground bass in many of his works, even in the classical works whose surface optimism seems to be the very antithesis of such dark broodings. But, as real as this negative side of his personality was, Goethe was often at pains to keep it secret, especially as he grew older, preferring rather to present a bland, impersonal, and reserved personality to the outer world than to reveal his as a personality torn by extremes. And Goethe's reluctance to lift his own mask has been respected by many a critic. Even when critics set out to probe beneath the surface and to examine the "secrets" Goethe so frequently alludes to, those very secrets emerge simply as benign and integral elements in a total and unified personality which sought, above all, clarity and clearness of perception. Ernst Bertram, for example, in an essay entitled "Goethe's Doctrine of Secrets," makes the following conclusion:

> We can say that Goethe's predisposition towards secrets ultimately originated in the drive of his clear and active nature to save everywhere the secret of life without which all human activity, all human nature would degenerate into soulless aridity and would be destroyed.[17]

Bertram never specifies what these "secrets" are, but says simply that such as did exist were necessary parts of the overall lucidity of his nature. For Bertram, and for many critics, the very tendency toward mask and secrecy which Goethe so often demonstrates is itself subverted into a support for the very opposite, a humanistic image of clarity. Even in a critical project like that of Bertram's which takes as its explicit task to burrow beneath the surface and to discover what has been "secreted," the imposing image of a classical humanism becomes too overwhelming, and the project is aborted into more of the same bland impersonality. Like Goethe's own Sturm und Drang personality as we have seen it in the passage from the *Italian Journey*, the drive toward secrecy had to be neutralized because it does not accord well with the image the poet wanted to create for himself. Critical attempts like Bertram's are direct continuations of the classical imposition begun by Goethe himself. But to demystify the mysteries like this is to lose much of the poet, for Goethe the enlightened humanist is only half, or less than half the story.

During the century and a half since his death, there have been a number of historical reasons for Goethe's classical facade proving to be an especially persuasive, even necessary image of the poet. In the nineteenth century, it was this imposing and authoritative image which allowed Germany to accept Goethe as its greatest poet despite the questionable amorality which was seen to lie behind much of his work. In the early twentieth century, it was to a large extent this classical facade which Goethe created for himself that enabled psychologists like Jung to see in the poet a model of integration within the personality and so to hold Goethe up as the exemplary path taken by a near-perfect balance of inner and outer, of conscious and unconscious elements of personality. The need for a convincing and accessible model of psychic health added a measure of support for the classical facade the older Goethe manufactured from his own experience and granted to this image, when necessary, the benefit of the doubt. Finally, in the mid-twentieth century, the image of Goethe as the eminently sane older man, creating rational order out of ambiguous experience, has served as a necessary and cherished model in an age of political and social turbulence. The many popular publications of the 1950s and 1960s which use passages from Goethe as daily text for fortifying reading, the many Goethe calendars, and the "Through the Year with Goethe" attest to this need. No other author, with the possible exception of Schiller, has been so ransacked for salutary quotes, and it is doubtful that any other author could have stood up under such assault. It is interesting here to try to imagine what a "Through the Year with Kleist" would be like.

But does Goethe's classicism still hold the essential power to convince? Are we still willing to interpret the man, and especially his literary works, strictly in the light of the classical lamp the old poet so carefully created and left behind for us? It is in response to this question that the following chapters are offered. I believe that, coexistent with Goethe's drive for the "classical" and for the perfection of form, there was a drive equally strong toward disruption and disunity and that this other drive is as evident in *Faust* as it is in the works of the "classical" frame of mind. It is this second and opposing drive which subverts the classical form so consciously crafted and which renders it a faulty facade. But, while this second impulse may spoil the serene monumentality of the classical works, it is this very force that elevates them above mere imitation and lends to them an irresistible vitality. Like the works of Thomas Mann's author, von Aschenbach, the classical works of Goethe have suffered the fate of becoming standard fare for the high school curriculum, and most readers do not pick them up again because the harmonious ideals of classicism these works supposedly proclaim have come to seem irrelevant in an age as preoccupied by intensity and energy as our own. But, it is just possible that—again, like the works of von Aschenbach—these works have unfairly been raised to this high level of cultural admiration and do not deserve their hallowed reputation. It is possible that beneath the polish of their surface these works reveal a moral ambiguity which is of greater interest to contemporary readers than the cool monumentality Heine found so decorative and uninspiring. It is to such an unclassical reading of these works, a reading in the light of *Faust I* rather than in that of the later Goethe, that the following chapters are devoted.

In exploring the disunity present within these literary works, it is useful to begin by examining a paradox which is central to all Goethe's intellectual and creative endeavors. Goethe himself was well aware of the paradox and gave it its most appropriate and poetic name: "Permanence in Change." In a world of endless transformation, what can be permanent? Art comes first to mind, but art can only promise to *lend* to transient moments a kind of durability:

> Be grateful that the Muses' favor
> Promises immortality:
> Meaning in your heart,
> And form in your spirit.[18]

Unfortunately, as Goethe well knew, works of art are themselves the products of a heart and mind which are also subject to the historical necessity of change, and they will be appreciated or neglected by a public also subject to the same historical necessity. Whether a work becomes a classic or is forgotten depends on an audience to reexperience it, and art, like anything living, can die.

If art does not possess immortality, what does? Goethe's studies in the metamorphoses of botanical and zoological form and his study of alchemy[19] tell us of his persistent preoccupation with the problem of change. The words of Heraclitus, philosopher of change, are embedded in the poem already quoted:

> And with every downpour of rain
> Your lovely valley has been changed;
> And, oh, in the very same river,
> You may not step a second time.[20]

It is within the context of this pessimistic preoccupation with the process of change and transformation that the effort to impose a classical edifice upon his own personality and upon the form of many of the works he created is best appreciated. In optimistic moments, the stable classical form seems to serve as reassurance that change and transformation will at least take place within determinable laws; Goethe puts this forward in the highly didactic poem "Metamorphosis of Plants":

Now, beloved, turn your gaze to the colorful throng
Which no longer moves confusingly before your mind.
Every plant now proclaims to you the eternal law,
Each flower speaks to you with ever clearer voice.[21]

Just as the calm elegiac form remains constant throughout the poem, so too beneath the transformations of plant life there is a perceptible law that no plant may violate. In this poem, Goethe tries to apply those same laws to man: "You see these laws every-where . . . Man himself will re-form his malleable yet determinate shape."[22] But, such laws as are clearly revealed by the study of plants are only very tentatively applied to the realm of men and women. The fusion of classical form and didactic message which seems so flawless in a small poem like the "Metamorphosis of Plants" is not so easily achieved in a purely human work such as *Iphigenia* or *Hermann and Dorothea*, because the laws of human change are not so easily perceived. And in the passage cited above from the *Italian Journey* we may perceive that the retrospective attempt to place a teleological and classical meaning on the simple experience in As-sisi violates to some extent the nature of the experience itself. The laws which govern the development of the human mind are simply not comparable to the laws of plant development, and even though he often attempted, as in the elegy above, to impose laws onto experi-ence within the work of art, Goethe could just as easily demonstrate a considerable skepticism toward such an enterprise. If we consider, for example, the chemical laws of attraction which are tested in the crucible of human relations in *Elective Affinities*, we find that their applicability is anything but simple. They apply and do not apply at the same time. As far as *Faust* is concerned, it was Goethe's doubt whether the whole of Faust's development could be adequately de-scribed by any external law or "idea" that led to a mild disagreement with Schiller[23] and which finally led to his famous outburst to Eckermann:

They come to me and ask what idea I was attempting to embody in my *Faust*. As if I knew that myself and could articulate it! . . .In general . . . it has not been my way as a poet to strive for the embodiment of something abstract . . . the more incommensurable and incomprehensible for the rea-son a poetic production is, the better it is.[24]

A more succinct refutation of the purpose of the "Metamorphosis of Plants" could hardly be found. If, then, the classical form adopted by Goethe is to be understood as formal support for an underlying and abstract idea, to which the artifice of the work is to be subordinated, such an interpretation must be limited to a very small number of strictly didactic works, such as the "Metamorphosis of Plants" and its companion piece, "Metamorphosis of Animals." In these short poems, the classical form is the support and exemplification of a classical content—that is, a content which stresses the predictable in the process of development, and the form helps make that content accessible to the faculty of reason. But this does not hold true for the form in the larger classical works. In works such as *Iphigenia*, the classical form serves a purpose diametrically opposed in that it functions to increase the "incommensurability" of the work rather than to reduce it, and it does this by providing a fundamental discrepancy between the surface and the inner content of the work.

We must return then to the question of the relationship between a preoccupation with change and the classical effort. This question has been posed recently, not in a Goethean context, by Leo Bersani in his investigation of character and desire in literature, *A Future for Astyanax.* A fundamental question for Bersani is "what is the place of personality in a psychology of metamorphosis?"[25] Bersani suggests that much of the best of nineteenth-century literature is "less interested in the psychological continuities which make personality possible than in those radical discontinuities and transformations which explode the myth of personality."[26] The terms Bersani offers are very useful to a study of Goethe, and we may apply his statement to the literary works of Goethe to the extent that the "classical" works present the "myth of personality," by which we mean the myth of the integrated or harmonious personality, while his *Faust* explodes that same myth. But, as we will see, even the presentation of the myth is fraught with the anxiety of its own impossibility. The wholeness, the balance of character and personality which seem to characterize the "classical" works, as it characterizes the persona Goethe tries to achieve for himself in the *Italian Journey*, is a myth whose insubstantiality is revealed by the poet's own consciousness of his endeavor as one of artifice. The self-consciousness which any work of art must display is a major article of the classical aesthetic worked out by Goethe in the last years of the eighteenth century; "every work of art must announce itself as such," he asserts in the Laocoön essay of 1798.[27] Because of the work's recognition of its own status as artifice, Goethe, in his classical works, presents the myth of wholeness, but at the same time he reveals this myth *as* myth, and this act of self-recognition within the project itself compromises the classicism of the works and places them within an atmosphere which is much closer to that of his later novel *Elective Affinities* and in general to the literature of the present century.

The persistent awareness of the paradoxical relationship between continuity and transformation, which lies behind all of Goethe's works, becomes especially acute when we come to an examination of the classical works, because the very classicism which these works attempt to perpetuate carries within its own nature a fundamental contradiction which makes its use problematical from the outset. Peter Szondi formulated this contradiction most succinctly; for him it is "the contradiction between the perceived uniqueness of Greek art and the role postulated for it as an ideal, that is, its reproducibility."[28] Not long after Winckelmann had exhorted his generation of artists to follow the example of the Greeks, the literary works of the ancient world had already begun to lose much of their status as normative models because a new and vigorous historicism had captured the best minds of the age and had brought about a virtual revolution in the interpretation and appreciation of all cultural products. Thanks largely to the work of Herder, it was now generally acknowledged that all art was the product of a historical context and that each cultural era was unique to itself. The inevitable recognition that classical art was also the unique response to unique historical circumstances could not help but undermine the possibility of using ancient, classical works of art as models for modern artistic productivity, and for an age in which historical understanding of cultural phenomena was rapidly replacing moral understanding, the search for a normative poetics in the products of past ages could only be a futile one.

Herder had been the first in Germany to introduce historical considerations as criteria for the understanding and evaluation of all art, and, although for him the ancient classical world remained a kind of lost paradise,[29] he realized that no age or culture could possibly reproduce the circumstances and conditions of another. No matter how strong the will, Germany could never be another Greece, and yet the exhortation which had come from Winckelmann, and was felt by all German artists of the late eighteenth century, was suggested by the very title of his first important work: *Thoughts on the Imitation of Greek Works*. What could this call to imitation mean to a generation which also read Herder? Where earlier ages could have accepted such an exhortation to receive the works of the past as examples of a normative poetics and could have happily plundered the ancient world for viable and imitable models of form, the age of Goethe was troubled by the insight that these ancient works were the historical products of a world long past and were as irreproducible as the world which gave them life. When we consider how powerful the initial impetus toward historicism was, it seems improbable that a thinker like Goethe would have even attempted the resuscitation of classical forms at all. And if we compare the last decades of the eighteenth century with the historical period that gave rise to French classicism, we can only conclude that the historical conditions that produced these two forms of the classical were very different. Where the Paris of Racine and Corneille was relatively stable, large, and cosmopolitan, the Weimar of 1790 was a small provincial island in a Europe torn apart by political and social upheaval. Where French classicism reflects a mature society at a point of political equilibrium, Weimar classicism can only dream of such stability and is in many ways the very product of this dream.[30] Where French classicism shows an awareness of its own normative status for its culture, Weimar classicism demonstrates none of this confidence, and where French classicism left behind a large and coherent series of dramas, the products of Weimar classicism are only a handful of literary works, each in a genre by itself, each a brilliant and unique response to an awareness of its own impossibility. Given this very unusual nature of German "classicism," it is no wonder that Nietzsche, comparing the literatures of France and Germany, could ask if there had even been a German classicism at all.[31] Goethe's own morphological thinking would seem to rule out the possibility of successful imitation: "Every existing thing has its existence in itself. A living, existing thing cannot be measured by anything which is outside of it."[32] If each organic creation contains within itself the unique criteria by which it is to be understood and evaluated, what can provide a normative standard? If each authentic existence is unique in itself, what role can there be for progeny? As we shall see later, the entire problem of progeny, literary and human, was a deeply troubling one for Goethe. It is, then, against the background of this essential contradiction in the very notion of classicism that all of Goethe's classical works were written, and it was above all the poet's own sense of history that undermines the concept of the classical as model.

It was Herder who sparked in Goethe an awareness and an interest in the historical, and this interest never waned throughout the poet's lifetime. It was his fascination with the historical that prompted

Goethe to choose the material for his first major drama and his *Götz von Berlichingen* is not simply a historical drama—it is the first historical drama to show a fascination with the very process of history itself. Herbert Lindenberger writes of *Götz:* "What makes Goethe's play historical in a profoundly new way is its concentration on the very process of change, its sense of time passing, of one set of human values gradually, though inevitably, giving way to another."[33] As historical drama, *Götz von Berlichingen* differs from its immediate predecessors of the German Baroque or Enlightenment in that it does not present historical fact as exemplification of moral truth which possesses some universal applicability; moral value in *Götz* is relative to historical context. And *Götz* differs from the Shakespearean histories which inspired it in that it does not present history for its relevance to the present; where Shakespeare's kings were all of importance because they helped to explain or justify the political regime current in the playwright's own time, Goethe's hero is a man whose historical significance will die with him. Götz is the last of his line, a man without progeny and with no enduring political significance. Goethe's interest in *Götz* is not grounded in a moral or political idea; it is an interest in history *as* history for its own sake, and the history Goethe puts on the stage is in fact a literary document in Götz's own hand. The original title of Goethe's play makes this dependence on the earlier text clear: *The History of Gottfried of Berlichingen with the Iron Hand, Dramatized.* As Goethe himself puts it, he has dramatized the very words of the old knight himself, "just as the brave and hearty man had presented himself, pretty much to his own advantage, in his own story."[34] In a radical departure from earlier historical drama, Goethe's drama calls attention to itself as historical by announcing itself as the resuscitation of a historical text. In the course of the play we even see, in a scene that anticipates Romantic irony, Götz sitting down to write the autobiography which we are seeing put onto the stage.

It is important to emphasize that Goethe's very first literary project was a resuscitation of a literary text from the past, for this is an activity in which Goethe will engage himself again and again. From the very beginning of his literary career to the end of his life, Goethe "rewrites" literature of the past—literature of the ancient world, Renaissance autobiography, drama and verse epic, Persian poetry, even his own journals from an earlier period of his life—and while the literature rewritten is taken from completely different places and times, the impulse to rewrite remains the same. It is difficult to imagine two more different literary works than *Götz von Berlich-*

ingen and *Iphigenia in Tauris,* but *Götz,* no less than *Iphigenia,* is a rewriting of literature of the past, and both are bound together as acts of literary resurrection. Szondi refers to the radical differences between these two dramas and the power each exerted over the imagination of the times:

> Schlegel and Herder were encouraged by Goethe's poetry to speak of a new epoch of poetry. However, Herder had *Götz* in mind, while Schlegel was thinking of *Iphigenia.* They were referring to two different poets.[35]

But are these two poets really so different? Despite the classical facade which it presents to the world, *Iphigenia* is perhaps closer to *Götz* and the Sturm und Drang than Szondi realized. The schizophrenia implied in "two different poets" is perhaps not schizophrenia at all, but a conscious refraction of one artistic drive into the most diverse literary expressions. Perhaps the new epoch in literature which both Herder and Schlegel saw could be heralded by *either Götz von Berlichingen* or *Iphigenia* because it was to be an epoch in which the autonomy of the literary text would be called into question and in which various forms of literary parody would become dominant. *Either play* could serve as a forerunner of a literature preoccupied with its own literariness.

It is important that the drama *Götz von Berlichingen* announce itself as autobiography (or history) dramatized because it is the presence of his hero within his own literary presentation that Goethe wants to offer to his audience. It is therefore Götz's own book, the actual historical document, which, like the autobiography of Benvenuto Cellini that Goethe will translate some years later, that Goethe brings to the view of his audience. This does not mean that Goethe's play is nothing more than the autobiography put word for word onto the stage (in fact, the drama is at considerable variance with the book), but what is important here, because it is completely new, is that a certain relationship of literature to historical fact is established with Goethe's first real literary work and this relationship can throw light on our understanding of many of Goethe's later works. *Götz von Berlichingen* is a vivid drama of a strong giant of a man, but it is also a documentation of life's transformation into art, and of art back into life. This adds a further dimension to Goethe's reconstruction of the traditional historical drama, and this dimension consists in the awareness that the historical fact, once it has become history, can only live within the realm of the aesthetic—for example, either in the highly fictionalized autobiography of Götz himself, or in the drama Goethe will make of that literary text. The consequence of this realization is a pronounced appreciation for the complex relationship between the historical and the aesthetic, for the dependence and opposition between art and life, an uneasy relationship which can itself become the very theme of the literary text:

Alexander and Caesar, Great Henry and Great Frederick,
   Gladly would yield up to me, each of them, half his garnered
     fame,
If in return even one brief night in this bed I could grant them:
   But, poor souls, they are dead; Hades imprisons them all.
Therefore rejoice, living man, in the place that is warm with your
   loving:
   Cold on your shuddering foot Lethe's dread waters will lap
                            (Roman Elegies, X)[36]

If by "garnered fame" we understand the literary representations which have kept the memory of these men alive, the relationship of history and literature in the poem becomes readily apparent. Without the literary transformation of these men's lives, these great men would have been entirely forgotten, but even the literary achievement which insures for the men some kind of permanence, is nothing when compared to a simple hour of life itself. The substitution of literature for life is an unhappy resolution to the problem of permanence and never ceased to be a dark preoccupation for Goethe, a preoccupation that would often undercut even the poet's happiest moments. The subsumption of lived experience into art becomes a thematic element in most of Goethe's literary works and is a corollary to the Goethean aesthetic which emphasizes the awareness of artifice in any artistic creation.

    Human experience becomes history; that history, like the lives of the four emperors mentioned above, may be relived if it is converted into literary artifact, but the experience of history as art is essentially different from the actuality of history itself. Like human experience, works of art from the past may themselves become part of history and they too may be recovered and reexperienced as living organisms by a process of conversion into a new work of art. It was congenial to Goethe, from his earliest poetic attempts, to treat earlier literature as historical material which, like personal experience, could be brought once again to life through its reintegration in a contemporary work of art. Speaking particularly of Goethe's use of several French poets in his early poem "Lili's Park," Ernst Beutler says of Goethe in general: "It was Goethe's way to throw whatever material he came upon into the crucible and to re-cast it; he always admitted this and claimed it as his poetic right."[37] Goethe seems never to have been troubled by the thought that his adaptation of earlier literature might be judged as lack of originality, nor was he disturbed when other poets took scenes from his works and used them in their own creations. For Goethe, the work of art became, like the historical fact, unalterable, and therefore eminently usable: "What has been created by poetry asserts its rights, just like what has happened in life."[38]

The appropriation of an artistic artifact as poetic raw material was no different from the use of a bit of personal experience or an episode from history from which to create further works of art, and for Goethe the ease with which experience or history could be transformed into a new artistic form was a boon for his own creativity, but could also be a source of anxiety as he saw his own life being transformed even as it was lived. Perhaps it was this anxiety which led Goethe so often to cast his own experience into works of art which are themselves "imitations" of older works of art. Works of the past, and especially those of a classical past, have already achieved a kind of permanence; to unite his own experience with these durable objects would be to absorb for himself a measure of their permanence and stability. Nevertheless, if the poet's works are, as he said in an oft-quoted remark, all fragments of one great confession,[39] it is strange that so much of that confession is revealed in the form of literature recovered from the past.

It is true that most of Goethe's greatest literary achievement is directly derived from literary works of the past. The works we will consider are all openly dependent on established literary texts for their own existence: *Faust I* on the various earlier versions of the legend; *Iphigenia in Tauris* on the play of (nearly) the same name by Euripides as well as the many Iphigenia plays of the eighteenth century; the Roman Elegies on the work of the Latin poets Catullus, Tibullus, Propertius, and Ovid; *Hermann and Dorothea* on Voss's *Luise* and on Homer. This borrowing of earlier material to fashion new was by no means a naive borrowing; all these works depend for their very sophisticated effect on our awareness of their status *as* appropriation and reworking of earlier material. "In . . . reflected light we have our life"[40] could apply as easily to these works as to the newly risen Faust. Goethe was not only a great poet, he was a great editor, and he loved to translate (*Reineke the*

Fox, Benvenuto Cellini) as much as he loved to edit (Euripides' *Phaethon* fragments, his own notes from Italy), and these talents are an integral part of his poetic creativity. Beneath the interpretation offered in this book for the four works listed above is the assumption that both sides of Goethe, the classical and the Faustean, share equally in this attitude toward literature as a form of "repeated reflections" ("wiederholte Spiegelungen"),[41] as a continual process of oscillation between lived experience and its representation in art. Beneath both literary masks Goethe adopts, there is the common anxiety which fears the literary transformation of life while at the same time there is the recognition that such transformation is essential to the preservation of the primary experience and is necessary if past experience is to become the historical material to which later artists will give further transformation.

The works considered here all come from the middle period of Goethe's life. *Faust I*, in its final form, is the product of over thirty years of intermittent work, but much of that work was done in the period in which Goethe was creating his classical works, and for the sake of the argument, I have generally treated *Faust I* as a single printed text, not as an assorted collection of disparate layers of production. I will argue that there is great disunity in *Faust*, and while one common explanation is to attribute that disunity to the long and complicated history of its composition, I wish instead to suggest that the disunity within the work is in fact an integral part of the work's conception, not an accident nor the result of indifferent piecing together of scenes. It is this fundamental disunity within *Faust* which is the explosion of the myth presented in the classical works, and if we read the classical works in the light of *Faust*, we see that they reveal themselves to be myths already ripe for explosion. For purposes of organization, I have divided my discussion of *Faust I* into two chapters—one devoted to Faust and one to Margarete. Each half of the play presents a specific problem which I wish to raise separately for its relevance to the other works examined in this book, but I do not intend this division to imply that the two halves of the drama are not necessary to each other.

It is possible that Goethe's classical works were written in conscious response to the fragmented world as it is represented in *Faust*, that they represent an attempt to mold modern experience into classical form and thus to overcome the fragmentation of the contemporary world through an artistic vision of wholeness and completion. But the classical works do not entirely succeed in dispelling fragmentation or disunity, and in fact reveal beneath their carefully polished surface those same attributes we see in the character of Faust, attributes that become all the more disturbing because of the attempts to disguise them. It is this discrepancy between surface and depth that makes these works exciting; the scene, for example, in which Iphigenia abandons the measured flow of classical tragic form and breaks into the freely constructed song of the Fates is chilling and exhilarating in a way few scenes in modern drama can be. Such a scene as this is possible because the fragmentation of the world is as implicit in *Iphigenia* as in *Faust;* it is only that the recognition of this fragmentation is located in the discrepancy between surface and depth rather than being treated thematically as it is in *Faust.*

Winckelmann, in his *Thoughts on the Imitation of Greek Works* (1755), recognized the essential difference between the ancient and modern world as one of wholeness against fragmentation, and he recommends the ancient as a means of improving the modern: "The concept of wholeness, of completion in the nature of the ancient world will make the fragmentation in the nature of our own world all the more apparent and can purify it."[42] Undoubtedly, Winckelmann intended something optimistic with these prophetic and programmatic words—that the study and imitation of the ancient works of art could actually *heal* the fragmentation within the nature of the modern world, that by "making more apparent" and then "purifying" the nature of the modern world, the modern artist will be able to approach the wholeness of the ancients in the realm of the aesthetic. But the statement may also be taken to mean almost the reverse: that the study of the ancients can only make the fragmentation of the modern world all the more apparent and clear, and that any sense of healing can take place *only* in the artificial realm of the aesthetic construct. It is as though Goethe had set out to take Winckelmann's exhortation in the sense he had originally meant it, but had, in the course of the classical project, come around to the other, less optimistic reading of the injunction; in the end, Goethe fulfills faithfully the program set out by Winckelmann—he shows the fragmentation of the modern world through an imitation of the ancient form, but in doing so he does not reestablish the classical sense of wholeness for the modern age, but simply reveals all the more clearly the fragmentation and disunity perceived in his own world. The comparison implicit between ancient and modern, which is the inevitable result of a modern imitation of classical form, turns out for Goethe not to be so salutary as Winckelmann had imagined, and this was true because for Goethe the absolute distinction between art and life meant that whatever wholeness was envisioned in the aesthetic work must imply its opposite in the realm of lived experience.

I am searching, then, for the kinship between *Faust* and Goethe's classical works. I will not, however, attempt to suggest a healing resolution between the two Goethes, but simply to relocate the sense of dichotomy. *Faust I, Iphigenia in Tauris*, the Roman Elegies, and *Hermann and Dorothea* all share a sense of the disunity of the modern world, and this sense is conveyed in each case through a rewriting of literature. Faust is no longer in the world of the chapbooks or of Marlowe; he is no longer in a world where moral certainties give meaning to concepts like redemption and damnation. He is now trapped in a new world where all earlier distinctions have been blurred; his contours as a personality as well as the existence of any external moral order have all been rendered ambiguous. Margarete, the victim of Faust's fragmentation of the self, begins her literary existence as a whole and healthy individual, but concludes her life as torn and fragmented as Faust himself. Implicit in this trajectory from wholeness to disunity is the growing awareness that her life is being made the material of a literary transformation, and like so many of Goethe's characters, she dies a death without progeny, and a death that is fraught with dimensions of consuming literariness. No less than Faust, Iphigenia now finds herself in a world where the ancient moral order has been relocated from the external to the internal, and this new interiorization has obscured the old order. It is no accident that there is no chorus in this new *Iphigenia*, for a chorus would have provided that external point of reference that is as absent here as it is in *Faust*. The absence of a chorus is a conscious element of the literary rewriting of this ancient play, and we are meant to notice it. The Roman Elegies raise the literariness of *Iphigenia* to a higher level as Goethe makes his own awareness of his relationship to the literary traditions of the past a constituent element of the text itself. No less than Faust or Margarete, the poet of the *Elegies* is revealed as a man caught in the meshes of literature, unable to make a clear distinction between art and life, and so condemned to a reflected existence within an ambiguous frame. Unlike the flesh and blood poets of the elegiac tradition whose work the poet purports to continue, the poet of the Roman Elegies is a passive lover whose passion is greater for literature and literary fame than for life. Finally, *Hermann and Dorothea* is a brilliant subversion of an optimistic idyll of middle-class German life, Voss's *Luise*, which is itself an ironic adoption of Homeric epic form. The happy life of the German burghers is revealed by Goethe to be as problematic as the attempt to portray them in grand epic form. The result is an ironic comedy where resolution is proclaimed while at the same time disunity and disharmony are revealed to be as powerful as ever. The pessimism behind the work emerges as the poem undermines the optimistic tradition it claims to perpetuate.

A common theme throughout all these works is that of fragmentation and the resuscitated literary text. Each treats the theme differently and ingeniously; it is a theme that brings *Faust* squarely into the critical preoccupations of our own day and it renders the classical works less formidably monumental and therefore more readable for us.

1
Faust: Secular Anxieties

There is a lake which one day simply refused to let its water flow out of it and built a dam at the point where until then the run-off had taken place. Since then, this lake has risen higher and higher. Perhaps this very act of renunciation will enable us also to bear a similar fate and perhaps from then on man will will rise ever higher to a point where he no longer flows out into a god.

—Nietzsche, *The Joyful Science*

GOETHE'S *Faust* rests secure as one of the handful of major literary monuments of the Western world which will be read and reread, interpreted and reinterpreted, by every new generation. Like all great works of art, *Faust* seems to bring to a culmination both the preoccupations of the historical age which brought it to light and the thoughts of the author who created it, while at the same time the work looks beyond to a meaning larger than was imagined by the author or the audience for whom it was originally intended. Like the *Aeneid*, the *Divine Comedy*, or Shakespeare's *Lear*, Goethe's work is virtually inexhaustible, and the meaning one finds in it will depend to a large extent on the method adopted for the search. The Earth Spirit conjured up by Faust tells him that what he sees is simply a reflection of himself, and the reader of *Faust* must apply this admonition to himself, for it seems that the answers offered by the text he is reading reflect precisely the nature of the questions asked of it. It could be argued that the search for meaning in *Faust* is bound to be a far more subjective enterprise than a similar search in the other masterpieces named because *Faust* is the product of an age which for the first time in the West consciously articulated an aesthetic of indeterminacy, an age which for the first time recognized a plurality of truths and methods which were coexistent and exclusive at the same time. The refraction of Truth into truths is announced in the text as a premise for its own existence.

Goethe himself was well aware of the implications contemporary philosophy had for any expectation of absolute truth, whether in science or in matters of artistic judgment; he was well aware of the personal and historical limitations which had come to be recognized as the inescapable restraints on human understanding. His essay "The Experiment as Mediator between Object and Subject" (1792) explores just this topic, and in a later essay, "Experience and Science" (1798), Goethe describes the self-reflecting nature of observation:

> The observer never sees the pure phenomenon with his eyes, but rather so much depends on his own state of mind, of the condition of his perceptive faculties in use at the moment, of light, air and weather, of substances and methods; it is like drinking an ocean dry if one attempts to confine himself to the uniqueness of the phenomenon and to observe, measure, weigh and describe it.[1]

Since a completely objective observation of phenomena is never possible, all such attempts must be recognized as interpretations in which the limitations of the observer are an inevitable component. Interpretation is limited truth, but it is all that is possible. Morse Peckham describes the shift which took place in the second half of the eighteenth century, a shift which rendered the hope for objectivity and absolutes futile:

> A single step was taken and all the world was changed. All previous world views had assumed that the mind had access, whether through revelation from God or from study of the world, to the real nature and character, the true essence, of what was not the mind; and this assumption was unconscious. . . . The new attitude was not a simple assertion that we cannot know the world. Rather, it realized that we cannot know whether we know it or not . . . We can get out of one system only by gliding, whether we are aware of it or not, into another.[2]

In a world where a plurality of systems can and does exist, and in the absence of any absolute criteria for judgment, the act of knowing has no choice but to become an act of interpretation.

Goethe's *Faust* is a monument to the age that produced it, not only in that it is a work that demands interpretation at every step, but also because it is a work that has as one of its major thematic

patterns an articulated concern with the act of translation and interpretation itself. From Faust's attempts to interpret the Bible, to Margarete's anguished cry—"There's an old song that ends like this, /
But who gave them the right to interpret it like this?"[3] (4449–50)—
the text itself shows a conscious preoccupation with the very problem of interpretation which is also demanded of the reader. It is this
awareness of its own status as an object for interpretation that distin-
guishes *Faust* from earlier works of literature. Just as the Kantian
revolution made forever impossible the return to an epistemology of
certainty, *Faust* brings literature to a heightened stage of self-
awareness, but this new degree of self-consciousness must be purchased at a high price, and that price is the security of unambiguous
meaning. While earlier literature may confidently hope to be understood by the superimposition of external systems onto the text itself, that is, by assuming the text to be part of a larger system which
is comprehensive in its totality, *Faust* deliberately seeks to destroy
the possibility of such external reference and to frustrate attempts at
interpretation from without. It is no coincidence that the very first
words Faust utters are a condemnation of the conventional epistemo-
logical categories of understanding, while the image of Faust sitting
in his dark study attempting to come into contact with the larger
world may serve as a metaphor for the relationship between the
reader and the world of this text.

The enigmatic character of the drama and the difficulties it poses
for the reader are also no coincidence, for Goethe consciously created the text to be the object for interpretation, leaving for future
readers to find in it or to deny to it the existence of an overall unity
of purpose. It is quite possible that Goethe intended the text of *Faust*
to be inconclusive and contradictory. This seems to be the thought
behind a remark made to Karl Friedrich von Reinhard shortly after
the publication of *Faust I* in 1808. Writing specifically of the "Dedication" of the *Faust* text, Goethe writes:

> In the course of my life, this much I've been able to observe—
> that the public doesn't always know what is going on in po-
> etry, and very seldom does it have any idea of what is going on
> with the poet. In fact, I won't deny that, because I learned this
> very early on, that it has always been fun for me to play a
> game of hide-and-seek.[4]

To conceive of literature as a game of hide-and-seek is certainly to
implicate the reader in the construction of meaning for the text. The

hypothetical ideal reader would no doubt be able to extract from the text even here an unambiguous meaning, but the possibilities of such a reading at "degree zero" are for Goethe as remote as the possibility of scientific observation where the subjective limitations of the observer have been transcended. In short, both are impossible.

In an earlier letter to Schiller,[5] Goethe jokes about his game of hide-and-seek with his readers; his poor reader, he writes, never knows what to make of his poetic productions, and such a reader would never have taken up a book of his, if the author had not understood very well how to "put one over on the reader's abilities, feelings, and his thirst for knowledge." Just as Faust can discount the conventional categories of knowledge as modes of understanding the world because they have not brought him anywhere near the truth—"Here I am, a poor fool, / No wiser than before!" (358–59)— so Goethe claims to have defrauded the reader's faculties for understanding his works. Clearly, certainty of interpretation is not to be hoped for in a literature consciously created as a joke on the reader's quest for knowledge. Instead, this literature, and Faust in particular, presents itself as a work aware of its own insubstantiality and its own resistance to final understanding. Faust and the reader are drawn together into a search for meaning in a world where the very faculties of understanding are obscured.

In its strategy to convey its own awareness of its status as an object of interpretation, the text of Faust also calls attention to itself as a literary artifact. This is surely one of the major functions of the Walpurgisnight's Dream, with its satire on contemporary literary figures, including the author himself. This is also the purpose of the Prologue in the Theater, which points our attention to the fact that Faust is a reworking of a story already well established in an entire tradition of texts. Goethe's Faust is the self-conscious reworking of material already familiar; no reader comes to his text in the belief that the learned doctor is Goethe's own creation. The very reading of Goethe's Faust demands some acquaintance with the Fausts on which his is built, and it is to draw our attention to the relationship between this Faust and earlier Fausts that Goethe opens the play with his Faust doing what is most characteristic for the historical figure of Faust—demonstrating his dissatisfaction with conventional human knowledge. From the first lines of the Night scene we know that this is the Faust of literature whom we already know, and Goethe does not try to wrench his Faust from the grip of the past by placing him in a wholly new context (at least not yet), nor by having him do something entirely new or out of character. After all, Goethe could have introduced his Faust to us by having him return from a walk or by placing him in the kitchen preparing an omelette, but he begins by pointing to the very Faust-ness of his Faust and this is especially important because in the Margarete episode, the confrontation between the two lovers will in many respects be a confrontation between literature and life. As we will see, in the course of the drama the very nature of literature will be shown as an arid and infertile alternative to life, yet this very aridity will prove to possess a deadly attraction, and will triumph over life as it is represented in the drama. This triumph is part of the tragedy of Faust.

By revealing its awareness of its relationship to earlier literature, Goethe's *Faust* immediately raises questions of interpretation. How will this Faust differ from those of the past? What is the meaning of those elements in this Faust which do not appear elsewhere in the traditional legend? Similar questions are raised each time one literary text refers back to an earlier text for meaning, but what is radically different here is that while interpretation is demanded, the categories and outside points of reference which could ground an interpretation are put into question by the text itself. Faust's translation of the Bible becomes in fact a model act of modern literary criticism and interpretation that draws the critic-translator so far from the original text that it becomes unrecognizable. Can this be regarded as a model for interpretation of the *Faust* text as well? Is the critic who attempts to interpret *Faust* forced to be as bound by the limitations of his own perception in reading *Faust* as Faust is in interpreting the Bible? Is this scene a healthy warning to readers and critics, or a simple statement of inescapable fate? Certainly, in his act of translation, Faust proves to be wholly caught up within his own preoccupations, and it is precisely this carceral aspect of the Faust drama that will be the focus of my interpretation.

Before looking at the text of *Faust*, we must ask, what text? The history of the composition of *Faust, Part One* is long and extremely complicated. Many critics, most recently Albrecht Schöne,[6] have felt that the text as it was finally published in 1808 does not fully represent Goethe's intentions for the drama, and that the function of criticism is to ascertain and secure the conscious intentions of the author out of the published versions and unpublished fragments. It will not be my primary purpose, however, to search for the conscious intention of Goethe behind the *Faust* texts, but rather to show that, in the text as it was finally published, there is a pattern of preoccupation which, whether conscious or unconscious, and while perhaps not sufficient to argue for any real unity in the work, nevertheless provides a strong basis from which to compare and discuss the "classical" works of Goethe written in approximately the same years as those in which Goethe completed his *Faust I*. I am in search of a less optimistic Goethe than the one usually seen behind the classical works; the Faust text reveals this darker poet in almost every aspect of the drama, and we will find him in the classical works as well. In *Faust*, this pessimistic side of the author is revealed in a pattern of self-imprisonment, parody, and solipsism, and it is to that pattern that I propose to turn.

The text of *Faust I* is permeated from its beginning to its conclusion by an obsession with incarceration. In the "Dedication" to the work, the poet's insistence on his own passivity in creation, the comparison of his song to an Aeolian harp, and, above all, the mention of "the erring, labyrinthine course of life" (14), already prefigure an immobility of the self which is to receive much fuller symbolic representation in the character of Faust. The strands which connect the person of the poet with his creation become apparent as the poet declares that in his work on the drama he undergoes the act of rejuvenation through magic: "My heart is shaken again as in youth / By the breath of magic that follows in your train" (7–8). Like Faust in the Witch's Kitchen, the poet seems to be the passive recipient of emanations rather than the active creator of his own work. Only once in the opening poem does he refer to his work in the active mode, and this comes in the form of a question: "Shall I try this time to hold you fast?" Elsewhere in the poem, the poet speaks only as the passive observer of forms outside himself: "You come near . . . ," "You bring with you . . . ," "I am shaken . . . ," "a shudder takes me . . ." In his creativity, the poet seems more of a captive than a free agent. This motif of incarceration is repeated in a slightly different register when, in the dialogue among the director, the poet, and the jester (Prologue in the Theater), the poet expresses his longing for the "Himmelsenge" ("the confines of heaven," 63) and the theater is referred to as "ein enges Bretterhaus" ("a narrow house of board," 239). After this somewhat whimsical introduction of the theme, it is with the first appearance of Faust that we find it given full treatment.

We first see Faust, restless and dissatisfied, within the confines of his study, a high-arched, narrow Gothic interior. The very setting is symbolic of Faust's mental imprisonment—while the vault soars high above the man as if to promise a corresponding flight of thought, in fact the doctor sits uneasily at his desk, oppressed by the narrowness and darkness of the chamber; the Gothic arch, once the symbol of man's aspirations to the eternal, is now a prison: "Where even the sweet light of heaven / Breaks darkly through the stained glass" (400–401). The light which shines only dimly through the stained glass serves only, like the candles in the cathedral scene of Kafka's *Trial*, to intensify the darkness of the room, and is but a parody of the heavenly light which filled the stage in the scene just previous, the Prologue in Heaven. At the opening of the second part of the Faust drama, Faust will awaken in a pleasant landscape to say, that "we have our lives in a world of colorful refraction" (4727), and perhaps (but only perhaps) at that point Faust will have grown to accept the limitations and peripheral existence here so graphically represented by his incarceration in the dark study. However, the opening of Part Two is a great way off, and here there is no such genial accommodation to surrounding circumstance; here such light as enters is rendered into colored distortion by ancient stained glass, whereas in that pleasant landscape it is a rainbow, a symbol of man's reconciliation with nature, which refracts the light into its many hues.

It is important to remember that the stained glass, which symbolizes Faust's distance from the light, is an architectural element with a long history of ecclesiastical use as a didactic tool. What for centuries was used to order neutral light into meaningful shape and message is the very thing which now for Faust distorts the light. We see that the world which Faust inhabits (or which is created by him—it is difficult or impossible here to distinguish projection from external reality) is one existing on the very periphery of the traditional orthodox Christian community. The forms and the symbols of the traditional world are still extant, but their purpose has become obscured, or worse, they have been transformed into the very opposite of what they were originally intended to be. This sense of living on the edge of, or even isolated from, the center of Western tradition and culture, expressed in the new meaning ascribed to the stained glass, is given further palpable representation in the Bible-translating scene where Faust, like Martin Luther, sets himself the task: "To translate into my beloved German / The holy Original" (1222–23). With every attempt to render the opening sentence of Saint John's gospel into German, Faust wanders farther and farther from the surface meaning of the "holy Original": "Im Anfang war das Wort . . ." ("In the beginning was the word . . ."), "Im Anfang war der Sinn . . ." ("thought"), "Im Anfang war die Kraft . . ." ("power"), and finally: "The Spirit helps me! And all at once I find advice / And write consoled: In the beginning was the deed!" (1236–37). The translation has moved with almost systematic precision from the word *logos* to its very opposite. Even Mephistopheles, who is witness to this scene, but is still in the guise of a poodle, cannot sit still for such a perversion of the original text, and Faust must quiet him down:

> If I'm to share my room with you,
> Poodle, then leave off howling,
> Quit that barking.
>
> (1238–40)

But, whether the dog's response is actually one of gleeful approbation at Faust's thorough distortion of the original text, of shock at Faust's boldness of interpretation, or of disgust at Faust's quasi-religious undertaking in the first place, we cannot know for sure. If in fact Mephistopheles is delighted at the perversion, which is perhaps the more probable explanation for the dog's agitation, then we are reminded that the Devil himself can pervert Scripture by quoting it, and we will see Mephistopheles do just that when he writes into the student's commonplace-book *eritis sicut deus scientes bonum et malum* (2047). It must warm Mephistopheles' cold blood to see Faust quoting Scripture to *his* own purpose, for this draws the two together in that for both, to quote Scripture in this way is to quote the self. In Faust's translation, the "Original" is still perceptible, but only barely, for the willful wrenching of the word *logos* to encompass the significance of "deed" imputes a meaning far too distant from the original meaning to be considered as anything but the very mind of Faust himself.

The translation is such a perversion of the original text that we are impelled to ask who the spirit can be who Faust believes has come to prompt the translator's mind. Is there in fact a spirit actually present to Faust as he translates? Perhaps Faust believes that in his updating of the Gospel he has been witness to the agency of the Holy Spirit as it unfolds further revelation. This would be an interpretation of the spirit which would imply that idiosyncratic interpretation is the appropriate response to divine revelation in the modern age. But it is equally possible that the "spirit" referred to here is very much like the Earth Spirit conjured up by Faust himself in the first scene, and who disappears, telling Faust, "You approximate the spirit you can conceive of, / Not me!" (512–13). If these two manifestations of spirit can be compared, then the spirit Faust sees helping him translate the Bible may also be only a reflection of Faust himself and not some herald from transcendental realms.

The very ambiguity we encounter when we attempt to define the spirit is characteristic of the world of *Faust:* divine intervention and willful indulgence of the self look strangely similar. What might be a reference to a realm outside the self (if "Geist" were "heilige Geist") can easily become just another manifestation of the self, as the Earth Spirit points out to Faust. There is a good deal of humor in both these "spirit" scenes—certainly the notion of having the spirit himself point out that the spirit Faust can see is a projection of his own mind is whimsical and perplexing. Does the spirit exist or not? Later we will ask the same question of Satan in the Walpurgisnight riots. If the spirit Faust conjures up is from a world antithetical to Faust, how is communication even possible? Or, is the spirit merely a part of a world created by Faust within himself? The spirit asks Faust:

> Where is the heart that made a world within itself,
> Bore it, cared for it, trembling with joy,
> And swelled itself to rival us spirits?
>
> (491–93)

How, then, could it reproach Faust for doing that very thing which brought the spirit to form? This spirit proves as difficult to define as the spirit that aids Faust in translation. The confusion and humor, however, do not belie a more serious truth here, for Faust's very ability to recognize something outside himself is called into question.

The potential solipsism which lies at the heart of this system of quoting and self-quoting, reflection and self-reflection, does not mean that the first half of the drama is completely without intimations of a salvation outside the carceral self. Here again, the vaulted, arched study is the perfect emblematic representation of Faust's situation; the arch may still hold reminders of its ancient and archetypal connotation of aspirations to a higher realm, but for Faust the vault nevertheless remains merely an architectural expression of his prison. What once was the house of God is now the prison of man. Another intimation of salvation comes from the Prologue in Heaven, where the Lord, even if he is portrayed in stagey sententiousness, is actually present for at least one scene. Here at least there seems to be the promise of outright salvation for Faust:

> Since now he serves me, if only in a confused way,
> I will lead him soon into clarity . . .
>
> (308–9)

A good man, struggling in his darkness,
Will always be aware of the true course.

(328–29)

The Lord's words invite us to look at Faust *sub specie aeternitatis* and thereby see his ultimate salvation. But why does this promise seem so remote, and why is the Lord's presence here not more comforting? For one thing, the Lord we see on stage is too perfectly a parody of the serene old man who too often serves, for want of a better symbol, as the Christian personification of God. His calm sententious style would probably grate on Faust's ears as much as it occasions Mephistopheles' cynical humor. Mephistopheles rightly points out that the Lord has in fact had to teach himself to maintain this high seriousness:

My pathos would surely make you laugh,
Had you not learned to do without laughter.

(277–78)

How has it come about that God has forgotten how to laugh? Did God once have a sense of humor? The humorlessness he now demonstrates emphasizes his distance from the world because the Lord's cultivated high seriousness threatens in the end to dissolve into Epicurean indifference. After his brief interview with Mephistopheles, the Lord turns to his Archangels (and we sense that in this turn he also deflects his immediate attention away from Faust and the problems of the here and the now) to say:

But you, who are the true sons of gods,
Take your delight in the richly living beauty!
May what is in progress, eternally alive and active,
Surround you with the beautiful bonds of love,
And what hovers in wavering appearance,
You will make firm with enduring thoughts.

(344–49)

"Sons of gods" are not the "children of God." The reference to gods in the plural is strange and vitiates the credibility of "*the* Lord," while the divine preoccupation with beauty points to an Epicurean detachment and displaces the moral function of the Christian God. Faust is himself a part of that "which is in progress," that which, from a viewpoint sufficiently removed, can be enjoyed as an aesthetic, not a moral, phenomenon. From a less exalted viewpoint, however, Faust's sufferings cannot be regarded so abstractly and must remain what they are—human sufferings. It is from such a viewpoint that all the drama outside the Prologue in Heaven is seen. The concluding stage directions of the Prologue establish the dramatic world as it is to be for the rest of the play: "the heavens close; the archangels disperse." This is not a promising sign for the possibility of Faust's salvation.

In *Faust* criticism, the Prologue in Heaven is almost universally read as a frame for the entire play which sets the acts and feelings of Faust into a more benign perspective where culpability is reduced and redemption assured, but surely such an unambiguous reading is hardly consistent with the mode of reading suggested by the rest of the drama. Neither the poet's "Dedication" nor the other prologue has clarified the meaning of the work; on the contrary, each has raised doubts and questions regarding the nature of the drama which is about to unfold, and the lack of agreement between the three persons in the first prologue could be seen as echoed in the fundamental difference in outlook between the Lord and Mephistopheles. There is no reconciliation in the first prologue, and perhaps we should not assume that in the second prologue either perspective is to be regarded as dominant. Only if we grant the Lord status as representative of a truly transcendental realm may we accept his judgments over those of Mephistopheles, but nowhere in the play are we led to suspect that Faust himself believes in such a realm (in fact, like Prometheus, he denies the relevance of such a realm, even if it were to exist), and the external point of reference that would be offered by a truly divine manifestation on stage is seriously undermined by our doubts (and Faust's) as to whether such a thing is to be taken seriously within the context of this drama. This Lord is *too* serious and too perfect a caricature of the clichéd Enlightenment philosophy, which saw in every manifestation of evil a higher good. This optimistic philosophy had pervaded the thought of European philosophers from Christian Wolff to Soame Jenyns, and had already been thoroughly parodied by Voltaire and Samuel Johnson for the facile treatment given human suffering under such a regime of easy optimism. Goethe gives the parody a final ironic dimension by depicting the benign guarantor of a beneficent teleology on stage and then having him disappear with no word of consolation directed to the human whose sufferings may contain in themselves the promise of salvation. A further dimension of parody in Goethe's Lord is his resemblance to another literary figure of ineffective goodness, to King Canut, in the play of the same name by Johann Elias Schlegel. In this play, the well-meaning king, who is all kindness and rational optimism, is incapable even of understanding the mind of his evil subordinate Ulfo, let alone being capable of changing it. Like Mephistopheles and the Lord in *Faust,* Ulfo and Canut hardly speak the same language, and the language Canut speaks reminds us very strongly of Goethe's Lord in its impersonal, optimistic sententiousness; his line—"A soul that thinks and feels will err only a short time"[7]—is probably the source for the Lord's genial lines—"Man will err so long as he strives" (317) and "A good man in his dark drives / Is always aware of the right course" (328–29). *Canut* was a play well known to Goethe from childhood; he had even played the role of the king in a little production given in the Goethe household.[8]

The literary and philosophical parody which lies at the basis of the Prologue in Heaven do much to increase the unreal, dreamlike nature of the scene, and in a play like *Faust* where self-projection and reality tend to blur into one another, a reading of this prologue as the dream of a despairing man of his own salvation seems as plausible as accepting on faith that the Lord as he is here depicted is truly the firmly established and benign divinity imagined by the eighteenth century as guarantor of ultimate mercy and goodness. And even if the Prologue in Heaven is intended to be more than an ambiguous vision, such a distant promise of salvation can be of little comfort to Faust in his confinement in the here and now. And even if Faust *were* able to view himself as the Lord can, *sub specie aeternitatis,* and could see his own salvation as a future reality, how would he accept the Lord's offer of "the beautiful bonds of love"? Does he in fact wish to be "made stable," as the Lord says to his angels? The very words remind us of the "holy bonds of slavery" which hold an unwilling Iphigenia in her role as priestess to Diana. It is precisely these bonds she seeks to escape. Is it not also the very opposite to these bonds that Faust longs for—a release from confinement and limitation? The salvation suggested by the Lord seems to be the very antithesis to what Faust is in his innermost self; it is a salvation in which Faust would cease to be Faust.

The incommensurability which exists between the Lord and Faust is reflected in the relationship between Faust and the spirit which appears to him in the Night scene. When the spirit speaks of the world in eternal process, his words are a variation of the Lord's last lines: "Thus I work at the humming loom of time / And weave the living garment of God" (508–9). And here the spirit seems to be not a projection of Faust but the representative of a world outside. But Faust seems not even to understand what the spirit is referring to. Rather than accommodate himself to a dispassionate and impersonal view of the cosmos as a "living garment of God," he speaks instead from the depths of a very personal need, and reiterates his desire to identify on a personal level with something more than himself: "You who swirl around the whole wide world, / Active spirit, how near I feel to you!" (510–11). And for this attempt to rise above himself, he is rebuffed by the spirit and thrown back even more violently upon himself. Disinterested observation of the macrocosmos seems as impossible for Faust as the belief in a transcendental realm. That this brush with a grand theological concept should result in frustration rather than comfort should come as no surprise; we have known from Faust's opening lines in the drama that the study of theology, like the study of every other discipline, has provided him with no release from his incarceration:

> Now, alas, I have studied philosophy,
> Law and medicine,
> And unfortunately theology too—
> Studied them well, sweated over them,
> Yet here I am now, a poor fool,
> Exactly as wise as I was before.
>
> (354–59)

How strong a contrast is provided by Faust's impassioned outcry against his present condition ("*here* I am *now*") to the calm vision of Faust *sub specie aeternitatis* we have heard the Lord articulate in the scene just previous. The Faust *we* see is not the Faust whose end is already disclosed to us, but the Faust who is caught in the sufferings of his own here and now.

The contrast between these two Fausts could hardly be more pointed and gives the text from the very beginning a deep sense of disunity. The historical reasons for this contrast are well known: The Night scene was written some time before 1775 while the Prologue in Heaven was written a full quarter of a century later. Within those years, Goethe himself changed, and it is possible that the perspective of the Lord in the Prologue reflects those changes; it may be that Goethe's original intention was to condemn his Faust (the *Urfaust* shows us a Margarete who was likewise unredeemed, for the "saved" spoken by the offstage voice was added much later), but by 1800 the poet's judgment of his character had changed, or at least become considerably more complex, to the degree that he was able to create the Prologue which offers a theoretical salvation to the man. Yet, even if this addition to the Faust drama was a genuine attempt to create a perspective of (belated) Enlightenment optimism from which to view the character of Faust, the result is certainly ambiguous: the Sturm und Drang Faust remains intact as he was for the *Urfaust* text, which was incorporated largely unchanged into the later *Faust*. It could even be argued that the one-dimensional and parodistic Lord who assures us of the ultimate salvation of Faust is so unconvincing as to be a bitter hope which can only intensify rather than ameliorate the situation of Faust. To the passion of a Faust lashing out against his search for knowledge and the academic prison which surrounds him is added the irony of a shallow god dwelling inaccessibly above Faust's personal turmoils in serene indifference. The very lack of depth in this Lord throws into ever sharper relief the profundity of Faust's tragedy, for if this is the Lord of salvation, who could communicate with him? In view of the contrast between these two early scenes, it is possible to read Goethe's attempts to soften the conditions of his Sturm and Drang Faust by the addition of this Prologue as a misfire in which the intended effect is subverted and the opposite actually achieved, but I for one do not believe Goethe would have been unaware of the irony created by the juxtaposition of these two scenes. Rather, I believe that he knew the best way to intensify our sense of Faust's existential isolation was to frame the miseries of the human being with a bland promise of eventual redemption revealed in words that bear a strong resemblance to another literary text (*Canut*) where the same offer of redemption is rejected. We will see that in the Easter promenade (Before the Town-Gate), our sense of Faust's isolation is actually intensified by the presence of the one-dimensional characters who surround him. Perhaps something like that effect is achieved here in the unreconciled juxtaposition of the temporal and the "eternal."

The world we see Faust inhabiting is certainly not one in which man is aware of his own salvation, but is rather one in which an indifferent nature or an indifferent god remains deaf to the immediate concerns of man. Goethe delineated a similar view of the world in Werther's letter of August 18 in which he describes nature as a "wiederkäuendes Ungeheuer"[9] ("a regurgitating monster"), and in a poem written probably in 1783 ("The Divine"), Goethe once again gave expression to this negative sense of nature which always stood just on the periphery of his more positive moments:

> For nature
> Is unfeeling;

The sun shines
Both on good and bad,
Moon and stars
Shimmer for the criminal
As well as for the best.[10]

This is also the world of Faust, and it is unrelieved by the later overlay of Olympian optimism. In a recent book on *Faust*, John Gearey has demonstrated that "of all the characters in the early major works, Faust is most strikingly like Werther."[11] Both are bound within themselves, yet each dreams "himself king of infinite space."[12] For each, the indifference of nature plays an important part in the creation of this self-incarceration.

The imprisonment of Faust has more than theological implications; there is a social dimension to his isolation as well, and this dimension is brought out most fully in the scene "Before the Town-Gate," written, like the Prologue in Heaven, around 1800. Here too the characters surrounding Faust have the one-dimensionality of the Lord and his Archangels; they are merely archetypal representatives in a masque of quotidian life. In this scene, we find Faust surrounded by what seem at first to be the warm everyday people of a small German town on their Easter promenade, but on closer inspection, we find here too the same indifference which characterizes Werther's nature and Faust's Lord. Eudo Mason, in his book on *Faust*, sees the scene as a kind of relief to the scene in Faust's study:

> From the confined atmosphere of the Gothic study in which Faust had appeared always alone or with one sole companion . . . we are here, a welcome contrast and relief, transported into the open air, to the countryside before the walls of Wittenberg. After the introspective broodings of an exceptional individual, isolated by his strange powers, aspirations, visions, and despair, we are given a broad panorama of everyday human life.[13]

It is true that here we are in fact in the open air, a rare atmosphere in *Faust*, but it is difficult to find much relief in the scene. For one thing, the entire scene, from the opening lines to the peasants' song "The Shepherd Dressed up for the Dance," is dominated by the complementary themes of raw sexual attraction and ultimate betrayal:

Servant Girl: No, no; I'm going back to town.
A Second: We're sure to find him by those poplars.

The First: O, that's a great thrill for me;
He'll be by your side,
He'll only dance with you on the floor.
What's your fun to me?
The Second: He's sure not to be alone today,
He said the curly-haired fellow would be with him.
Student: Hell! Look at those girls go!
Come on, brother, let's catch up with them!
A strong beer, tobacco that bites,
A girl all decked out, that's what I like!
A Middle-class Girl: Just look at those cute boys!
It's really a shame—
They could have the best of society,
And yet they run after these servant girls!

(820–35)

The round dance being performed here by this cross section of
society is no pleasant interlude from *Freischütz* or *The Bartered
Bride,* but is a grim chain of pursuit and abandonment aptly summarized by the last stanza of the poem sung in chorus by all the
peasants:

How many a man has not lied
And betrayed his bride!

(974–75)

The depiction of everyday life in this archetypal small German
town is oppressive in unrelieved sexuality (a characteristic which
draws this scene into a possible comparison with the Walpurgisnight's scene later in the drama), and it gives concrete expression to
that sense of nature as an endlessly creating and destroying monster
which Goethe had envisioned so explicitly in *Werther,* again from the
letter of August 18: "it is as though a veil had been torn away from
before my eyes, and the scene of unending life changed before me into
the abyss of an eternally open grave."[14] Just as the beauty of nature
changes for Werther into an arena of violence and destruction where
every step he takes costs hundreds of living creatures their lives, so
here too the conventional surface of lightness and whimsicality falls
away as a mask for something much more sinister. Beneath the simple, ordinary tone of the scene, there is a world of desire, aggression,
infidelity, and indifference, a world of Weislingens and Clavigos.
The chain of attraction and abandonment is given no redeeming

aspect. At first, Faust, like many a reader, is taken in by the apparent fullness and variety of life presented here, and he breathes a sigh of relief—

> Here I am a man, here I may dare to be human
>
> (940)

—but soon he is disillusioned and returns to his old broodings:

> Happy the man who can hope to emerge
> From out of this ocean of folly and error!
>
> (1064–65)

It is no coincidence that Faust's description of the alchemical process by which he created the poisonous medicine which he had hoped would cure his townspeople of the plague is laden with sexual imagery:

> There a red lion, bravely courting,
> Married the Lily in a warm bath,
> Then both above an open flame
> Were tortured from one bridal-chamber to another
>
> (1041–45)

Natural process and social ritual are both characterized in this scene by desire and pain. The result of both, like the result of Faust's scientific experiment that purports to heal, is poison and death. What is prefigured here is precisely the ritual that Faust will reenact with Margarete.

The world depicted in the scene Before the Town-Gate is the world of futility and meaninglessness summarized in another of Goethe's poems written in the early 1780s:

> What divides
> Gods from men?
> That before their eyes
> Pass many waves,
> An ever-rolling stream:
> We are raised by the wave,
> Thrown down by the wave,
> And we drown.[15]

Schopenhauer could hardly have put it more bleakly. Faust realizes he is ill at ease in these "mackerel-crowded seas" and so he walks away from the crowd to gaze on the city from a vantage point high above it, an act which parodies the Epicurean distance of the Lord from his creation. From this point of removal, Faust may momentarily share the divine view of the world as an aesthetic object. Faust is right to leave the crowd behind, for his salvation among these cardboard figures is no less distant a prospect than his salvation through the theatrical heaven portrayed in the Prologue.

Although at first this scene may seem to provide a "contrast and relief" to the preceding scene, on closer reading we find, as Faust finds, that there is none. Only if we read the scene as we might read a "realistic" novel where all characters are assumed to be equally conceived as authentic representations of life can we interpret this scene as portraying a Faust among society. But Goethe does not deal with his readers here as a more conventional author might; he is playing hide-and-seek with his audience, just as he explained to Reinhard, and he does not draw us together with himself into a community of shared moral consensus where we may be confident that the opinions of the creations presented are the author's own. Such a consensus between author and reader would imply an external standard of reference by which actions observed in the text could easily be understood and categorized by both, but it is precisely this sense of security and its requisite external frame of reference which are consistently withheld from us throughout the entire first half of the drama. In this scene, for example, such a consensus is far from obvious: The colorful townspeople are presented singing and enjoying themselves on a bright Easter morning, yet the subject of their concerns and song is not a joyous praise of God's world but an expression of the oppressive cycle of seduction and betrayal which we will later see Faust himself fulfill with Margarete. How are we to interpret this? Is the scene just a representation of *natura naturans,* just nature and a natural society being itself, or is this a representation of the meaningless "regurgitating monster" Werther saw in nature? Furthermore, once we have decided for ourselves how we are to interpret the scene, how then are we to evaluate these nameless types in relationship to Faust? Is he to be interpreted as the "exceptional individual," the one among many, whose extraordinary emotional range we can better appreciate and judge within a context of conventional society? But can we really call these shallow types a true depiction of society? There seems too great a degree of incommensurability between Faust and these flat archetypes for this scene to be interpreted as truly showing us Faust in the context of the real world. This scene, like the Prologue in Heaven, proves far too shallow a creation to counter the power and solipsism already revealed by the Sturm und Drang Faust. Instead of providing us with an external Archimedean point of view from which we as readers could judge Faust, these scenes do the very opposite; they intensify the feeling that Faust is the only real character we have. And, since we lack a genuine sense of otherness apart from Faust, we are thrown together with him into his world of entrapment.

If Faust's incarceration is thus thrown into sharper contours by the superficiality of the theological context and the social milieu which are delineated at the periphery of his existence, it is intensified even more by the parodistic nature of Faust's closer companions, Wagner and Mephistopheles. Like his mentor Faust, Wagner aspires to be a Renaissance man of learning, and, in his baldly acknowledged greed for knowledge, he is a pale parody of his teacher's aspirations. But where Faust is a true scholar, Wagner is a mere pedant and as such has few thoughts of his own; instead, he is a series of quotes of others. His "O God! Art is long / And our life is short" (558–59) is a simple translation of Hippocrates' famous phrase, *ars longa vita brevis*, while his pathetic outcry "How difficult are the means to attain / By which we mount unto the sources!" (562–63) is an abstract parody of Faust's far more concrete and passionate question "Where might I seize you, limitless Nature? / Where, you breasts, you source of all life . . . ?" (455–56). By simply mirroring in an unimaginative way the learning which surrounds Faust as his natural element, and by citing back to Faust his own sentiments and words, Wagner's companionship can only reflect and intensify the frustrations of his teacher's sense of self-imprisonment. With Wagner, Faust finds only the same lack of depth that he finds elsewhere; in Wagner he sees himself reflected in a very shallow pool.

Mephistopheles is a much more complex character, but he too is in many ways a parody of Faust. Like Faust, he appears to us first in the guise of a man of learning—"dressed as a travelling scholar"[16]— and in this parodistic reflection he literally fulfills the wish expressed by Faust for a magic cloak with which to travel to foreign lands (1122–23). When Mephistopheles proposes to conduct Faust to Auerbach's cellar in Leipzig, we learn that he in fact does possess the magic cloak dreamt of by Faust, although Auerbach's cellar proves to be anything but a foreign land. The illusory spell Mephistopheles casts on Brander and his drinking buddies in the cellar, convincing them that they are in a land of plenitude and beauty, is only a parody of the method Mephistopheles has of fulfilling Faust's desires. In Mephistopheles, Faust sees his most inward desires reflected and parodied. His new companion is indeed a traveller, as Faust would like to be, but the tone of black humor which surrounds Mephistopheles prompts the question, just where has this scholar travelled from? And there is some humor in the fact that the cloak longed for by Faust only takes him as far as Auerbach's cellar, a chamber even more confining than the study he is so eager to leave behind.

The notion of casting Mephistopheles as a traveling scholar probably came from an account of the historical Faust which Goethe read while stopping in Nürnberg on his return from Rome in 1788: *ex illa schola (Druidica) prodierunt, quos vulgo Scholasticos vagantes nominabant, inter quos Faustus quidam, non ita pridem mortuus, mire celebratur* ("they came out of that Druidical school which the crowd calls the wandering scholars, among them was a certain Faustus, now recently dead, whom they were wild about").[17] Goethe jotted this description of Faust in a notebook which otherwise contained the most disparate of observations from his Italian journey. Eventually, it was Mephistopheles, not Faust, who would emerge as the traveling scholar. That in creating Mephistopheles Goethe gave him the outward appearance of the historical Faust points to the original parodistic function Mephistopheles was intended to play. And, since Faust is parodied in Wagner, so Mephistopheles will also parody Wagner. Mephistopheles' self-depiction, "I'm not all-knowing, but I do know a good deal" (1582), is a reflection of Wagner's "I know a great deal, but I want to know everything" (601). If poor Wagner were present, he would hear his quote from Hippocrates quoted in turn by Mephistopheles: "Time is short, but art is long" (1787). Of course, Wagner is not present to see himself parodied, and it is interesting in that regard to note that in *Faust I* Mephistopheles and Wagner never appear in the text simultaneously; perhaps this is because they fulfill similar parodistic functions. Between the two of them, they provide an ever-present house of distorting mirrors for Faust where parody and the parody of parody (Mephistopheles quoting Wagner quoting Hippocrates) surround the doctor with endless fragmented images of himself. Neither can offer Faust a genuine way out of his imprisonment, either through companionship or true intellectual exchange; on the contrary, each seems to be merely a partial projection of Faust's own self (or aspects of Faust's ego) rather than achieve a genuine independence of character. Yet, despite the self-reflection they present to Faust, and despite the fact that through them Faust is constantly thrown back upon himself, neither can give him a clue to the nature of his own identity. Neither can bring Faust closer to the center (if there is one) of his being. They stand at the periphery of Faust's existence in the same way Faust stands at the periphery of Western culture.

In assessing the parodistic function of Mephistopheles, we must recognize that he is also a parody of the earlier Satans of the Faust legend as well. It is important to recall that Goethe's Mephistopheles is not himself the Devil with whom earlier Fausts have made their pacts; he is not the embodiment of sheer evil, nor does he have any very great powers, demonic or otherwise. There has been a drastic reduction of power since the Mephistopheles of Marlowe. It is, after all, to Mephistopheles, the second-rate citizen of Hell, that the Lord refers when he says, "Of all the spirits who deny, / The Joker is the least troublesome to me" (338–39). And Mephistopheles characterizes himself as "not one of the great" (1641) when he offers his services to Faust. We have seen Faust depicted on the border of a once united and unified culture which he himself destroys when he shatters the "holy Original" text, which had provided the basis for the culture, into the multitude of possible translations. This same process of decentralization in the sphere of evil must have also taken place before we see the emergence of Mephistopheles. The spirit of evil we encounter in him is only a fragment of a once powerful antipode to goodness. In the Witch's Kitchen when the witch attempts to address Mephistopheles as "Junker Satan," Mephistopheles is adamant that the name no longer applies—"that name, woman, is forbidden to you" (2505). In other words, Mephistopheles knows he has undergone a severe reduction in stature from the greatness of his older relatives in Marlowe and the *Faustbuch,* and Goethe is at pains to insure that this diminution is not lost on his readers. There are perhaps several reasons that this change in the traditional material had to be made. To begin with, there are the reasons of parody. To cast Mephistopheles as a reflective parody of Faust intensifies the tragedy of Faust which is his self-entrapment. That entrapment may be translated as the lack of an Archimedean point from which Faust might view and judge his own existence. Goethe denies that point of reference to Faust just as he denies it to us. Satan, the absolute embodiment of evil, whose powers were great enough to represent a serious temptation to Christ, whose realms are vast, and who in literary form is the most compelling character in Milton's influential epic, would naturally have provided just such an external point of reference by his unqualified nature. Confronted with absolute evil, we could anticipate an absolute good, but such a simple polarity is not given to us. Goethe's Mephistopheles is assigned a position far too low on the register of devils to lend to the drama the security of any external anchorage through metaphysical polarization. While Marlowe's Faustus pledges his soul to absolute evil in exchange for a specified length of intense life, Goethe's Faust makes an ambiguous pact with a creature of limited powers who looks disturbingly like Faust himself. There is more than a hint that, far from being the embodiment of anything absolute, Mephistopheles is Faust's *personal* devil:

> I am *your* companion,
> And if I suit *you*,
> I'll be *your* servant, *your* slave!
>
> (1646–48; emphasis added)

Mephistopheles is as far from his own "original," Satan, as Faust's translation is from the original Bible. Mephistopheles will quote his "original" to the young scholar—*eritis sicut deus scientes bonum et malum*—but where Satan's temptation of Eve would result in a complete change in the order of the universe with the fall of man from grace and innocence, the student on whom Mephistopheles perpetrates his act of temptation is already a fallen cherub whose innocence is from the very outset dubious. To tempt Eve, God's own innocent creature, was an act of tremendous power and daring; Mephistopheles' pale reflection of that primordial act of evil is but to confirm what is already a foregone conclusion—the young scholar is a lost soul. Mephistopheles, like Faust, suffers the impotence of distance, and so instead of giving Faust greater insight and power, he can only throw Faust even more in upon himself.

Nowhere is Mephistopheles a greater parody of Faust than in the scene with the student where he actually assumes the role of the learned doctor and is accepted as such. When the young student inquires of the scholar he assumes to be Faust how best to use his time, Mephistopheles replies with a catalogue of the four faculties, and we remember that the first thing we have heard from Faust's own lips was just such a disparaging catalogue of the four faculties that *he* has studied. Mephistopheles' monologue is thus a parodistic variation and expansion of the monologue with which Faust opened the drama.

The scene with the student goes even further in elaborating the self-reflective prison created for Faust, for not only does Mephistopheles act as a surrogate for Faust himself, but the student too is in his own way a parody of Faust. The young student's expression of his own academic desires—

> I'd like to become truly learned,
> And like to grasp what's on earth
> And in the heavens,
> The natural sciences and nature itself
>
> (1898–1901)

—is a parody of those same lines of Faust (455–59) which have already been parodied by Wagner. Moreover, the student shares with Faust the distaste for the confining walls of the Gothic study:

> To tell the truth, I'd like to leave:
> I'm not at all comfortable
> In these walls and corridors.
> It's a downright confining space.
>
> (1881–84)

Superficially, the scene is one of the most comic in all of Goethe, but there is another aspect to it which makes it one of the most chilling as well. This scene, more than any other in the drama, is constructed to dissect the character of Faust into various and opposing segments, each represented through parody by one of the two characters on stage. This dissolution of the unity of character into conflicting components which may even deceive one another (as Mephistopheles deceives the student) brings into question the fictions of personality essential to the maintenance of the realistic drama. If Faust is incarcerated in the self, and if that self is at the same time capable of dissolution, the situation is tragic indeed. But it is precisely this tragic situation which Goethe intends with his Faust, and this intent may be substantiated by a comparison with an earlier version of the scene. In the case of both passages cited, there is a considerable variation from the corresponding passages in the Urfaust text, each indicating that as Goethe reworked the scene his purpose was no longer simply to parody the quest for knowledge in itself as embodied in the overzealous but lazy student, but also to parody in the most merciless fashion Faust himself. In general, a comparison of the Urfaust with the final text of 1808 reveals the evolution of Goethe's increasing preoccupation with the theme of Faust's self-incarceration through parody and self-reflection.

From the very first segments of the *Urfaust*, however, there is ample material to convince us that Goethe's plan to incarcerate Faust in a prison of self-reflexiveness was present there too, if only in a less elaborated and systematic form. There exists already in the *Urfaust* all the symbolic material whose subsequent ramifications would only make more manifest with far wider-reaching implications this obsession with incarceration. Again, we may look to the setting of the Night scene itself to provide a primary symbolic representation of Faust's miserable state. Where once there was one original text, the Bible, there is now an ocean of texts and interpretations; we see Faust himself contribute to the proliferation through his highly eccentric translation of the original text. Such a translation as Faust's will of course demand further commentary and interpretation, and in no time there will be another sea of books and papers such as that already represented by the collection in his study. Faust in this early setting is literally buried in texts; his opening monologue returns again and again to the theme of encirclement by books:

> Confined by this pile of books,
> Gnawed by worms, covered by dust,
> Which, reaching right up to the high vault
> Where smoke-stained paper clings.
>
> (402–5)

And, by a cruel irony, in his attempt to flee this bibliomaniacal imprisonment he actually turns to yet another book:

> And this book, filled with secrets,
> From Nostradamus' own hand—
> Is not this sufficient for you?
>
> (419–21)

But this book, and all Faust's magic as well, does little to bring him out of his entrapment. In fact, magic actually effects the opposite result: all the feats of magic or alchemy performed, observed, or recounted by Faust, serve only to cast the doctor back into himself all the more. His own invocation of the Earth Spirit ends with a disappointed Faust hearing that he can comprehend only his own projection. Later, when he recounts how his father, like his son an adept at alchemy, attempted to connect himself with the outer world through a benign act of wizardry, we find that he succeeded only in annihilating the very people he had hoped to save (1034–55), thereby intensifying his own isolation and bequeathing to his son a sense of failure and guilt. Perhaps Faust's greatest feat of magic which we observe is the invocation of Mephistopheles, and, as we have seen, this spirit is far too much a parody of Faust himself to be any great asset to him in his attempt to flee "out into the far-flung lands."

Faust's acts of magic in Part Two of the drama hardly get him any further. In his attempt to create wealth for the Emperor (wherein he re-enacts the archetypal role of alchemist), Faust actually creates only paper money, and in doing so proves himself not only a financial fraud, but also once again merely encircles himself with the curse of printed paper. Printed paper bears the same relationship to gold that the books in Faust's study bear to the primal text, the "holy Original." Moreover, in the act of creating paper money, Faust is once again a translator, and once again in this role, rather than bringing himself closer to the source of value or meaning, he actually manages to make more manifest the vast distance between himself and the original. (It should be noted that, while it is undoubtedly the Renaissance alchemist who provides the literary archetype in whose mold Faust is cast, Faust himself is in truth an alchemist in reverse. The goal of the true alchemist is to create gold from substances of less value; by creating paper money, Faust does just the opposite. An alchemist, judged from the viewpoint of modern science, may seem a charlatan, and when we realize that Faust is a fraudulent alchemist, we once again have the uneasy feeling of being in a hall of distorting mirrors. Furthermore, when we add to this the fact that the gold which Faust is translating into paper money is itself as yet unmined and may in fact be purely imaginary, we add yet another dimension to the fraudulence of Faust's undertaking and yet another degree of distance between Faust and the original source of value.) In each act of translation, Faust subverts the original, and the result of this betrayal is in each case greater remoteness from the center.

To continue the line of self-incarceration further, we may suggest that insofar as Mephistopheles is the product of Faust's invocation, he too is Faust's own creation and is in many respects only another projection of Faust himself. Faust at first hopes that Mephistopheles will prove to be a force which could teach him what "life truly is" and what it means to be "unrestrained and free" (1542–43), but his new mentor cannot succeed in bringing Faust out of his prison at all. His first attempt, the journey to Auerbach's cellar, is a complete fiasco, ludicrous in fact because the means and place of escape are so incommensurate with the desires for escape expressed by Faust. It is as though someone with a strong longing for exotic, tropical lands were handed a trip to a circus sideshow as satisfaction for the desire. For Faust, the urge to flee is so strong that death at times becomes a possible means of escape to his mind, and he expresses this wish for flight through death in the most high-flown poetical language:

> O blessed is he, whose temples are wreathed
> By death with the bloody and glorious laurels of victory,
> He whom Death finds, after a madly wild dance
> In the arms of a girl!
>
> (1573–76)

Every description Faust gives of possible flight is figured in similar, highly metaphorical language, and a great deal of Faust's dialogue in the second Study scene is composed of just such highly wrought, death-intoxicated depiction of flight from the self. After such poignant and eloquent sentiments, Mephistopheles' choice of Auerbach's cellar as a fit initiation for Faust's life beyond the study is truly farcical. Not only is the cellar simply another place of confinement, hardly the "far-flung lands" Faust has envisioned, but in place of Faust's dreams of a perfect death in the arms of a lovely girl, he is given instead a fraternity brawl where women are just the source of crude humor. The cellar scene as it stands—in which Faust speaks only two lines—could be read as a demonstration of the extreme difference between Mephistopheles and Faust. We can imagine Faust merely standing to one side watching with contempt the low antics of his "mentor." Yet, if we compare the scene to its original version in the *Urfaust*, we find that it is Faust who performs the acts of magic which in the later version are assigned to Mephistopheles. In other words, Mephistopheles becomes here again what he was in the previous scene, a surrogate for Faust, and magic here, which for Faust is otherwise a serious pursuit, becomes simply a low parody in the mimicry of Mephistopheles. Faust is still surrounded by distorted reflections of himself; the incarceration here is no less than it was in his study. Eudo Mason suggests that Faust is "bored by the whole proceedings and might just as well not be there at all,"[18] an interpretation of Faust possible only if we ignore the *Urfaust* text. In the later version, Mephistopheles is only a surrogate Faust doing what Faust was intended to do. Faust's silence could be interpreted as horror at seeing the reality of the self in contrast to the hopes and fantasies the self can produce. Faust's last line is spoken not so much out of boredom as of weary desperation, and Faust has every reason at this moment to despair; the companion who has promised to give him a new lease on life—"I congratulate you on a new course of life" (2072)—and to bring him "out of isolation" (1632) has simply placed him in a situation where his isolation is even more painfully apparent.

In the following scene, the Witch's Kitchen, Faust again has at least as much cause for despair, for here too he finds himself incarcerated; the cellar has been exchanged only for the smokey den of a witch. Stuart Atkins points out the similarities between the two scenes:

> Witch's Kitchen is the supernatural companion piece of the stylized naturalism of Auerbach's Cellar, many of whose motifs it elaborates satirically. Of these, the most important is the motif of erotic desire.[17]

But the scene contains analogies with more than just the scene previous; the Witch's Kitchen with its "walls and ceiling covered with the most fantastic of witch's apparatus" bears striking similarities to Faust's own study as Faust has described it:

> Surrounded by glass and containers,
> With instruments crammed in everywhere,
> Inherited clutter of centuries past—
> That's your world! That you call a world!
>
> (406–9)

Where in Faust's study, the clear light from outside is prevented from entering by the colored glass of the windows, here it is smoke and steam that make the atmosphere murky. And here too Faust finds the alchemistic magic, which he had hoped could bring him out of confinement into the "far-flung lands," hopelessly parodied by a pair of apes skimming a witch's brew in the archetypal cauldron.

The close relationship of the characters in the scene has been well described by Atkins when he says of Faust's speech (2429–40):

> Faust's innate nobility is emphasized by the fact that this section of the scene is a playlet with parallel actions. One culminates on the imaginative plane to which Faust has been trans-

ported; the other reaches its simultaneous climax as the Apes break the crown of misgovernment and folly. . . . And when the Apes proclaim the triumph of the uncreating word . . . Faust, still engrossed in the mirror, cries, "Alas, to madness I'm transported!"[20]

Not Faust alone, but everyone in the scene shares in the peculiar madness inherent to the place, and I am not convinced that the general theme of madness functions here primarily to set off Faust's "innate nobility." To Faust's "Alas, to madness I'm transported," Mephistopheles answers, "Now even *my* head is beginning to swim" (2456–57), and the witch echoes, "I practically lose all reason / When I see Lord Satan here again" (2503–4). All the characters in the scene are drawn into the frenzied excitement that is the atmosphere of the den. Note the meaninglessness of the witch's magic multiplication table:

> Pay attention!
> From one get ten,
> Drop the two, then three,
> Now make it even, and see,
> You'll be rich . . .
> That's the witch's one-two-three.
>
> (2540–52)

This is a repetition of the kind of hocus-pocus practised by Mephistopheles when he tells Faust that spirits like himself must leave by the same place they entered (1410–11), or when he makes Faust repeat three times his invitation to enter: "You have to say it three times" (1531). The setting of the scene, the parody, the repetition of parallel actions, and the meaninglessness of the magic all show Faust to be as imprisoned as ever in distorted reflections of himself. Whether or not Faust displays "innate nobility" in this scene seems less important than the fact that he is becoming increasingly desperate to escape as scene accumulates upon scene to bring the inescapable message home to him that Mephistopheles is not going to prove an effective means to flight. That this imprisonment is more precisely an entrapment within the self is given unmistakable graphic representation by the fact that throughout the first part of the scene Faust has been staring into a mirror. Although the mirror eventually reveals to him a vision of beauty which has the power to transport Faust out of himself—"Lead me into her fields" (2432), he says in

variation of the "far-flung lands" motif of the opening monologue—
the fact still remains that it is a mirror, the most obvious of all
symbols of self-reflection, into which he has been staring.

As a corollary to the triviality of the witch's hocus-pocus, which
only reveals her own distance from a true adept of black magic,
Mephistopheles once more emphasizes his own distance from the
original source of evil. When the witch asks why he objects to being
called Satan he answers,

> For a long time, he's only been creature of fable;
> But men are no better off for it—
> Free of the Evil One, evil ones remain.
>
> (2507–9)

An earlier unified and absolute sense of evil has been reduced to the
triviality of the witch and Mephistopheles by refraction from the
original into the many and the derivative. By dissecting original evil
(Satan) into many fragments (*"die* Bösen"), Goethe has shown the
destruction of its unity, and thereby removed from the drama the
Archimedean point of view which such a sense of any absolute
might have established outside the work, or outside Faust. As it is,
we are in no better position to judge Faust than Faust himself, and
just as Faust expresses complete indifference to the question of an
"afterlife"—"I care little for what's on the other side" (1660)—so we
too are hardly invited by the text to a concern with these issues.
Heinz Politzer, writing of the last scenes of *Faust II*, describes the
unchanging indifference which is an important aspect of Faust's
character:

> In directing his eyes from what is nearest at hand to what is
> furthest from him, Faust remains to the end his old restless
> self. His deepest guilt is also his most profound victory; his
> last triumph over reality is at the same time his greatest hu-
> man disgrace. Faust is always capable of redemption and
> never capable of redemption.[21]

The resistance of Faust to change certainly does call into question
any possibility of salvation, and it confirms the unreality of the
supernatural forces as they are construed in the play. If Politzer is
correct in judging Faust's salvation to be a matter of literary indifference, then what is left is precisely the permanence of character and
the hopelessness of Faust's self-imprisonment. Certainly through-

out the Witch's Kitchen scene Faust does remain the same, and in this regard it is interesting to remember that, although the witch's brew is intended to rejuvenate him as well as to make him see a Helen in every woman, in fact the text does not present us with a visibly younger Faust; rather, the very sameness of Faust is emphasized by the similarities between the ending of this scene and that of Auerbach's Cellar. Atkins points these out:

> Faust's ordeal ends with two motifs from Aucrbach's Cellar: student drinking ritual—"a man of many degrees is no novice in drinking rites"—and flame from liquid . . .[22]

Similarly, the inanity of the students' games is here replaced by the circle of the witch's hocus-pocus. Faust and Mephistopheles both express their doubts that the magic the witch performs is anything but silliness. Rather, both seem to accept the hocus-pocus as perfunctory to the role they play; the legend says that Faust is to be rejuvenated, and so Goethe's Faust and Mephistopheles go through with this ritual although they show every sign of incredulousness. Faust asks, "What is this nonsense she is saying?" (2573), and Mephistopheles is anxious to have the rite over with: "Enough, enough! most excellent sibyl! / Let's have your drink . . ." (2577–78). The rite is performed because it is required by the literary background of the legend, but Faust feels uneasy and says he hears a chorus of a hundred thousand fools. As far as we can *see*, the rite is merely perfunctory pedantry; there is no evidence in the text that any transformation has been accomplished. We simply see Faust step out of the circle and move on to fall in love with Margarete, a girl who bears the same relationship to her "original," Helen of Troy, that Mephistopheles bears to his "original," Satan. There is little reason to believe that anything more than a strong aphrodisiac has been administered to Faust.

To speak of Faust's unchanging nature is but another way of speaking of his entrapment in the self. The greatest opportunity for transcending the self will be offered to him in the second half of the drama through love of another person, but Faust will fail to achieve that love and will remain what he has been all along—a personality at war with itself within the inescapable boundaries of its own existence. Before turning to a discussion of the Margarete episodes, it would be helpful to explore some of the implications of this world which holds Faust chained to his old self, since this is essentially the same world which will serve as background for Goethe's classical works as well.

To begin with, it is a world where God has withdrawn to inaccessible heights and has forgotten how to laugh. Mephistopheles' observation that God has become humorless is evocative, for it implies that a great distance has evolved between God and his fallible world. In his removal from the world of men, God has become an irrelevant pomposity as untouched by the prayers of mankind as he is by their emotions and despairs. The Lord in *Faust* resembles the Zeus of Goethe's "Prometheus," a god to whom childlike souls could once pray, but who now, to a world grown wiser, has become an enigmatic memory which it seems better simply to ignore. Concomitant with this elevation of God to impossible heights is the refraction of evil into countless lesser forms. Mephistopheles is one of these many forms and the text of the drama strongly suggests that he is the *personal* devil of Faust, a private evil whose powers are so constituted as to conform to Faust's own contours as a personality. It is Mephistopheles' function to torment Faust with the hope that the self can be transcended and at the same time to be the very force that frustrates that hope; Mephistopheles' capacity for evil is restricted to this very specific role. Faust's tragedy is one truly beyond good and evil, for in the world he inhabits, both moral poles have been rendered irrelevant—good through exaggerated elevation, evil through ridiculous reduction. In the world as we see it in *Faust*, it is just possible that good and evil do still exist, but Faust's existence is so played out at the periphery of these moral certitudes that in effect they might as well not be there at all.

The metaphysical world of *Faust* is one with which few critics or readers have been comfortable. A world in which "every living-thing creates the norms by which it is to be judged"[23] is not easy to accept, nor is it inhabitable by real human beings. But this is the world we have in *Faust*; he cannot be judged by any criteria outside the self, and this world makes the question of his salvation something of a red herring. According to what external point of reference is Faust to be saved or damned? The text of *Faust* has worked to reveal external standards as obsolete or irrelevant. This is why a critic like Gundolf could find the final scene of *Faust Two*, which depicts Faust's salvation through the "Eternal Feminine," so deplorable:

> That Faust's salvation is achieved through the Eternal Feminine, the all-encompassing Love, is grounded neither in the plot of *Faust* nor in the problem of Faust. It contradicts the

attitudes and mentality of the Titanic and Promethean man; it is not a resolution inherent in Faust's strivings and transformations. In fact, it deviates from the point of the Prologue in Heaven. One would have expected that God the father, the creator of the world and its judge, would have been the one to pronounce judgment on Faust's creative soul. The Eternal Feminine, although it might have played a great role in Goethe's own life and thought, emerges in *Faust* more or less as a *dea ex machina*.[24]

Like most critics, Gundolf wishes to see Faust's salvation confirmed by some principle external to Faust; he would even like to have seen the Lord come on stage once more, but of course this is exactly what does *not* happen. The Lord has made his appearance, already a literary parody, only once and that primarily to underscore his absence from the rest of the drama. Faust's salvation through the Eternal Feminine is, as Gundolf sees, not prepared for in the text and is inconsistent within the context of the play. But perhaps those are the very reasons Goethe chose to have Faust saved in this way. Because there is no resolution to Faust's tragedy in itself, a patently artificial and unsatisfactory resolution is stuck onto the end of the play, announcing by its very artificiality (and the final scene of Part Two is nothing if it is not self-conscious art imitating art) that it is inappropriate to the purpose it plays. All this points with greater emphasis to the irresolvable nature of Faust's tragic destiny.

There is a further dimension to Faust's tragic situation which argues for its irresolvable nature, and this is its historical dimension. In the few passages we have discussed where a past spiritual condition has been alluded to, it seems that the text posits a prior time in which Satan had not yet been consigned to the book of fable and where God still knew how to laugh. We may assume that this was a time of orthodox belief, a time when credible external standards, represented by a God intimately involved in the affairs of the world which he had created, ruled the human mind. As we will see, Margarete still lives in that more archaic world. But Faust does not; in fact, the modern world which he inhabits may be viewed from one perspective as Faust's own creation. When Faust sits down to his task of translating the Bible, he begins to look like the literary surrogate for Martin Luther. Luther's own translation of the Bible may serve as a symbolic point in Western history, the point at which interpretation becomes the supreme mode of understanding. With Faust/Luther's translation of the "holy Original" out of its original form, the unity and domination of the medieval worldview was shattered into a multitude of refractions. As Goethe wrote in his early essay on religion, "Letter of the Pastor at ***":

> Luther worked to free us from intellectual slavery; may all his descendents keep as much disdain for the hierarchy as the great man himself felt. . . . He gave the heart its freedom back and made it more capable of love. . . . Luther made enthusiasm into emotion.[25]

In this early characterization, Luther looks very much like the founder of the German Sturm und Drang, the first man of "Empfindsamkeit" ("sentiment"), and a Promethean of intellectual freedom.

This continued to be Goethe's assessment of Luther throughout his life. In one of the poetic aphorisms of his old age he wrote again of the liberation Luther had brought to medieval servitude:

> They merely lay in half slumber
> Until Luther translated the Bible so well. . . .
> Freedom waked in every heart
> And we all gladly became Protestants.[26]

Faust, as he reenacts the historical role of Luther, represents the emerging human type whose newly won intellectual freedom brings with it the anxieties of a decentered universe. Just as Bruder Martin represents the coming order in Goethe's first play, *Götz von Berlichingen* (and is another literary representative of Luther), so too Faust represents the new man which is emerging into history. Against these new historical forces, the representatives of the past order—Götz and Margarete—have no chance of survival. The world characterized by Faust is aptly summed up by Goethe in a later essay, "Eras of the Intellect," where he describes the modern age:

> Instead of teaching with understanding and working calmly in the world, one throws indiscriminately seeds and weeds at the same time in all directions; there is no longer any center which can be looked up to. Every individual presents himself as a teacher and leader. . . . And so the value of every mysterium is destroyed; even the belief of the common people is desecrated. Qualities, which once developed naturally out of one another, now work against one another like conflicting elements, and so we have . . . a world in confusion which is

headed for destruction and extinction, from which the spirit of God himself could hardly rebuild a world worthy of him.[27]

This is the dark side of the brave new world for which Luther stands as a symbolic beginning, and it is a historical perspective internalized by the character of Faust. Once the door has been opened, every man becomes an interpreter and the world is forced to move from a logocentrality to an egocentrality.

Faust's symbolic position as initiator of the new age and destroyer of the old is emphasized by the chorus of unseen spirits who sing to Faust of his deed:

> Woe, woe!
> You have destroyed
> The splendid world
> With a mighty fist.
> It shatters and falls!
>
> (1607–11)

These spirits do more than simply register the fact of this destruction; they also propose a remedy to the world which has fallen into pieces through Faust:

> Build it again,
> Build it more magnificent,
> Build it within your heart!
>
> (1619–21)

Where these spirits come from is not clear. Mephistopheles claims them for his own—"They are the little ones of mine" (1627–28). Reinhard Buchwald finds this assertion of appropriation untenable and compares them rather to the spirits who appear to Faust on the Easter Vigil when he almost takes his own life. For that reason, Buchwald sees them not as belonging to Mephistopheles, but as "good spirits."[27] But can the message to rebuild a shattered world within the self be construed as a truly good message? Especially when the message is delivered to a man whose tragedy is already the inability to escape the self? Buchwald is surely correct in seeing these spirits as related to those who saved Faust from suicide on Easter night, for here too they pull Faust back from a similar sense of despair. Yet the suicide Faust seeks that night would have been a flight from the self, and it is precisely that escape which it is the intent of both groups of spirits to prevent; in each case, Faust is brought back in upon himself and to an inner self. Here in the later scene, Faust is told to rebuild the shattered world inwardly (hardly the message a man trapped in himself longs to hear), just as on that earlier night the spirits recalled Faust to himself through personal memory of his own past. In that earlier scene, it was definitely not religious belief (which we might expect to be especially strong on Easter morning) that called Faust back from the deadly "brown juice," but rather the memory of how once before

> . . .with a thousand burning tears
> I felt a new world rise up *for me*. . . .
> Memory afresh with childlike emotion
> Keeps me from this last decisive step.
>
> (777–82; emphasis added)

Such a religious belief as one might expect in this situation would posit an "other" outside the self, but the choir of angels does not direct Faust to anything like this "other" but recalls him again to himself, just as the spirits in the later scene recall Faust to his self-regenerative capacity. Can we apply any moral categories to such an injunction to self-absorption? Such an injunction could not be the Lord's exhortation, but on the other hand, Mephistopheles shows that he completely misunderstands the message of these spirits when he says

> Out into the wide world,
> Out of your isolation . . .
> This is where they want to lure you.
>
> (1631–34)

This is not at all what the spirits have advised. Mephistopheles here reveals himself as capable as Faust of untrustworthy translation. It seems the spirits belong to neither world. Perhaps it is not unfair to say simply that these are the spirits of the age who reflect the contemporary metaphysical concern with the self and its projections. The remedies that flow from these spirits—healing through memory of the past and through self-creation—are neither good nor bad, but are simply the answers Faust, as representative of the new world, would give himself; the answers characterize Faust's greatness as well as his tragedy. The effect of both choruses is the same: Faust stays securely within himself.

In the second half of *Faust*, Part One, we leave the dark and self-reflective world of Faust's self-incarceration to enter a more conventional world as Goethe pits a figure familiar from an entire corpus of literature against a person who not only seems to be real flesh and blood, but whose very destiny Goethe was able to model on that of a real woman, known to him, in all likelihood, through his activity in the law courts. The destinies of Doctor Faustus and of a young girl accused of infanticide seem as remote to one another as those of Hamlet and Patty Hearst, but it was just this jarring juxtaposition Goethe was after. The results of his unlikely match form the content of the Gretchen episodes.

2
Margarete: The Dangers of Literary Transformation

What in Poetry may find its life, In life, must die.
—Schiller, "The Gods of Greece"

WITH the introduction of the character of Margarete into the drama of Faust, the so-called "scholar's tragedy" comes to an end, but the problems raised by the first half of the play have not been resolved. The scholar's tragedy is one of solipsism and parody; that must naturally end as a second real person enters the stage, but the elements of Faust's tragedy are only left in suspension as the opportunity is offered to Faust to escape the self-entrapment which has characterized his dramatic existence to this point. Unlike Mephistopheles or Wagner, Margarete is more than a mere reflection or parody of Faust, and her character is not confined to the one-dimensionality of the townspeople of the earlier scene "Before the Town-Gate." She is a genuine character outside the context of Faust's study, and she brings with her onto the stage an entire world, the natural realism of which makes the earlier scenes appear as a kind of science fiction. The shift in dramatic modes between the two halves of the play is as striking as the difference between the philosophies of realism and nominalism, and this shift is a dramatic necessity because the two dramatic parts are intended to contrast in every possible way with each other. Eudo Mason describes the shift:

> The technique of stylization, fragmentariness, incoherency, omissions, laconic hints, and eloquent silences, by which Goethe strove to assimilate the Gretchen theme to the world of

Faust and to prevent Gretchen from imperilling the ideal
unity of the mystery play, proved unavailing. Once Gretchen
appears, and whenever she appears, she concentrates all the
limelight upon herself and Faust loses in stature. She brings
her own world with her, and the kind of interest that belongs
to that world.[1]

Mason believes that Goethe's attempts to assimilate the Margarete
scenes to the rest of *Faust I* are a failure because Margarete has too
much of a life of her own. But, it could be argued that the connection
between the two halves of the play is in fact one of the major tri-
umphs of the work. What better way to expand the tragedy of Faust's
incarceration than to have him actually meet a genuinely independent person, one who does not reflect or parody himself, one who is
presented in a completely different dramatic style, and yet with
whom he ultimately fails to connect? And how better could the
tragedy of Faust be intensified than by drawing in another person
whose destruction is directly related to Faust's own self-imprisonment? The "Gretchen tragedy" is in fact the necessary expansion
and culmination of the "scholar's tragedy," and this expansion of
tragedy is possible only because Margarete and the world she brings
with her are in every way a contrast to Faust and his world. We sense
the shift immediately: after a series of scenes set in small, dark
chambers, we are suddenly out in the fresh air of the street.
Margarete literally brings a breath of fresh air into the drama.

There is of course a relatively simple dramatic reason Margarete
takes on a life of her own—she appears in many scenes alone or with
persons other than Faust. Throughout the first half of the drama after
the appearance of Faust on the stage, there is no scene in which he is
not present, if not the major character. As we have seen, in
Auerbach's Cellar, Mephistopheles plays out the role originally assigned to Faust, and in the scene with the student, Faust's personality
is symbolically present in the two parodistic surrogates. Even if we
consider only those short scenes of the Margarete episodes where
Faust or Mephistopheles is totally absent—Gretchen's Room, At the
Town-Well, Zwinger, and Cathedral—there is still enough independent characterization to establish her as a complete person in and for
herself. If Goethe had wished to assimilate the Margarete material to
the first half of the drama, as Mason suggests he wished to, he would
have had only to introduce another genuinely independent character
into the scenes where Faust dominates, thereby vitiating the theme of
Faust's isolation and preparing us for the introduction of yet another

person outside of Faust. But the actual structure of the text persuades us that such assimilation was not at all what Goethe wanted; the text as he let it stand in the edition of 1808 consistently frustrates the expectations of the reader searching for a conventional drama, and the sudden shift from Faust's tragedy to that of Margarete is certainly the greatest, if only one among many such frustrations.

Margarete is indeed a real person within the context of the drama and she brings with her a whole world of petit-bourgeois conventions and fears, all of which introduce into the drama a realistic dimension lacking to this point. Yet, as abrupt a shift in style as her entrance initiates, still her appearance has not been entirely unanticipated. In the scenes which immediately precede her actual appearance in the Street scene, there are a number of allusions and intimations which prepare us for her entrance. In Auerbach's Cellar, the theme of sexuality has been introduced in a very vulgar mode, and Mephistopheles' song about the king who has the great flea anticipates with its similar beginning Margarete's own song about the king of Thule whose most prized possession is something not so insignificant as a flea, but a golden chalice given to him by his one true love. Later, in the Witch's Kitchen, the theme of sexuality which was begun in Auerbach's Cellar takes on greater specificity as Faust stares into the mirror and sees the world's most beautiful woman. The scene ends as Mephistopheles tells him:

> Soon you will see the model before you
> Of all feminine beauty.
> With this drink in your body, you'll see
> In every woman you meet Helen of Troy.
>
> ˮ(2601–4)

After such symbolic preparation, the reality of Margarete comes less as a complete change of direction than as the realization of a promise. The emergence of Margarete from the experiences and visions of Faust is a literary, one might almost say parodistic analogue to the emergence of Eve from the body of Adam. She is entirely different from him, yet there is a visceral link between them which probably accounts for the speed with which the relationship between them is formed. As Heinz Politzer has pointed out, much of the story of Faust and Margarete is a reenactment of the myth of the archetypal parents and their fall;[2] here we have one more analogy to that original text which Faust has attempted to translate. In their reenactment of the world's first couple, Faust and Margarete give validation to Mephistopheles' observation in the Prologue in Heaven that man is still made from the same old mold.

The independent reality of Margarete must be strongly emphasized, for while the first half of the play provides us with the tragedy of a man caught up within himself, the second half is the projection of this solipsistic vortex onto another. The "Gretchen tragedy" is not the tragedy of an innocent love betrayed, but the horror of a systematic contamination and destruction of one person by another. The violence of this section of the drama has often been disregarded by critics who emphasize the spiritual or sentimental nature of Faust's love for the young girl. Stuart Atkins represents this prevalent opinion: ". . . in his love for Margarete, however profane it may be, there is implicit some measure of that sacred love which is the Lord of Prologue in Heaven."[3] Here Atkins imputes the divine love which is the essential nature of the Christian God to Goethe's Lord, but there is little textual evidence to support this supposition. Above all else, the Lord of the Prologue seems a disinterested spectator to the ways of the world. And it cannot be assumed that his love, if it is indeed one of his attributes, extends to man. One thing is certain: The Lord's love, if it exists, is most conspicuous in the Faust drama by its absence. Furthermore, Faust's love for Margarete is not just "profane"; it is also very violent. The aggressiveness of his attraction to her is clear in his commands to Mephistopheles: "Listen, you have to get me that wench" (2619) and "Unless that girl with her sweet young blood / Sleeps in my arms tonight, / We part at midnight" (2636–38). And in the stage direction given to Margarete in her first encounter with Faust there is the suggestion that Faust has accosted her physically as well as verbally. His violence and the aggressive character of his invitation to accompany him at the beginning of the Margarete episode are repeated in the violence of the final scene, as Faust once more attempts to induce Margarete, now completely given over to her own madness, to accompany him out of the prison. Only the superficial courtliness of "May I dare to offer you my arm as escort?" (2605–6) has been transformed into the desperate "Come! Follow me! . . . just follow me; I ask only this!" (4498–4500). The second half of the play thus begins and ends with Faust pleading that Margarete come with him, that is, with Faust's attempt to attach himself to another person. The fact that he fails to make this connection outside of himself places the tragic burden just as heavily on Faust as on Margarete.

Faust's love for Margarete is often interpreted as an extension of his sentimental feelings for nature, as though Margarete were somehow the representative of an unspoiled and uncultivated Rousseau-ean innocence. But she is far from such cultural and moral isolation; she enters the drama and brings with her an entire world made coherent by a complete code of cultural orientation including familial, ecclesiastical, and societal mores. It will become Faust's project systematically and inexorably to estrange Margarete from each of these threads of attachment to the world outside herself, and to leave her in the profoundest form of self-incarceration, madness.

Unlike the characters who appear in the scene Before the Town-Gate, who are little more than conventional social types one might encounter in any such small city, Margarete is *both* a conventional type *and* an independent and integral personality. This is realism in one of its classic definitions: a proper and convincing balance between the particular and the general.[4] When we first see Margarete, this balance is maintained and harmonious; as the play progresses, a wedge is driven between the two sides of the balance so that ultimately the personal will stand in opposition to the transpersonal. And the portrayal of her personality is all the more realistic because as the play progresses we see her actually attempting to reconcile her individual thoughts and acts with the conventional world of culture and custom which surrounds her. This is something we never see Faust do; whenever he comes into contact with culture or tradition outside himself, as in his attempt to translate the Bible, rather than accommodate himself to that external world, he construes or perverts the received tradition to conform to his own preoccupations. The destructive Titanism which characterizes his relationship to the external world will eventually be extended to Margarete, and, despite his sentimental attachment to her, the violence he shows in the relationship and the destruction he eventually brings to her will be as complete as the violence he does to the Bible text which he also claims to love.

Margarete brings into the drama a human world where theological concepts such as sin and redemption make sense, concepts which, Faust claims, have no meaning for him. Because the world she brings with her is a serious one which does not admit a principle of nihilism, Mephistopheles is speaking truthfully when he says, "over her I have no power" (2626). He has no such power because she is a part of a world of substantial and shared beliefs and values. Mephistopheles is only truly in his element when he can reduce the external world to meaninglessness and parody, and for this reason he is the complementary side of Faust's Titanism. Where Faust would build a complete world of his own, Mephistopheles would destroy one. The two work as one, Mephistopheles through parody and Faust through despair, to perpetuate the state of self-imprisonment where no Archimedean point is possible from which to view the self in perspective. Margarete's world is the precise opposite of this; in her world there exists an established point of view from which human acts may be judged and evaluated as good or bad, and when Margarete is brought to the point at which she can no longer reconcile her own actions with the world as she has accepted it, the world falls apart for her, and she is confined in the prison of her own madness.

Margarete's is a world which believes in established ideals, and it is just such an ideal that stands as the foundation of the folk song she sings to herself to quiet her mind as she prepares for bed. It is important that the song, "There was a King of Thule," is a folk song; it is not Margarete's own, but comes to her from a body of generally accepted beliefs and cultural ideals which constitute an important part of her world. The song speaks of fidelity in love, a beautiful ideal and one which is nowhere realized in the drama. The sexual frivolity of the young men and women in the scene Before the Town-Gate is only the lighter side of the pathetic story of Bärbelchen which Margarete hears from Lieschen by the town well (3544–86). And, of course, Margarete herself fares no better with Faust than Bärbelchen with her nameless lover. Nevertheless, however poorly the world may live up to the ideals it establishes for itself, those ideals are always present in the world of Margarete to provide for her and her companions a reference point outside the individual self, and to supply them with a means of judging their own actions.

Since it will be Faust's destiny eventually to sever the filaments which bond Margarete's personality into a unity with itself and with its world, it is important that in Margarete's opening scenes a clear and carefully contoured identity be established for her. Thus it is not by chance that her first words are not merely a surprised response to the unexpected encounter with a nobleman she does not know; in rejecting his offer to accompany her, she states clearly who she is, and so differentiates herself unequivocally from Faust, socially and emotionally. She shows her complete independence, and it is this very attribute which initially attracts Faust:

> She is so modest and virtuous,
> Yet with a little pertness there too . . .
>
> (2611–12)

Her short way of talking
Fills me with ecstasy!

(2617–18)

Margarete's insistence on her own class distinction from Faust (she is perfectly certain that he is a nobleman) presents Faust with his first line of attack. Margarete comes from a tidy, middle-class home, and in the imagination of Faust, she resembles closely Werther's Charlotte, surrounded by children (not her own) in a home well established in the community. Although Margarete refers to herself as poor (2804) and refers to her mother's scrupulous household economy (3083–84), still there are enough resources in the family that Margarete's first thought upon seeing Faust's gift of jewels is that it must be collateral on which her mother has lent money (2786–87). Much more could be said of the details by which Margarete is situated unambiguously in the middle-class setting, but here it is sufficient to observe that her sense of identity is clearly grounded in a solid economic situation. The strong roots of her identity within the structure of a specific community is in sharp contrast to the insubstantial references to Faust's position in the world. In his opening monologue, he describes himself as having neither goods nor money, neither honor nor glory. Yet on the Easter Sunday promenade, he is treated by the townspeople with a great deal of respect, as though he were the visiting local dignitary. We never really know whether he is truly destitute, as he says of himself, or whether he is the local nobleman. There is, however, no question in Margarete's mind but that Faust is of an upper class, no matter how Faust conceives of himself. In brief, the text presents us with a great contrast between the rootless unascertainable relation of Faust to the external world and the concrete and unquestioned integration of Margarete to her surroundings. It will become Faust's project to abolish this contrast and to bring Margarete into his own world of insubstantiality.

Faust's very words to describe Margarete reveal the direction of his project—"mein schönes Fräulein" and "die Dirne." Margarete knows that she is no "Fräulein" ("lady") and she would undoubtedly object as vigorously to being called a "Dirne" ("wench"). By conscious linguistic distortion of Margarete's actual position in society, Faust begins the process of dislodging her from that secure place. Just as Faust's own self-conception vacillates between worm (653) and god (516), he proposes a wide spectrum—whore to noblewoman—within which Margarete's own self-conception may fluctuate. Beyond the obvious differences in social standing, one further dimension of the difference between Faust and Margarete lies in the degree of self-consciousness possessed by each. While Faust's un-yielding self-consciousness leads him to question every aspect of his identity so that the result is a perpetual blurring of the barriers that separate his self from the external world and a constant sense of self-distortion and self-parody, Margarete, when we first see her, shows none of this painful self-scrutiny. Her immediate reply to Faust's offer, "neither a lady nor pretty," leaves no room to doubt her un-questioning acceptance of the role nature and society have given her. The temptation Faust puts before her in the form of the jewels is designed precisely to dislocate her own sense of security and the limits of her identity and to make her want to be more than she is. Ironically, she begins by wanting to be a lady and will end her life seeing herself as a whore.

In order to understand the truly demonic nature of Faust's love for Margarete, we must take at face value Faust's own description of himself:

> I'm not troubled by doubts or scruples,
> Nor afraid of hell or the devil.
>
> (368–69)

Not only must we accept the unscrupulousness of Faust, we must also rid ourselves of the notion that Faust's love for Margarete is only idealized, ennobling, and possessed of transcendental intima-tions.[5] Nor should we oversentimentalize or idealize the personality of Margarete; the fragility of her innocence, the very ease with which she succumbs to Faust's temptation, make dubious any criti-cal exaggeration of her virtuous character. Schöne goes so far as to suggest that in his original concept, Goethe may have conceived of Margarete as a witch. He points out that Margarete commits every one of the seven deadly sins:

> These offenses from the medieval catalogue of vices taken together constitute the doctrinal background of the Gretchen scenes, in the foreground of which we see the death of her mother, her brother, and her child; they show how deeply this girl, tempted and seduced by Mephisto, has fallen to the Evil One. . . . Gretchen a witch? Even more important than the reasons for suspicion, accusation and judgment so far men-tioned, one should remember how much weight was given in

the procedures of the inquisition to the subject of killing children. Already in the trials of heretics, but more emphatically in the persecution of witches, the murder of new-born, unbaptized children was among the most central of accusations and confessions.[6]

Schöne provides the necessary counterbalance to critics who have seen Margarete as a sweet and innocent child, but his Margarete too cannot be the whole character. It is difficult to bring his suggestions into line with the girl we see in the Zwinger scene praying to the Virgin Mary. As a realistic creation, Margarete is somewhere between the two extremes—witch and saint—found in the criticism. Whatever greater than human dimensions there may be in her character, as a personality, she is characterized by a very human fragility and a strong potential for seduction.

This fragility is at the very heart of her existence; Goethe himself summed up this aspect of innocence in a letter written in 1769: "That every young innocent heart is unreflecting, gullible, and for that reason easy to seduce—that is simply the nature of innocence. Deny that if you can!"[7] It is in the nature of her character that Margarete be eminently seduceable, even that she encourage her own seduction by being somewhat coquettish, as when she plays the game of "He-loves-me-he-loves-me-not," conscious that Faust is watching (3179–86). But the sexual seduction which Faust commits on Margarete is only the beginning of the project of dislocation; he must alienate Margarete from her moral awareness, her religion, her social and family ties. Margarete is imprisoned, not in a web of solipsism, but in a world of strict conventions and moral expectations. Where Faust is aware of his entrapment and of his powerlessness to escape it, Margarete is not. It will be his task to open her eyes, and the project fills him with a kind of ecstasy.

Faust's monologue, spoken after Mephistopheles has smuggled him into Margarete's room, is worth examining in some detail, for it throws a good deal of light on the relations of these two characters. It comes as no surprise that Faust is here once again in a small confining space and that it is nearly dark. The very darkness appears to illuminate the room for him: "Welcome, sweet twilight glow, / That permeates this holy place!"(2687–88). The preceding scene, the Street scene, seems to have taken place in the full sunlight, which makes it one of the very few scenes which occur in full illumination, but the scene of their encounter is all too brief—four lines—and we next see Faust, not with the object of his desire, but alone with his fantasies about that object. He seems to be very much at home in the absence of the subject of his desires and to enjoy the opportunity to refract his desire through language; for that reason the twilight is welcome to him. Faust actually seems to prefer the absence of the object to its presence, for it is not long after he imagines the fulfill-ment of his desires—looking at Margarete's bed, he says he could linger there for hours on end (2710)—that fear seizes him and he becomes alienated to himself: "Pathetic Faust! I hardly know you any longer" (2720).

At the moment Faust imagines his desires to be fulfilled, he is no longer himself because he is only truly in his element when in the suspended animation of unfulfilled desire, and he even sees this state of unfulfillment as something holy. Margarete's room, with-out her in it, has become for Faust a shrine, a place like his study where he can be his most Faustian self, always following the prom-ise of a new knowledge but never attaining it. Just as on that Easter morning when Faust was brought from the act of suicide by memo-ries of his past life, which were tinged with a kind of sanctitude, so here in his freedom to fantasize, Faust feels he is in a shrine. Is the holiness here the holiness of the self, conscious of itself only through its desires and imagination? The word "durchweben" ("weave through") is a strange one to use to describe the dying rays of the sun as they partially illuminate, partially conceal the actual room in which Faust finds himself. Here we are reminded of one of the most striking metaphors in *Faust*—the image of the world as a living fabric, as the Erdgeist describes it: "Thus I work at the rus-tling loom of time / And weave the living garment of God" (508–9). The metaphor is repeated near the end of Faust's monologue in Margarete's room when Faust describes Margarete herself as a part of this fabric: ". . . here with holy pure weaving / Was created the image of god!" (2715–16). This image of Margarete as herself part of the living fabric receives an unsettling twist when later we see her at an actual spinning wheel, lost in thoughts about Faust and begin-ning to sense her own isolation from the world she knows. While a loom as a symbol may embody images of fertility, plenitude, and creation, the spinning wheel constantly turning in the same path is far closer to a darker vision of nature as eternally churning, indiffer-ent, and destructive.

Just how Margarete actually forms a part of the living fabric of reality is of less importance than the fact that in this monologue Faust fantasizes about her in this way. He throws himself on the leather chair by the bed and says

How often a band of children has played
Around this paternal throne!
Perhaps here my sweetheart, thankful for a gift
Of Christmas, with full childlike cheeks,
Kissed her grandfather's wrinkled hand.

(2697–2701)

(Am I the only reader who finds the idea of such a family reunion in Margarete's small bedroom slightly preposterous?) This is nothing but pure fantasy. The truth of Margarete's situation is completely different; far from being surrounded by a crowd of children, Margarete has only a rather strict mother, an elder brother who is a soldier, and a younger sister who died shortly after birth. But Faust creates his own reality, and it is to this self-generated vision rather than to external reality that he attaches himself. Surely it is for this reason that the half-light of the chamber is so welcome to him. Here, just as in the scene with the Erdgeist, in both of which scenes the metaphor of the living fabric is an important part of the imagery, Faust sees not reality but his own projections. That he is perfectly willing to do so is made clear by his own words: "Seize my heart, you sweet pains of love / That live in yearning on the dew of hope" (2689–90). Like the narrow Gothic chamber, these lines provide us with a graphic representation of the self-incarceration of Faust. Ostensibly, he is speaking of his love, his desire for the beloved object, but the words "pain" and "yearning" make it clear that, however much he may be infatuated with Margarete (whatever such infatuation can be after such a short exchange of words), he is at least as equally in love with his own loving. The phrase "the dew of hope" is a brilliant stroke—it establishes for Faust a limit, a horizon of expectation, and at the same time withdraws it by pointing out its ephemeral quality. The dew of hope can promise, but *only* promise that which can never be fulfilled. Faust is once more imprisoned, but imprisoned with the illusions of escape—"In this prison, what bliss!" (2694).

It is only after the appearance of Margarete that we may hope for any criterion according to which Faust may be judged. In the first half of the drama we are given no external point of reference from which to make such judgments, and, although we as readers may decide for ourselves whether or not Faust is condemned, the text itself does all it can to render these private codes irrelevant. With the introduction of Margarete, the text itself offers an alternative to the bewildering complex of moral issues in the first half, and, while we must use a great deal of care to qualify the situation appropriately

(Goethe is certainly not proposing seriously the world of sixteenth-century Roman Catholic codes and conventions as anything like an ideal standard), we are nevertheless given some sort of world within whose context the self-incarcerated Titanism of Faust may be seen and judged.

The question of Faust's salvation or damnation has understandably been one of the major points of controversy in *Faust* criticism. Eudo Mason aptly sums up the situation:

> Faust criticism has all along tended to be one endless, often acrimonious debate on the question, whether Goethe intends to glorify or to denounce the Faustian superman, to justify or condemn his self-centredness and ruthlessness, to represent Faust as being saved *because of* what he is or *in spite of* what he is. It is assumed that one or the other of these two views must be the right one, and each has its violent partisans. But whichever side is chosen in this debate, one is faced with serious difficulties.[8]

Mason's own proposed solution is subtle and sensible; his is a reading that attempts to encompass the entire text and not reduce it to justification of an opinion:

> The paradoxical view is here proposed that Faust is in equal measure a glorification *and* a denunciation of the superman, that his self-centredness and ruthlessness are in equal measure justified and condemned, that Faust is saved both because of what he is and in spite of what he is. The work is in this respect ambivalent and is meant to be so, as *Werther*, *Tasso*, and the *Wahlverwandtschaften* are ambivalent, and as Goethe himself felt human existence and his own ego to be ambivalent.[9]

Certainly, Mason is in line with current literary discourse in positing an ambivalent solution as the most acceptable one, and is close to Politzer's position that the issue of salvation in Faust is one of "literary indifference." However, I submit the qualification that this ambivalence (to which I fully assent) is not so much a result of an equal measure of glorification and denunciation as of a total lack of material within the text to provide adequate grounding for valid judgment. Here, even the world of Margarete, and Margarete herself, are far too limited to provide such a basis. To support his idea of

ambivalence, Mason must see the aim of *Faust* as a "synthesis between amoral individualism and esoteric Christianity":

> In *Faust* the two opposed principles confront one another in
> undiluted intensity, the one represented, of course, by Faust
> himself, the other chiefly by Gretchen, and no mild conciliat-
> ing humanism mediates between them.[10]

Here is the weakness of the argument. To read the text as positing
such a confrontation demands that we see the two sides as of equal
force and importance, but the very structure of the work is too
asymmetrical to allow us to accept this view, and the "opposing
principles" seem not so much opposing as mutually exclusive. Opposing principles seem to allow the possibility of forensic debate, a
dialogue on commonly accepted *terra firma* with established rules
of conduct, but with worlds mutually exclusive of each other, there
is no such possibility. The difference between the world of Faust and
that of Margarete is characterized in an aphorism of Kafka:

> The crows assert that a single crow could destroy heaven.
> That is beyond doubt, but proves nothing against heaven, for
> heaven means: the impossibility of crows.[11]

Where Faust is possible, Margarete cannot exist; and where Margarete can live, Faust cannot. Furthermore, the fundamental commitment we sense on the part of Goethe to his Faust is not matched by a
similar commitment to "esoteric Christianity," so that any contest
of equals is out of the question. In Goethe's Faust drama, the outcome is so overwhelmingly on the side of Faust that it is impossible
to see the conflict as one between opposing but equal forces.
Titanism and a religious worldview are simply not comparable
enough to be regarded as equal but opposing principles. Faust is, in
most essential ways, the modern man, while the world of Margarete
is an anachronism. A dialogue between what exists and what has
ceased to exist is an impossibility.

There may well be a historical dimension to the confrontation
between Faust and Margarete which could be summed up as the
view that history is irresistible and inevitable. Margarete, with her
anachronistic religious faith, is as little a match for Faust, with his
dynamic antitranscendentalism, as the American Indians were for
the technologically advanced Europeans. Later in his life, Goethe
described the subordinate role of religion in a work of art:

Religion stands in the same relationship to art as does every other higher aspect of life. It is simply to be regarded as material, which has the same rights as all the other material taken from life. Belief or the lack thereof are in no way the proper faculties with which to comprehend a work of art.[12]

Religion is just another element of the world of Margarete which Goethe is attempting to portray realistically. It is not an opposing principle to Faust's Titanism. It is true that Margarete's world is one which *is* dominated by belief and unbelief, but this is a world of the past and, as Goethe puts it clearly in the passage above, these are not the criteria with which to judge an aesthetic concept. Far from establishing an alternative, equal to the Titanic self-imprisonment of Faust, Margarete and the world she represents are a fragile construct, all too vulnerable to the destructive power in the vortex of Faust's self-incarceration.

The incommensurability of Margarete's world with Faust—and it is this incommensurability that accounts for the feeling of asymmetricality in the work—is most clearly expressed in the scene in Martha's garden where Faust and Margarete discuss religion. The placement of this scene is important; it comes after the scene in the gazebo where Margarete declares her love for Faust and after the scene in Margarete's room where her song at the spinning wheel tells us clearly that Faust's project of dislocation has already begun to take its effect. It is interesting to observe that in the spinning scene Margarete is already beginning to see her personality as fragmented:

> My poor head
> Is in a spin;
> And all my thoughts
> Are in pieces.
>
> (3382–85)

Margarete has become aware of the gulf which separates her world from Faust, and in the garden scene (the last, incidentally, in which we see them together until the final scene of the play), she tries fervently to bridge this gap by eliciting from Faust an admission that he is after all a part of the world she knows. But the answers she receives to her ingenuously direct questions show that any such commitment on the part of Faust is not to be hoped for. Margarete adheres to an external, culturally rooted system which gives her identity substance and coherence, and she would like to believe

Faust also is a part of this larger unity: "Now tell me, how do you stand with religion?" (3415). Faust's reply is a calculated subterfuge designed to appear as an answer, but intended strategically to dislodge the discussion from its external and objective framework: "Let that go, my child; you can feel that I mean well by you" (3418). He does not even speak in an unequivocal fashion of *his* feelings and intentions, but rather invites Margarete into the subjective and unrooted world of *her* feelings. Where Margarete hopes to hear a firm answer, she receives instead another question:

> *Margarete:* Do you believe in God?
> *Faust:* Dearest, who can say
> I believe in God? . . .
> *Margarete:* So you don't believe?
> *Faust:* Don't misunderstand me, you lovely creature:
> Who could dare to name him?
> And who could declare:
> I believe in him?
>
> (3426–34)

By consistently rejecting any authority outside the self and insisting again and again on the validity of feelings which can neither affirm nor deny any external order, Faust throws Margarete back upon herself and destroys the external point of reference from which she has until now viewed the world.

Critics, eager to find in Faust's character an innate nobility, have wished to see in his speeches in this scene a kind of "credo"[13] and a "pantheistic confession of a belief in God,"[14] and have generally neglected to view this "credo" within the rhetorical context of the desires and intentions which drive Faust at this particular moment. Erich Trunz, for example, seems either disingenuous or at least naive when he says of this scene, "the moral imperative, to which Goethe later attributed such great importance, is not mentioned here,"[15] as if somehow such a moral imperative were in fact implicit in Faust's intentions, but simply "not mentioned." But why should it be mentioned here? The moral imperative is not only "not mentioned," it is deliberately absent, even denied by the insistence on subjective feeling as the only measure.

We must not forget that in this scene Faust has come to seduce Margarete, and he has even come armed with a sleeping potion for her to slip into her mother's bedtime drink. It is ludicrous even to consider the possibility of his mouthing some moral imperative in this context. And if Faust's words constitute a credo of faith, surely it is the only one ever formulated entirely in the form of questions:

> Does not the heaven arch up above?
> Does the earth not lie here below, firm and fast?
> And do not the eternal friendly stars
> Shine down as they rise in the heavens?
>
> (3442–45)

This credo is less an acknowledgment of God's presence than an "argument of insidious intent" whose logic is as irresistible to Margarete as the temptation of the jewels; and it has its effect, for it succeeds in dislodging Margarete gently but surely from her religious security: "That is pretty much what the priest says also, / Only with a little different words" (3459–60). Margarete wants to believe that what Faust is saying to her can be fitted into the fabric of her life, and so she convinces herself that Faust and her priest really say the same thing. But it does not require a theologian to recognize that what Faust proposes is as far as possible from any interpretation of Christian dogma. Yet, as much as she wishes to be convinced of the acceptable nature of Faust's argument, Margarete is dimly aware of the danger posed to her personality by Faust, and she locates the danger entirely in his companion, Mephistopheles, whom Faust actually defends to her, telling her that there have to be "odd birds" like him in the world (3483). She recognizes that Mephistopheles is not a part of her community and that his perpetual cynicism and negative view of man keep him always an outsider to human society. His presence is itself enough to destroy the love and faith which are the bases of this community:

> It overcomes me so, that
> When he just comes near us,
> It even seems to me that I don't love you any more.
> And, when he is present, I could never pray.
>
> (3495–98)

By placing a hindrance between Margarete and her prayerbook, Mephistopheles also dissolves the bonds which hold the separate elements of her world together. Yet, despite the fact that Margarete recognizes so clearly the danger presented by Faust and his companion, she openly acknowledges that she is a pawn in Faust's hands; almost like an automaton, she speaks her final lines to him:

O, dearest of men, just to look at you,
Something, I know not what, drives me to your will.

(3517–18)

It may be that these lines could be construed as an expression of
love, but the language itself, especially the phrase "drives me to your
will," leads us to believe that what we are witnessing is not a love
story but a violent power play in which it is a foregone conclusion
that Faust will win because there is really very little to resist him.
Margarete has done all that she has for Faust because she has accepted on faith the final article of his "credo": "Feeling is everything" (3456), and a belief in feelings is a belief in the self.

In three brief subsequent scenes we see the progress of Margarete's
isolation and madness: By the Town-Well, Zwinger, and Cathedral.
A close examination of these scenes reveals how carefully this progression is worked out. In the first scene, we see Margarete in her
familiar world, in the timeless social world of women, as it is symbolized by the town well. The first we learn of Margarete in this
scene is that her isolation has become constant: "I don't go out very
much" (3545). The world the girls discuss is the world of forbidden
yet accessible sexuality which was somewhat abstractly represented
in the earlier scene By the Town-Gate and is here given very concrete, if brief, realization. The names of the girls are clearly given:
Bärbelchen, Lieschen, Gretchen. This concreteness contrasts to the
anonymity of type which characterizes the earlier scene. And just as
concrete is the justice meted out by society to those who break its
rules: poor Bärbelchen will have to do her penance at church in the
"sinner's shirt," and even if she succeeds in legitimizing her as yet
unborn child by marrying the boy who made her pregnant, the townspeople will make a mockery of the marriage ceremony. Of course,
the thematic importance of Bärbelchen's plight is that it reflects
Margarete's own. Margarete now identifies herself, not with the society from which Bärbelchen has fallen, but with Bärbelchen herself.
Where once she would have been the first to censure a fallen girl like
Bärbelchen, now she recognizes that her own surrender to Faust is
no less culpable than the other girl's to her soldier. In Margarete's
sense of identity with the fallen girl, there is also a real sense of
compassion, and this makes her own fall so poignant and touching,
for compassion is a virtue not often encountered in *Faust*.

It is the recognition of her own sin which begins to separate
Margarete from her community and which brings her to a lonely
spot along the town wall where at a shrine to the Blessed Virgin she

offers up her prayers. Here she identifies herself, not with a fellow sinner, but with the religious archetype of the sorrowful woman, the Mater Dolorosa. The sword in the heart of the Madonna finds a corresponding symbol of pain in Margarete's "pain . . . in my bones" (3598). It is Margarete's realization of her sin that has drawn her out of the crowd of townsfolk with whom she has until now shared her life; now, alone and tearful, she stands before the religious and literary archetype of herself, and the prayer she utters is a loose translation of the liturgical texts she has known. We can be fairly certain that these traditional prayers are well known to Margarete since the evil spirit who sits beside her in the cathedral refers to her "well-worn prayerbook" (3779). The verse form and much of the content of her prayer is derived from two medieval Latin sequences, the *Stabat Mater* and the *Planctus ante nescia*. We do not know to what extent Margarete is aware that the words she utters are not her own, and we do not know exactly what led Goethe to put these ancient words into Margarete's mouth, but the use of the Latin hymns is very evocative. The *Stabat Mater*, a depiction of Mary at the foot of the cross, invites comparison between the mother of Christ and Margarete, soon to be the mother of an illegitimate child. Are we to see her guilt diminished by her prayer or by her sense of identification with the Virgin Mary? Or, do we simply see a young girl falling back on the worn texts of her religious heritage in a vain attempt to redeem what she knows to be her fallen state? Gradually, the *Stabat Mater* gives way to the *Planctus*, a poem written in the first person, in which Mary describes her own grief and pain in unadorned, direct verse. Margarete's own words are not a direct translation of the Latin, but are close enough for us to recognize clearly that her own language is being infiltrated by the literary texts which constitute her religious tradition. Whether Margarete draws comfort from these other voices we do not know, but we can see that, as she begins her painful course into madness and death, her language loses the freshness and immediacy of individual expression that it once had.

In the Cathedral scene, the act of translation becomes more precise as Margarete's madness takes its final form to the words of yet another Latin hymn, the *Dies irae*. This ominous text—it is significant that only the opening verses, with their words of doom and damnation, and not the final verses, which speak of salvation, are used—is translated directly and personally into Margarete's own language. The evil spirit, interpreted almost unanimously by critics as

Margarete's conscience, whispers this personal translation into her ear. The chorus sings

> Dies irae, dies illa
> Solvet saeculum in favilla
>
> (3798–99)

and the evil spirit translates this into

> And your heart,
> Made whole once more,
> Trembles forth
> Out of the peace of ashes
> Into the flames of hell!
>
> (3800–3804)

Where the Latin hymn describes the general destruction of the world, the evil spirit translates this into a personal sense of destruction; the objective *saeculum* becomes "your heart," the "ashes" of the hymn become the "peace of ashes" of the translation, and the general destruction of the world becomes in the translation the flames of hell which represent the eternal destruction of Margarete's soul. The chorus sings another stanza:

> Judex ergo cum sedebit,
> Quidquid latet adparebit,
> Nil inultum remanebit
>
> (3813–15)

which the evil spirit translates in turn:

> Hide yourself! Sin and shame
> Will not remain hidden.
>
> (3821–22)

Where the Latin speaks of a general situation, a day of final judgment presided over by the judge on his throne, a judge to whom all deeds of men are known, the evil spirit mentions no such external judge, but only the personal and paradoxical message that Margarete must hide herself and that such hiding will be futile. Margarete must become her own judge, and between the poles of such self-contradictory injunctions, Margarete's identity is dissolved into pieces which can no longer cohere. The utter helplessness of Margarete's situation is expressed by the chorus in their final lines:

> Quid sum miser tunc dicturus?
> Quem patronem rogaturus?
> Cum vix justus sit securus.
>
> (3825–27)

The patron and the just person, who is himself hardly safe in the time of such general retribution, become in the translation of the evil spirit the pure and saintly who turn their faces from Margarete. With no words of redemption to temper the message of absolute doom, the Latin hymn in the personal translation offered by the evil spirit stands as a literary symbol of Margarete's complete alienation from society and the rejection from her own religion. Thus, at the end of these scenes, Margarete's identity is completely destroyed:

> I feel as if the organ
> Were taking away my breath,
> As if the music had dissolved
> The depths of my heart.
>
> (3809–12)

Goethe could hardly have found a more successful image to convey Margarete's destruction and the encroaching literary presence which accompanies her death: the organ playing the *Dies irae* must have the air to fill its pipes; almost like a vampire, it preys on Margarete and literally steals her breath away, while the words of the poem dissolve the bonds of her heart and shatter its unity.

It was the impression of certain early critics of *Faust*, especially of Wilhelm Scherer, that the Cathedral scene was an early production, intended to be replaced by the scene at the Zwinger,[16] but such an opinion misses the rhetorical progression that depicts Margarete's increasing isolation and destruction. In fact, the three scenes serve as a kind of triptych, held together by certain thematic devices. In the first two scenes, Margarete begins to feel the increasing burden of her guilt (and the increasing burden of the child within her womb) and identifies herself with another—first with a girl much like herself, then, as the helplessness of the situation becomes more apparent, with the Virgin Mary, who was also helpless to prevent the most catastrophic and painful of events. In the third scene, there is no longer a sense of connection between Margarete and the world around her; consequently, there can be no act of identification, for the sense of guilt has become too crushing. In the first scene, we see life represented as relatively natural (the town well may seem to be a literary archetype, but it does not point necessarily to a specific text from the past); in the last two scenes, natural life becomes increasingly literary. While in the second scene, Margarete unconsciously repeats and reformulates bits of ancient Latin liturgy, in the third scene there is a far more conscious act of translation from a Latin hymn into a localized and personal meaning, and by this act of translation (which in its emphasis on a personalization of the text is as much a distortion of the original text as Faust's version of the Bible), Margarete is drawn ever closer to Faust and to the cycle of self-incarceration he represents. The sense of progression in these three scenes is intensified by their respective setting: the first takes place in the open air, probably in daylight; the second in a more confining space between the inner and outer town walls (the Zwinger); and finally in the third scene Margarete is in a space much like Faust's study—dark, Gothic, and confining:

> It seems so close here!
> The walls and pillars
> Hold me captive!
> The vaulting
> Crushes me!—Air!
>
> (3816–20)

In the Cathedral scene, we have the triumph of Faust's project. Margarete is as imprisoned as he, and her desire to escape reflects his own, albeit in a far simpler, far more terrifying form. And, like Faust, Margarete has acquired a companion, the evil spirit, who is a reflection and a distortion of herself as Mephistopheles is a reflection and distortion of Faust. The image of an externalized conscience is a graphic representation of the disunity of her personality.

As Margarete becomes dislocated from her social and religious context, and as she acquires her own Mephistopheles-like companion, she also becomes, like Faust, a much more consciously fictive creation. The Margarete we first saw seemed as unself-conscious and unreflective upon herself as any character in literature can be. Her lines are original, and when she sings a "folk-song" to quiet her mind, the song she sings is in fact a new song, written for this text and borrowed from no other. As she becomes more and more isolated from her world (or, more precisely, as her world disappears from around her in the text), the literary archetypes on which her personality is founded become increasingly apparent, and the fictive texture which comes to represent her becomes thicker with its own literariness. Her language is no longer original, but is a conflation of translations from earlier texts; with Mephistopheles' pronouncement, "She is not the first," she becomes just one more member of a long chain of "Kindermörderinnen" and other fallen girls and women of literature. The phrase itself was used earlier by Goethe in the original version of *Götz von Berlichingen*[17] and in his *Clavigo*;[18] he himself found it used in the 1725 version of the Faust chapbook. The phrase may also be a citation of a similar phrase in Wagner's *Kindermörderin*,[19] although here it would be difficult to ascertain who is quoting whom. The phrase marks an end to any claim Margarete had to originality as surely as it puts a seal to her days of innocence.

Finally, as Margarete approaches closer and closer to madness, another figure from past literature looms within the *Faust* text and this further intensifies the increasing literariness replacing the spontaneity of Margarete's character. This new figure is Ophelia of Shakespeare's *Hamlet*, whose own madness bears a number of similarities to that of Margarete. The "serenade" sung by Mephistopheles in the scene before her house confirms this literary association between the two texts since it is so closely modelled on Ophelia's song in the fourth act of *Hamlet:*

> *Ophelia:* Let in the maid, that out a maid
> Never departed more.[20]

> *Mephistopheles:* Er lässt dich ein,
> Als Mädchen ein,
> Als Mädchen nicht zurucke.

> (3687–89)

Late in his life, in a conversation with Eckermann and Riemer, Goethe discussed his use of a text by another poet, and this passage in Eckermann is one of the most important statements Goethe made regarding the issue of textual borrowing. Goethe's own conversational preface to the passage is interesting, for it sets the tone for what is to follow:

> The world remains always the same, Goethe said; circumstances repeat themselves. One people lives, loves and feels just like another, so why shouldn't one poet write poetry like

another? Life-situations are similar, so why shouldn't the situations in poetry also be similar?[21]

This sense of the continual sameness of things reminds us strongly of Goethe's dark vision of the indifference of nature, a vision which appears so frequently in the early works and which in the later days of his life helped bring the poet to his general attitude of "renunciation." It is this sense of eternal sameness which brings him then to discuss the use of Shakespeare in this scene from *Faust:*

> Walter Scott used a scene from my *Egmont* and he had a perfect right to it, and because he did it with intelligence, he is to be praised. Also, in one of his novels, he modelled a character on that of my Mignon. . . . Lord Byron's transfigured devil is a continuation of my Mephistopheles, and that is as it should be! . . . And if my Mephistopheles sings a song of Shakespeare's, why shouldn't he?[22]

Literature itself can become the house of mirrors whose parody and self-reflection are the literary components of a world which remains ever the same. The effect such knowledge can have on a character who is cognizant of her own fictive personality is clearly shown in the Helena scenes of *Faust II.* But Margarete, no less than Helena, becomes a consciously fictive character as she progresses into madness, the only difference being that Margarete is *not* aware of her own literariness while Helena is painfully aware of her own insubstantial and parodistic nature. With Margarete's last pitiable and unsuccessful attempt to make connection with the outside world—"Neighbor, your smelling salts!"—she has completed her own *via dolorosa* from a character filled with life to the shadow of a literary fiction, a composite of texts. She literally loses her life to literature.

Margarete is not the first of Goethe's characters to die a death strangely implicated with literariness. Goethe's first fully realized literary creation, Götz von Berlichingen, also dies a death closely connected with the act of literary transformation. Götz's death begins with the scene in which we see the old knight settling down to write his own story, to convert his own lived experience into words. As if he knew that the conversion would mean his death, Götz finds the task uncongenial in the extreme. The very act of writing seems to narrow the field of his existence:

> Alas, writing is just busy idleness; it makes me sick. . . . Idleness is not at all to my taste, and my confinement grows more confining every day. . . .[23]

Like the death of Margarete, Götz's death is not only implicated in a literary transformation, but it is also plagued with a kind of barrenness represented by a lack of progeny. In place of the many children sired by the real Götz, Goethe's Götz has only one son, and even he rebels against his father to become a monk. Goethe's hero thus dies virtually without heirs. In the autobiography scene, Götz's wife, Elisabeth, even makes an ironic reference to a progeny of readers: ". . . create for a noble progeny the joys of remembering you."[24] She is referring to his completion of the autobiography. The transformation of life into literature could not be more apparent than in this scene, and it is from this point in the drama (the last scene of the fourth act) that Götz's life becomes nothing but decline.

We see Götz for the last time in the last scene of the play. Götz is on his deathbed, bemoaning the fact that he is dying childless and that he is the last of his line. The literary project begun by his autobiographical writing has been completed, for the dying Götz is nothing but a pastiche of literary citation, mostly from the Gospel of Matthew and from the Psalms:

> I leave you in a corrupted world. . . . Close your hearts more securely than your doors. The time of deceit is at hand to do what it will. The ignoble will rule with trickery and the noble will fall into their nets.[25]

Even the last line of the play, spoken by Götz's wife, is a paraphrase of earlier literature; the line, "The world is a prison," draws our attention to the thickening atmosphere of literary quotation as well as to the Shakespearean inspiration of the play. As the old Götz pales into script, his very language is replaced by literary citation of external texts. At the end of the Cathedral scene, Margarete cries out that her very breath is being stolen by the organ, and the gathering clouds of literary atmosphere which surround her in this scene are as ominous a sign for her destiny as Götz's newfound Biblical voice is for his.

Götz is not the only character in Goethe to die a death surrounded by literary triumph. Ottilie, in *Elective Affinities*, drops the child of Eduard and Charlotte into the lake, where it drowns. She inadvertently kills the child because she is trying to balance it in one hand while in the other she holds the novel she has been reading. The balance is precarious, and it tips in favor of literature. Presumably the book is saved while the child perishes.

At this point in *Faust I*, the story of Margarete is interrupted as the triumph of Faust and of literature over life is celebrated in the Walpurgisnight. As he participates in the ghoulish revels, Faust does not even think of Margarete until some considerable time has elapsed on the Brocken, when, unexpectedly, he sees a vision of Margarete as already dead. Even then, his emotions are hardly those of a person who has had a vision of his lover's death, and Faust can still make time to watch the entertainment provided, the Walpurgisnight's Dream, before rushing off to save her. When Faust sees the vision of Margarete coming to him amid the riotous revels of the Satanic celebration, he describes what he sees in surprisingly detached and casual tones. Hardly impelled to action by the vision, Faust speaks as though he were in a state of anesthesia: "I must confess that it does seem to me / That she looked like the good Gretchen" (4187–88). In a brilliant essay on the Walpurgisnight, Albrecht Schöne shows the extent to which in this scene Goethe was indebted to the literature of the sixteenth and seventeenth centuries which described witchcraft and the trials of persons accused of being witches or heretics.[27] Schöne is primarily concerned with the formal structure of the scene, but he could easily have extended his argument and suggested that the language Faust uses at this point sounds very much like testimony extracted during these trials: ". . . this is the breast she offered to me; this is the body which I enjoyed. . . ." It is plain and unadorned, a simple statement of facts which are almost an accusation. In any case, the vision seems to mesmerize Faust, but does not cause him to leave the revels on the Brocken to test the vision for its accuracy in the real world. Instead, he seems to be describing an aesthetic object which demands only a neutral contemplation. Erich Trunz calls these lines "words of pure love,"[28] but surely there is little love shown in these curious lines:

> How strangely that one scarlet thread
> Would ornament her beautiful neck,
> A line no broader than the back of a knife.
>
> (4203–5)

These are not words of passion or love, nor do they reveal any haste on the part of Faust to be at the side of his lover.

Mephistopheles, to insure that the vision does not bring Faust out of his anesthetized state, seeks to draw Faust's attention from it by comparing the vision to Medusa (4194). There is more in this comparison than the allusion to an apotropaic warning. There is in fact a macabre parallel between the stories of Medusa and Margarete, in that both are women who suffer death by decapitation. Furthermore, Medusa, at the moment of her death, gave birth to Pegasus, the winged horse who, because he created the Hippocrene spring, was regarded by later tradition as the spirit of poetry; thus, by reference to the myth of Medusa, Margarete is likened to yet another figure from past literature, and indeed to one whose story reveals the triumph of literature over life. Apart from the more grotesque aspects of the comparison between Margarete and Medusa, there is also a rather dark irony: whose responsibility is it after all that Margarete has "lost her head"? If this "idol" (as Mephistopheles refers to her) is "lifeless" and can kill by turning all who have contact with her into stone, who was it that robbed her of her own life and gave her that terrible deathly power? Is it not Faust himself as well as Margarete who turns life into death? Is Goethe suggesting that Margarete, now that she has herself become a construct of literature, will henceforth possess the same deadly and attractive aridity that makes Faust and the world of literature which he represents so dangerous?

That the Walpurgisnight is a triumph of literature over life, and that the triumph is one characterized by aridity and barrenness, is seen most clearly in the figure of the Proktophantasmist and in the progression which leads up to his appearance on the stage. Although as perceptive a critic as Walter Dietze has denied any order to the events of the Walpurgisnight[29], there is in the scene at least the order of progression from the bottom of the mountain to the top, and there is, as I will show, a progression from the natural to the increasingly literary, a progression which culminates in the Proktophantasmist and the literary entertainment of the "Dream." In defense of Dietze's argument, it must be noted that Dietze wishes to draw a comparison between the Walpurgisnight and the Walpurgisnight's Dream in terms of order and disorder, and clearly, in his terms, the "Dream" posits an aesthetic order which is the very opposite of the apparent randomness and confusion of the Walpurgisnight revels. Dietze wishes to see in this relationship between the two sections a recapitulation of the myth of creation—from apparent chaos will emerge an artifact of precisely measurable order and form. This is an interpretation which stresses the highly literary "creational" aspects of the "Dream." However, in assessing the literary character of the

"Dream," we must not neglect the aspects of form within the Walpurgisnight itself which lead up to the evening's entertainment. The Walpurgisnight scene begins with Faust enjoying the natural setting through which he and Mephistopheles are making their way to the peak of the Brocken:

> Already, spring weaves amid the birches,
> And even the firs begin to feel the spring;
> Shouldn't spring also have its effect on our limbs?
>
> (3845–47)

They are joined by a will-o'-the-wisp, and the landscape loses some of its naturalness as it becomes tinged with art and magic. Faust is probably the one who, in the alternating lines of the "Round," sings

> Do I hear the rustling of trees? Is it song?
> Do I hear the lovely complaint of a lover? . . .
> And the echo, like the legend
> Of older days, sounds once more.
>
> (3883–88)

The rustling of the wind in the trees threatens to turn into art, yet the work of art which is about to be born is not a new creation but is an echo of older poetry (sagas and legends), a sign which points once again to the motif of literature as a hall of mirrors and to the prisonhouse of language in the self-reflexiveness of the work of art. Behind this nature are the legends and sagas of the north; in the classical Walpurgisnight, it will be classical poetry which informs the naturalness of the landscape. Finally, the landscape loses all the soft contours evoked by Faust's opening lines and becomes one of fantastic *un*naturalness: "How strangely a dark dawn-like red glow / Shines over the chasms" (3916–17). As Faust and Mephistopheles approach Satan, the denizen of the fable book, the landscapes become increasingly estranged from simple nature, as though transforming themselves to accommodate the Prince of Darkness.

With the masque of the witches, the unnaturalness of the scene is complete; the related themes of barrenness, infertility, and frustration are organized into a demonic counterpoint. Eternally condemned to be without progeny of any kind, the witches sing of their frustration at not being able to get to the top of the mountain and of their unending restlessness. Like figures in a medieval depiction of hell, these witches seem almost complacent in their resigned acceptance of their fate. They know they are caught in a ceaseless and meaningless turbulence (which reminds us of Werther's dark vision of nature as an eternally masticating monster), but they are helpless to do anything about it. The theme of infertility reaches its climax as Mephistopheles recounts his erotic dream (the printed text is coy, but Goethe left no doubt as to the rhyme-words which were to fill in the gaps):

> Da sah ich einen gespaltenen Baum,
> Der hatt' ein ———— ———— ————; [ungeheueres Loch]
> So ———— es war, gefiel' mir's doch [gross]
>
> (There I saw a tree, split in the middle,
> The tree had a [monstrous hole];
> [Large] as it was, it was fine with me.)
>
> (4137–39)

The mention of this inhuman and infertile place of sexual gratification evokes an equally vulgar response from an old witch with whom Mephistopheles has been dancing. She offers him her own body for sexual pleasure, and the implication is that she is no more fertile a receptacle for his sexual pleasure than the hole in the tree. This exchange, in which sexuality is taken to its lowest, most unidealized level, follows directly upon an exchange between Faust and a beautiful young witch in which there is the recurrent reference to the story of Adam and Eve and the tree of knowledge: "The little apple that you desire so much / Is the one that comes from Paradise" (4132–33). Here the literary background against which the drama of Faust and Margarete has been played is made explicit. To whatever literary elements already present in the constitution of the characters is added the extra dimension of the legend of Adam and Eve, the oldest and most primary of literary texts. Here, in the Walpurgisnight, the conflation of literary allusion and bestial and infertile sexual gratification could not be more obvious, and the four strophes sung by Faust, Mephistopheles, and the witches firmly establish this connection, which finally culminates in the appearance of the Proktophantasmist, the very embodiment of literary aridity.

There is no doubt that the Proktophantasmist is a parody of Christoph Friedrich Nicolai, the critic in Berlin whose enlightened principles of literary propriety led him to a violent rejection of *Werther*.

Ostensibly the parodistic character who appears on the stage of the Faust drama is called the Proktophantasmist because of a bizarre and well-known incident in the life of Nicolai: plagued in 1791 by ghostly visions, he effected a cure through an unusual form of bloodletting—by attaching leeches to various points on his buttocks. Nicolai himself delivered a report of this extraordinary catharsis to the Berlin Academy of Sciences.[30] There is no doubt that the grotesque nature of the story, coupled with Goethe's own desire for some sort of revenge on Nicolai, is adequate explanation for the appearance of this ridiculous figure at the Walpurgisnight, but it should be noted that *prōktos* is not really the Greek word for buttocks, but for the anus, which, like Mephistopheles' splitting tree, is yet another infertile place of sexual gratification. If Goethe had intended the figure to be simply an unambiguous reference to Nicolai and his unusual treatment, he might well have called the figure the Pygephantasmist (from *pūge*, "buttocks"), but instead he coins the word on the Greek *prōktos*, a term far more suggestive of unusual sexual practice. It makes perfect sense, then, that his appearance comes directly after the reference to the "grosses Loch." The Proktophantasmist thus completes the imagery of infertility which has been so prominent throughout the Walpurgisnight by bringing to it the literary element in the form of a current literary personality. And it is literature, specifically the arid parodies of the Walpurgisnight's Dream, that holds Faust back from rushing to the real-life tribulations of Margarete.

Goethe's inclusion of the literary parody, the Walpurgisnight's Dream, has been the consistent cause of much embarrassment on the part of *Faust* critics. Again and again, Goethe's judgment is called into question with regard to this section of the drama; translators regularly omit it or consign it to the obscurity of an appendix, producers almost never put these two hundred lines onto the stage. Yet there it is. Goethe placed it where it is in the text and apparently wanted it there for a reason. It is true that this satire on contemporary literature, philosophy, and politics was originally written as a kind of German sequel to the classically formed *Xenien* published by Goethe and Schiller in the fall of 1796. Goethe had expected Schiller to print these rhymed quatrains, written in much the same spirit as the *Xenien*, in his *Musenalmanach* for 1797. Schiller, however, convinced that they had already put their names to enough polemic satire, did not accept them for publication. He makes this point to Goethe in his letter of October 2, 1797.[31] On December 20 of that same year, Goethe writes back to Schiller:

You have omitted *Oberon's Golden Wedding* [the actual title of the Dream] with good reason; in the meantime the piece has grown to twice the number of verses and I should think that the best place for it would be in my *Faust*.[32]

The letter is interesting not only because it tells us that Goethe himself decided the Dream to be more appropriate to the context of *Faust* than to separate publication, but because in it Goethe also agrees with Schiller that the verses are indeed suspect. Grounds for this suspicion lie not with the quality of the verse—it is inconceivable that Goethe would have inserted a passage into his *Faust* because its quality was too low to have it published elsewhere—but with the devilish tone that the poet adopts toward literature and the poets who create it. The conflation of literature and devilry (which in *Faust* is almost always associated with the barren and the infertile) is a consistent theme in the Walpurgisnight, and it is surely this connection which led Goethe to believe that *Faust* was the appropriate context for the Dream, for throughout the final part of the Walpurgisnight, this theme is predominant. Toward the end of the revels, a young witch dances with Faust and sings to him; in the middle of her song a red mouse jumps from her mouth: Poetry is literally transformed spontaneously into devilry. The Proktophantasmist says in parting that he still hopes he will be able "to coerce . . . the devils and the poets" (4171). Poets and devils are mentioned in the same breath as if they were one and the same thing. After all these references to the connections between literature and devilry it is not surprising, then, to see the evening end in a cold satire on literature and intellectual endeavor in general. The very scene of the Walpurgisnight, the Brocken, is, as the "Quondam Genius of the Age" puts it, the German Parnassus.

Among the critics who would expunge the Walpurgisnight's Dream from the text of *Faust* is Albrecht Schöne. In his brilliant essay on the Walpurgisnight, Schöne argues for a drastic revision of the scene, one that would not only eliminate the Dream, but would also include the important Paralipomenon 50, a long passage in which Satan himself appears and holds court.[33] Schöne would also eliminate the "topical bits of satire, sprinkled within the Walpurgisnight scene itself."[34] Schöne argues that the inclusion of Satan as the culmination of the orgiastic scene was the necessary complement to the Prologue in Heaven, and that the entire Faust drama was conceived, in consonance with Goethe's polarity-oriented thought, within a context of absolute extremes.[35] Schöne would have Satan appear as a "heretical anti-god."[36] Without this important scene, he argues, the entire Faust drama loses its orientation, but the scene was simply too vulgar for Goethe to have left it in the body of the text. Bowing to the conventions of the day, Goethe omitted this crucial scene and so left us with a work whose center had been removed. Schöne, raising the intentional fallacy to an act of creativity, attempts to rewrite the Walpurgisnight scene and to restore it in its original form to the drama.[37]

Schöne's argument is compelling, and it is a well-known fact that the important scene, Paralipomenon 50, was indeed written for inclusion in the Faust text;[38] however, several assumptions made by Schöne must be examined carefully. First, if Goethe failed in the end to include the Satan scene for reasons of its obscenity, why did he not also expurge those passages already quoted here from the published text of 1808 which were as vulgar as anything in the Satan scene (the exchange between Mephistopheles and the witch, for example)? Second, would the relationship between the Satan scene, if it were included, and the Prologue in Heaven actually have been one of counterbalance? This presupposes the seriousness of the Prologue as theological grounding for the drama and demands a firm belief in this "Lord" as representing the god of love and goodness. But, as we have seen, the Prologue leaves too many questions unanswered about the nature of the Lord to convince us of his role in the drama as a guiding light of love. To be truthful, his absence seems to be of greater importance than his presence, and while Satan would have Mephistopheles throughout the drama as his representative, the Lord has no such ambassador, so that even if the Satan scene were left in the text, there would still exist a considerable imbalance between these two poles as they are represented in the text. Finally, the actual presence of Satan would have to be reconciled with Mephistopheles' insistence on the refraction of evil into the many smaller and separate elements (2507–9).

Even if Goethe's major reason for excluding Satan from the Walpurgisnight was a fear of social censure for obscenity, there are other, possibly more integral reasons the text, as it was published in 1808, contains only the vaguest references to the Anti-Lord who is supposedly in charge of the sacrilegious ceremonies on the Brocken. At first glance, there seems to be a great contradiction in the text with regard to the existence of Satan. On the one hand, we find the words of Mephistopheles explicitly relegating him to the world of fairy tale, while on the other hand Faust, in the midst of the revels, is made to say:

But it's up there I'd rather be!
Already I see fire and columns of smoke.
There the crowd throngs around the Evil One
Where many a puzzle must be resolved.

(4037—40)

And there is much in the Walpurgisnight (leaving aside Paralipomenon 50) to convince us that somewhere offstage Satan is actually
sitting atop the Brocken, the diabolical center of all the movement
in the scene. These passages are in direct opposition to one another.
Does Satan exist or does he not exist? I suggest that it is the question
itself, and not the answer, which is fundamental to our experience of
the Faust drama. To have consolidated evil into one figure would
have anchored the play in a firm and familiar context which would
have been antithetical to the nature of the text as we have it. It
would have established that Archimedean point of reference which
so much of the drama strives to destroy. The text as Goethe left it
gives Satan much the same kind of status as that possessed by
Margarete's mother; like her, he remains an unseen source of fantasy whose power is all the greater because his actual existence is
never confirmed before our eyes. The decentralized universe of
Faust is made even more ominous by the suggestion of these unseen
sources of control.

The appearance of Satan would have solved many a riddle for
Faust, and it would have solved many a riddle for the readers of
Faust, but it is more usual for the Faust drama to raise riddles than
to solve them, as Goethe suggests in his comment about "hide-and-
seek." Faust, too, seems to know that, as much as he longs for a face-
to-face meeting with Satan, it is his destiny to remain on the periphery of the action where little is certain and questions are never
simple. He complains to Mephistopheles that after all the trouble of
getting there, they are simply remaining on the sidelines of the
action (4032—33). And just as Faust has stood on the periphery of the
community in the Easter scenes, unable to participate in the rites
and customs of the others, so here too he proves to have an existence
only at the edge. The image of the crowd, thronging and swirling to
reach the top while Faust and Mephistopheles stand apart and con-
verse with other peripheral characters is one consistent with the
image we have of Faust in the majority of scenes in the first part of
the drama (Before the Town-Gate, Auerbach's Cellar, Witch's Kitchen, for example).

Mephistopheles himself is not sure that any riddles would be

solved by a meeting with Satan. He replies to Faust's desire to climb
to the top, where Satan is presumably holding court:

> Let the great world roar past,
> We'll be at home here in the quiet.
> It has long been the custom that, in the larger world,
> Man makes smaller worlds for himself.
>
> (4042–45)

The smaller world of private construction referred to here is a reflection of that world Faust is encouraged to build for himself by the
chorus of spirits that sings in his study when Faust has so vehe-
mently cursed the entire world. And so here, too, in the Walpurgisnight, Faust turns away from the greater world where a monarchical
Satan is said to hold sway and to a smaller world which is more in
keeping with the one in which we have seen him since the beginning of the play—a world dominated by literature (Erich Trunz calls
the entire scene from line 3988 on a "literary satire").[39] An unnamed
"author" appears on stage to complain of the contemporary literary
climate:

> Who is there nowadays who wants to read
> A book of even moderately intelligent content?
> And as far as the younger generation goes,
> They have never been so impertinent.
>
> (4088–91)

It is not difficult to see in this author the author of *Faust* himself,
complaining of his own work and its readers. The impertinence he
mentions may refer either to his readers or to the author's own game
of playing hide-and-seek with those complacent readers mentioned
in the first two lines. The atmosphere of the Walpurgisnight begins
to change from one of devilry and witchcraft to one of literary satire,
and the scene culminates in an arid literary diversion, the irrelevance of which has troubled every reader of *Faust*. But it is precisely
the magic of this highly contrived, pedantically literary masque
which holds Faust back from the much more pressing problems of
Margarete. The literary value of the Intermezzo is emphasized again
and again; the very title, "Oberon's and Titania's Golden Wedding,"
is a reference to Shakespeare, as are the characters Puck and Ariel,
who begin and end the diversion. The ephemeral yet seductive quality of this literary fantasy is the theme of the finale:

Ariel: If loving Nature
    And spirit gave you wings,
    Then follow my easy path
    Up to the hill of roses!
Orchestra: (pianissimo): Veil of mist and trail of cloud
    Are illumined from above.
    Breezes in the leaves and wind in the rushes,
    And all is blown away.

(4391–98)

This ethereal and ephemeral poetry, borrowed from the atmosphere of *A Midsummer Night's Dream,* stands here as part of a wedding celebration, and this puts the magical scene in sharp contrast with the reality of Faust outside the Walpurgisnight, for his relationship with Margarete ends, not with a marriage, but with murder and execution.

Certainly, Faust is seduced by the transient play of poetry just as he has been seduced by the books in his study. Like his Nostradamus, the literary diversion is for Faust an unsatisfactory but inescapable surrogate for real life. Yet, as trivial as the Intermezzo is, it nevertheless touches upon themes of real consequence for the drama as a whole. For example, the very question of Satan's existence is raised by the "Dogmatist":

I'll not let myself be shouted down,
    Neither by critics nor by doubt.
    The Devil must in fact exist,
    Otherwise, how could there be devils?

(4343–46)

In a way, this passage is a parody of the statement made by Mephistopheles about Satan in the Witch's Kitchen, and it rephrases the question Goethe leaves unanswered by removing the Satan scene from the Walpurgisnight and replacing it with this Intermezzo. The question is meant to be left open. Next, the very problem of Goethe's own game of hide-and-seek is brought thematically into the text of the Intermezzo by the poet placing himself, in an act of Romantic irony, into the text itself:

Northern Artist: What happens here today, I understand
    Only in a sketchy fashion.
    But in the meantime I prepare

For my Italian Journey.

(4275–78)

Even the separation of Faust from Margarete is brought into the context of the Intermezzo, although only in a very ironic way, by Oberon, who tells the audience that the best way to keep a couple together is to separate them (4243–46).

There is much more in the "Dream" which bears thematic relevance to the Faust text as a whole, but the most immediate impression created by this section is one of triviality, irrelevance, and artificial literariness. It is a scene in which the author plays the most elaborate game of hide-and-seek with his readers. Part of what is hidden here is what has been left out of the published text—the Satan scene. It is as though the text itself, conscious of its truncated nature, filled the void out of spite with the most unconvincing and even annoying of poetic passages. The question arises: Did Goethe create the Satan scene in the full conviction that it would be included in the final text of *Faust,* or was he certain, even while creating it, that it would ultimately be deleted from the whole? As we will see later, much the same problem exists for the unpublished Roman Elegies; the published text of the poems actually seems to play with the notion of its own incompletion. Possibly this was a part of the hide-and-seek game Goethe played with his *Faust:* to create an important scene only to leave it out and so to leave the text seemingly out of touch with its own center. Certainly, the text as it was published shows a decentralized world where all experience is open to interpretation and translation and where truth is difficult to detach from self-projection. Instead of the certainties of a possible Satan scene we are given an ambiguous literary parody, and I suggest that this was a deliberate choice. The "Dream" concludes. the Walpurgisnight with an exemplification of the conflation of literature and barrenness, and thus gives the author a chance to cast a self-conscious glance onto his own project, and indeed onto the whole enterprise of literary production.

It is against this background of literary aridity that we must read the final prison scene. In the short intervening scene, Dark Day. Field, Faust refers directly to the devilish diversions which have kept him from Margarete. Although the Walpurgisnight's Dream was written many years after this scene, it is easy to interpret its literary diversions as the distractions Faust refers to. Faust knows he has been led astray and he suddenly feels guilty for having neglected Margarete. Deaf to his anguish, Mephistopheles replies cynically,

"She is not the first," thereby ranking her with the thousands of girls who have been betrayed by their lovers. She is already on her way to becoming a literary cliché. The truth of Mephistopheles' words is more than Faust can bear, for he must cling to the illusion that Margarete is unique, separate from all the others: "The misery of *this one girl* cuts me to my life's marrow, while you grin calmly at the destruction of thousands" (emphasis added). But Mephistopheles is not deluded as to the true nature of the game Faust has been playing with Margarete; he recognizes the willful Titanism that has characterized Faust from the very beginning:

Do you want to seize the thunder? A good thing that you miserable mortals were not given it! So typical of the tyrant to smash the innocent bystander just to give himself a little room when he's in trouble.

The accusation Mephistopheles levels here at Faust—that like a tyrant he can ruthlessly destroy the innocent simply to satisfy a whim—could easily be the accusation of Prometheus against Zeus, whose empire is built on the smouldering corpses of the Titans, brought to their end by Zeus' tyrannical use of the thunder and lightning. The irony here, however, is that for all his Titanic striving and for all his willful use of an innocent person to achieve his goals, Faust is still no freer than he was in the very opening scene; in fact, the metaphoric prison of the opening monologue is soon to be replaced on the stage by the real prison of Margarete's incarceration.

As Faust enters Margarete's cell, he hears her singing an old song from a fairy tale, the "Märchen vom Machandelboom," the words of which draw a clear parallel to Margarete's own situation; she sings as though she were herself the murdered child: "My mother the whore, / She murdered me!" (4412–13). In words no longer her own (the song is a citation from an actual fairy tale), Margarete defines her own place in the long line of mothers who have killed their children. The trajectory established by the external literary texts cited by Margarete is now clear: from a devout identification with a religious archetype (Zwinger scene), through an identification with the generalized sinner of the *Dies irae* (Cathedral scene), to a position which admits of no externalizing perspective, and no transcendental dimension, a place where Margarete is alone with her own sins (Prison scene). Where in the earlier scene Margarete had identified herself with the Virgin Mary gazing at her dying son, here in the prison scene she is forced to the realization that *her* child was born of no virgin birth, and that she herself was the very murderer of that child. In a horrifying reversal of all the Madonna has symbolized, Margarete's perspective has by this point been systematically diminished and delimited; the external world, and with it the world of religious values, has been rigorously excluded from her vision, so that in her last scene she can identify only with herself and the child of her own body, who has been the victim of her own hand. Margarete's madness is the cruelest form of self-incarceration, and there could be no more chilling a representation of this self-imprisonment than the image of Margarete singing a song about herself and the child she has killed. Visually, the stage settings have followed this trajectory: from the early morning light at the Zwinger, to the half-light of the Cathedral, to the darkness of the prison. At the end of her song, Margarete voices her own fantastic desire to escape: "Then I became a little forest bird— / Fly away, fly away!" (4419–20).

Her imprisonment is the appropriate culmination to the second half of the tragedy, for now she is truly like Faust, her very words a parody of Faust's "Flee! Away! Out into the far-flung lands!" It is highly ironic that it is Faust, whose own incarceration in the self has found no release, who should come as rescuer to Margarete in her own imprisonment. Although he has come with a bundle of keys in his hand, Margarete is as unable to leave the four walls of her prison as Faust was unable to leave the confinement of his study. Unable to take the step toward freedom, Margarete is locked into a world of her own fantasies and desires. Just as Faust could create an entire world out of his fantasies in Margarete's room, so too Margarete can now only create a fantasy world of freedom while standing in the very midst of the most tangible refutation of those fantasies:

> It is he! It is he! Where now is all pain?
> Where now the misery of prison and chains?
> It is you! You have come to save me!
> I am saved!
>
> (4471–74)

Surrounded by the damp walls of her prison, Margarete fantasizes freedom, and here, too, just as in the opening scene of the drama, it is memory of the past which holds out the promise of life over death. No sooner has Margarete exclaimed "I am saved!" than memories flood in as the companions of her salvation:

Once again the street is there
Where first I saw you,
And the happy garden
Where I waited for you with Martha.

(4475–78)

Faust's desire for death in the opening scene of the drama was al-
layed by the presence of memory and for Margarete too it is memory
which holds out a promise of salvation. All these last-hour hopes,
however, of freedom and reprieve only give an intensified sense of
irony to the words Faust spoke in Margarete's room, "In this prison,
what happiness." Once again we are in a prison feasting on delusions
of happiness, but now it is Margarete rather than Faust who is the
author and victim of those illusions.

The final aspect of Margarete's incarceration to be mentioned is
her emerging status as a literary character and her own self-
consciousness of this transformation. The flesh-and-blood Margarete of the opening scenes of the second part of the drama has become, as we have seen, increasingly vulnerable to other literary
texts (and here it is appropriate to suggest that Faust, already a familiar figure in literature for more than two hundred years, is in this
sense yet one other external text which impinges on the "real"
Margarete). At last she too succumbs to literature and pales into
script. The passage in which Margarete recognizes her own literary
character is extremely important and should be examined in detail:

Now I'm completely in your power.
Only first let me suckle my child again.
I held it to me all this long night;
They took it from me, just to annoy me.
And now they say I killed it.
And I can never be happy again.
They sing songs about me! It's wicked of the people!
There's an old song that ends like this,
But who gave them the right to interpret it like this?

(4442–50)

Margarete has mistaken Faust for her executioner, and there is more
than a grain of truth in her mistake; the girl sees Faust entering her
cell and instead of the lover sees the man whose purpose it is to take
her life. In fact, Faust has been *both* lover *and* murderer to her.
Margarete begs to be allowed to nurse her child just once more, but

the dead baby in her arms proves her to be as barren as the witches on the Brocken. Once more a child has died under her care. She fantasizes her child is still alive and that some nameless group of people has taken it from her; the same "they" say that she killed it. This anonymous group plays a large role in creating the terror of the scene, and they occur again and again:

> What's the use of running? They're waiting for me. . . .
>
> (4545)

> It is so sad to wander as an exile,
> And they will still catch me. . . .
>
> (4548–49)

It seems as though the entire world outside the prison wants her blood, and, interestingly enough, it is this same anonymous "they" who are already at work translating the living Margarete into literature—"*Sie* singen Lieder auf mich!" Yet the song they sing is not new; it is an old tale into which the fate of Margarete is being woven. No matter how unfair her fate may be, and no matter to what degree Margarete's own unique situation may militate against her being placed among the long line of the "Kindermörderinnen"— and Goethe makes us feel this injustice deeply in Margarete's poignant words, "And yet I'm still so young, so young, and already have to die" (4432–33)—this anonymous "they," and with them the author of the drama himself, will have their way, and the real Margarete must die to conform to the fate of the literary character of the old tale being told about her.

Like Helena, whose role in *Faust II* is in so many ways a parallel to that of Margarete in *Faust I*, Margarete does not understand the reason for this translation from life into literature. She therefore asks the executioner who gave him the power over her life (4427), and more important, she asks who gave the crowd the right to interpret the old story in this way. C. F. MacIntyre's translation beautifully brings out this sense of the line:

> They sing songs about me! It's wicked of the people!
> There's an old tale ends so. . . .
> But why do they mix me up in it?[40]

Margarete's question is perfectly justified. She sees that her own living presence is being sacrificed to a literary tradition; what she

cannot know is that through her sacrifice she becomes the founder
of a special branch of that tradition, a branch peculiarly Goethean, a
separate line of mothers and surrogate mothers whose children will
die deaths strangely implicated with literary causes. Helena's child
by Faust dies because he tries to fly too high on poetic wings and
Ottilie drops the young son of Charlotte and Eduard into the water
where he drowns because she is trying to balance the child in one
hand and a book in the other. Little Otto becomes yet another child
sacrificed to literature.

We have seen Margarete sacrificed to the text's awareness of its
own literariness and its own place in a long line of literary tradition.
The only character in the drama with enough independent vitality
to draw our attention away from Faust (and the only character to
touch us deeply as she grows from a naive girl to a compassionate
woman) has been relegated to the status of one more manifestation
of the old tale that haunts the text like the old legends haunt the
woods of the Brocken on Walpurgisnight. Yet with her elevation
into the literary, she has achieved the permanence Leonore so desires to have from the poet in *Torquato Tasso:*

> His song will preserve what is passing.
> You will remain beautiful, blessed by fate, when long
> The tide of things has torn you along with it.[41]

Margarete has not died the death of Sussana Margarethe Brandt, the
unfortunate girl who murdered her own illegitimate child in 1771,
and who would be entirely forgotten today if she had not in some
way inspired Goethe's own literary creation. Margarete has been
given another life in art, and the "voice from above" who tells us of
her ultimate salvation may well be the author's own.

3
Iphigenia: Interpretation and Paralysis

The Lord whose oracle is in Delphi neither speaks out nor conceals, but rather gives a sign.
—Heraclitus of Ephesus, fragment B93

A T the very heart of Goethe's *Iphigenia in Tauris* there lies a paradox, as irresolvable as it is profound, and it is largely due to the nature of this paradox that interpretations of the drama have achieved very contradictory results. Schiller was probably the first (but certainly not the last) to categorize the play as "purely ethical":

> The play is so remarkably modern and un-Greek, it is difficult to see how one could even possibly compare it to a Greek play at all. *Iphigenia* is purely ethical.[1]

This ethical interpretation of the play has been curiously supported by Goethe's own comment to Schiller that the play is "ganz verteufelt human"[2] ("quite damnably human"). Critics have consistently placed far more emphasis on the "human" side of the quotation than on the "verteufelt" which qualifies it. And furthermore, "human" has most frequently been interpreted unambiguously as "humane," that is, as a catchword to the humanitarian ideals of the best in German Enlightenment. This has given the drama a comforting interpretation, and one that seems to afford a complementary corollary to Schiller's ethical view. But it requires a certain amount of critical determination simply to overlook the "verteufelt" and to accept the word "human" in its most attractive and benign meaning. This is doubly dangerous for a critic, since it is never wise to read Goethe's comments on his own art as though they were written without irony or as flatly unambiguous. The playfully ironic context of this famous passage should make any reader wary:

> Herewith comes the copy of the musifying play [*Iphigenia*]. I am curious to know what you will get out of it. I've looked into it here and there; it's quite damnably human.

Goethe here is certainly referring to the "humaneness" of the play, but the reference is ironic, and the qualification "verteufelt" points, not to the enlightened and confident humanitarianism of the play, but rather to the darker side of its humanness. The play *is* decidedly human, in that every element of the dramatic structure is designed to bring the transcendental realm of the gods into question. Schiller, in a letter written a few days later, emphasizes this secularized aspect of the play: ". . . you have already accomplished all that is possible from your material without gods or spirits."[3] But how are we to understand ethics in an anti-transcendental world? Can the two readings—"quite damnably human" and "entirely ethical"—really be so easily reconciled? And, if such a reconciliation is somehow possible, we still must admit that the equation of the devilishly human and the purely ethical can be at best an uneasy proposition.

It is this problem which lies at the core of the play and which makes the drama so "remarkably modern." The problem in its most compressed formulation is this: Can in fact the ethical be grounded in the purely human? And to this question the drama offers two opposing answers—yes and no. This is the paradox which runs through the entire play, and it is this that links this play to *Faust*. Furthermore, the theme of translation and interpretation, a thematic nexus organically tied for Goethe to the problem of human ethics, is as central to *Iphigenia* as it is to *Faust*. The question posed by Margarete—"An old tale ends like this, Who gave them the right to interpret it?"—could as easily apply to the oracle of Apollo in *Iphigenia*. Orestes and Pylades are confident they have interpreted the oracle correctly when they take the "sister" to be Iphigenia, but what is there in the play that confirms this decision? Who gives anyone the right to interpret? And who guarantees the accuracy of interpretation? Iphigenia offers a purely secular answer—the pure human heart—but there is much in the drama which militates against so easy an answer and which shows the author's uneasiness with it.

Despite the apparent discomfort with his answer (and I suggest that this sense of uneasiness is one reason he describes the play as *"verteufelt* human"), *Iphigenia* has seemed to many to be "the gleaming peak by which and from which the decline of the belief in humanity in the 19th and 20th centuries can perfectly be measured."[4] Above all, it is the form of the drama, the glistening classical surface it presents to the world, which has made this piece seem so supremely confident of the answer Iphigenia puts forward. *Iphigenia in Tauris* is as classical as any play written in the 1780s could be, and, although there is no chorus to elevate the particular characters' emotions and sentiments into the realm of the universal, the drama contains to a remarkable degree the classical qualities of balance, symmetry, and rhetorical elegance. The smooth, unbroken surface of the play is so seductive that at times it almost obscures the actual content of the action. In few dramas is the conflict between form and content so pronounced, yet here the conflict is intentional and is the direct expression of the paradox which constitutes the meaning of the play. This discrepancy is intended, and is extraordinarily effective. When Iphigenia, for example, at the lowest point of her self-confidence, at last breaks out of the blank iambic pentameter verse to sing her song of the Fates, the effect is astonishing; it is as though by contrasting these short breathless lines with the measured tread of the iambics, Goethe were consciously calling attention to the philosophical conflicts within the work. The surface breaks down at this point because it is no longer able to contain the violent emotions which lie at all times just below it. Only occasionally do we gain such a glimpse of the dark and irrational forces which lie concealed beneath the cool classical surface of the play, but when we do, the darkness seems all the more awesome because of the intense effort expended to keep it out of sight.

Above all, it is the highly formalized rhetoric that creates the elegant surface of the play. Goethe was well aware that the verse of the drama must have a calm and measured flow if it were to sustain the illusion of classical uniformity. The original version of the play, written in prose, was composed in what was for Goethe an extraordinarily short period of time. The first reference to the work is in a letter written to Frau von Stein and dated February 14, 1779.[5] Although he may have had the general outline of the play in his mind for several years before he actually began writing, when the writing did begin, it came unusually fast. By early April of 1779 the play was ready for performance. Shortly thereafter, Goethe began to feel that the drama was not quite what it should be, and on October 13, 1780, he wrote the following to his friend Lavater:

I would rather not allow my *Iphigenia* to be copied a number of times and circulated among people as it is now because I am busy trying to bring more harmony into the style of the play and am also changing things here and there. Be so good as to tell that by way of apology to those who have requested a copy of the piece.[6]

From that time until the end of 1786, when he wrote to Herder that he could finally say that his *Iphigenia* was finished,[7] Goethe was working sporadically at the versification of the play, attempting to bring more "harmony" into its style. The amount of time spent on the construction of this smooth surface for the drama far outweighs the amount spent on the original creation, and during the time of the re-writing, Goethe complains again and again of the difficulty of the task: "I have deluded myself with this piece in that I thought that the work would be easier."[8] When in 1826 Christian Moritz Engelhardt proposed printing an edition of the works of Goethe's youth in which the prose version of *Iphigenia* was to be included, Goethe rejected the idea completely: ". . . I cannot give my approval to this publication, and in fact must protest against it clearly and vigorously."[9] Seldom in Goethe do we find such adamant aversion to the publication of his own works, but here he is so intransigent because the harmonious surface of the play which he worked so hard to achieve is absolutely integral to the effect of the play as he wanted it. Of course he knew that the prose version would eventually be published (since every scrap he wrote was to be so destined), but he hoped to make certain that when it did appear, it would be strictly as an appendix, as a kind of preliminary sketch for the finished product, never as a play in its own right.

For it is truly as a finished product that *Iphigenia in Tauris* is to be read. In no other of his works does Goethe strain so for the elegant phrase, and nowhere does he strive so hard to achieve purely rhetorical effects. With its sheer clarity of form, *Iphigenia* seems at first to be the very antithesis of the fragmented and chaotic *Faust*, and in its own way, Iphigenia's opening monologue, with its highly formal structure, is as programmatic for this drama as Faust's opening monologue, with its abrupt shifts and changes, is for the drama of his name. The passage in *Iphigenia* is worth examining in some detail as an example of the technique which is to be used throughout the play.

The first twenty-two lines are constructed around a movement from the personal to the universal, a rhetorical movement that we find repeated again and again in the course of the play. The opening lines give a clear and rational expression to the intimate feelings which characterize Iphigenia's personal situation:

> Out here into your shadows, stirring treetops
> Of this thick-branching, ancient sacred grove,
> As in the goddess' own hushed sanctuary,
> I even now step with a shuddering awe
> As though my foot fell here for the first time,
> And here my spirit cannot feel at home.[10]
>
> (1–6)

The emotion which is the actual content of these carefully measured periods is the most anticlassical, the most romantic emotion imaginable: yearning ("Sehnsucht"). Goethe himself admitted that Schiller had convinced him of the play's close affinities with Romanticism on just these emotional grounds.[11] Like any romantic figure from Heinrich von Ofterdingen to the characters of Sir Walter Scott's *Waverley* novels, Iphigenia is not at home in the world she inhabits; like them, she dreams of a return to her real home—in her case, to the home of her childhood. If the ability to live fully in the moment, to live free of yearning and remorse in the here and now is an indispensable element of Goethe's classicism, Iphigenia as we see her in the opening speech, is anything but a classical figure. From the very beginning, then, we are aware of a discrepancy between the classical form and the characters who are embodied in it. If we have any doubts about the term "romantic" being applied to Iphigenia's personality, surely there are no such doubts with regard to her death-seeking brother, for he is truly as romantic a figure as any created by actual members of the Romantic school. It is interesting here, in the light of what we are later to discover, that Iphigenia says that she steps into the Taurian grove with the same fear and trembling with which she enters the temple of Diana, for in a sense both Diana and the Taurians have put her in much the same position: the Taurians have granted her a life which is a living death, while the goddess once granted her life only after demanding her death in sacrifice. A life which is death and a death which proved to be life—it is difficult to imagine a more romantic concept than this ironic equation of life and death, yet the rhetoric with its lucidity of diction is at pains to make such oppositions distinct and clear. The content tells us one thing while the form is at considerable pains to tell us otherwise.

The opening lines have given a clear and orderly account of

Iphigenia's tumultuous feelings at the first moment we see her; the subsequent passage steps back and assumes a historical, a distanced rather than a personal perspective, and we learn the actual facts which we assume have caused the emotion at the beginning:

> These many years I have been hidden here
> By a high will unto which I submit,
> Yet I am ever, as at first, a stranger.
> For, ah! the sea divides me from my loved ones,
> And by the shore I stand whole days long through
> With my soul searching for the Grecian land,
> And only muted tones amid its roaring
> Does the wave bring in answer to my sighs.
>
> (7–14)

In this, the second of the larger units of the speech, a greater degree of specificity is obtained. Where in the first part of the speech the subjective feelings seemed to have no bounds or limits, but simply to exist for their own sake, here we learn that Iphigenia's emotion is conditioned by space and time; that is, it is the direct result of the separation from her Greek home, an event which took place some years in the past. We learn, too, that nature, despite its beauty, is indifferent to the desperate plight of the heroine, for her own words and sighs, which are so full of significance and meaning, are answered only by the muted and dull sounds which are themselves without meaning. As in the poems, "The Divine" and "Limits of Humanity," here too nature is only an indifferent environment which can offer no solace to the sick at heart. And so, from the first two units of her speech, a picture emerges: Iphigenia, separated from her home and family in Greece, exists in a kind of limbo, thinking only of the past, unable to accept her existence in the present. She is in a perpetual state of inner rebellion and outer submission to the unspecified "high will" which holds her here. The discrepancy between the rhetoric and the emotions contained in it is a perfect parallel to the discrepancy between the outer submission and inner rebellion of Iphigenia's personality. But, to whom does this high will refer? To Diana? To Thoas, king of the Taurians? Or to both? Since both keep Iphigenia in a state of virtual slavery, it could well refer to both at once.

In the third larger rhetorical unit of the monologue, we move from the historical conditions of the subjective emotions to a gnomic passage which appears to elevate the experience set forth in the first fourteen lines into a formulation of universal validity:

> Alas for one who far from parents, brothers,
> And sisters leads a lonely life! From his
> Lips grief will eat the closest joys away,
> His thoughts forever go a-swarming off
> Towards the halls of his father, where the sun
> Revealed the heavens first to him and where
> At play those born with him bound firm and firmer
> The tender bonds that knit them to each other.
>
> (15–22)

Despite the gnomic form of the passage, Iphigenia is here speaking directly of her own experience—*her* thoughts constantly drift back to her home in Greece, *her* brother and sister are the ones she is thinking of, *hers* is the lonely life which is so pathetic. The use of the more universal masculine form serves rhetorically to elevate her own experience to a status of gnomic truth, and it masks, but does not entirely disguise, the personal truth behind the words. This movement from the particular to the universal has a comforting effect, like the placing of a balm on a painful wound. The rhetoric of the passage seems to gloss over the actual pain we know Iphigenia suffers and to give it a distanced, aesthetic form. The effect of the rhetoric here seems to be something like a bas-relief where a rigid one-dimensionality reduces all variation of gesture and emotion to an aesthetic stasis. I believe that this is the intended effect of the rhetoric, and on one level it succeeds, but there are holes in the smooth patina of the language. Against the one-dimensionality the rhetoric attempts to superimpose, there is the fact that Iphigenia's words tell us more than she intends. In the *exemplum*, for instance, with which she illustrates the situation of the person leading the lonely life, there is an unmistakable reference to Tantalus, founder and chief offender of the house to which Iphigenia belongs. The punishment meted out to Tantalus for his great sin was to stand up to his chin in cool water with a branch of ripe fruit just before his eyes; at each attempt, however, to quench his thirst or to satisfy his hunger, the water or fruit would recede just out of his reach. He is, quite literally, the one whose nearest pleasure is snatched from before his lips. Is Iphigenia aware of the implication of the figure she has used? Does she know that she has chosen a very personal example to illustrate what she is presenting as statements of universal applicability, an example which reveals her own link to the fate of Tantalus? The rhetorical turn to the gnomic is, then, not quite as impersonal as it would at first seem; the calming effect is, on closer inspection, not so calming.

There is, in other words, something suspect about the rhetoric employed in the drama, and our sense of uneasiness with it is only intensified by the clichéd, highly symmetrical contrast which follows:

> I do not argue with the gods; and yet
> The lot of women is a piteous thing.
> At home or in the wars a man commands,
> And in far lands he can still make his way.
> Possession gives him pleasure, victory crowns him.
> A death with honor will be his at last.
> How close restricted is a woman's joy!
> Even obeying a harsh husband is
> A duty and a comfort; but how wretched
> If hostile fate drives her to alien lands!
>
> (23–32)

The passage is painfully self-conscious in its balance and symmetry, yet when we penetrate the almost plastic surface, we find that here too the intended effect of the rhetoric is at odds with what lies below the surface. To begin with, the first two lines repeat, in a cool and composed way, the posture of outer submission and inner rebellion; if given a more vigorous expression, the sentiment would be worthy of a Prometheus: "I do not quarrel with the gods, *although I have every right to do so.*" The question comes to mind—does Iphigenia refrain from struggling with the divine because she feels that, as a woman, she lacks the strength? Would she fight if she were a man? Time and again we have the impression that Iphigenia is actually an inverted Prometheus, and, as we shall see, the rejection of the transcendental is as important an element in this drama as it is in *Faust* or in the poem "Prometheus." It is possibly this antitranscendental tendency that Goethe had in mind when he called the play "verteufelt human."

More than three decades after the completion of *Iphigenia*, Goethe wrote his most important comment on the play in his *Poetry and Truth;* speaking of his early attraction to the figure of Prometheus, he continues:

. . . the more daring of this race were my saints—Tantalus, Ixion, Sisyphus. Taken up into the company of the gods, they were not willing to behave themselves submissively enough and so they earned the anger of their generous hosts for being too spirited guests and they drew upon themselves an unhappy exile. I felt sorry for them; their status was already recognized by the ancients as truly tragic, and if I showed them as members of a monstrous opposition in the background of my *Iphigenia*, then I am surely indebted to them for a part of the effect which it was the good fortune of this play to bring forth.[12]

The Titans are the rough backdrop against which the smooth surface of the play is super-imposed, and they are the spiritual forebears of Iphigenia herself. Like them, she is unwilling to behave herself toward the gods (and toward her Taurian host) in the reverential and submissive way the gods deem appropriate. If we read the play keeping in mind the interpretation suggested by Goethe himself, the rhetoric of the piece becomes less an expression of "pure humanity" than a beautiful but somewhat ineffectual screen through which we occasionally glimpse the terrible antitranscendental "opposition" symbolized by Tantalus and his Titanic companions. The figure of Tantalus is somewhat obscured by the rhetoric in lines 16–17, but the passage gains its effects because he *is* there despite the camouflage.

The suppressed emotion of lines 23–24 is the result of the reduction of the Titanic struggle against the gods to the human level. The lines which follow, four devoted to the superiority of men, four to the inferiority of women, are couched in the language of a gnomic statement, but are in fact, like the gnomic passage beginning at line 15, only a generalized statement of Iphigenia's own situation. She senses her helplessness and puts this sentiment into the universal "the lot of women is a piteous thing." As an *exemplum per contrarium*, she then catalogues the advantages of being a man: he is glorified by his wars, by his home, by his possessions, and by his noble death. Ironically, every one of the glories attributed to the male as a typical being finds its contradiction in the particular and unique fate of Iphigenia's own father, Agamemnon. Of course, at this point, Iphigenia does not know what has happened to her father since he left Aulis, but we as readers do, and the truth as we know it undercuts the neat rhetorical contrast and once again renders the surface of the drama suspect. That her appraisal of what it is to be a man is totally contradicted by the facts of Agamemnon's fate makes Iphigenia's rhetorical move toward the generalized and universal faulty. Neither of her examples, male or female, proves to be a true gnomic statement of what it means to belong to a general class. When Iphigenia focuses on the disadvantages of being a woman, the catalogue of misfortunes fits far too closely her own fate for us to take these universalizing statements about "womanhood" as truly universal; although the ostensible subject of the sentence is "woman," the actual subject is too obviously Iphigenia herself. In fact, the very structure of the catalogue of disadvantages is carefully designed so that the last misfortune listed refers so unambiguously to Iphigenia herself that it functions as a kind of transition to return the speech to the particulars of the present situation in which Iphigenia finds herself: "Thus Thoas holds me here, a noble man, / In solemn, sacred bonds of slavery" (33–34). The very phrase, the "sacred bonds of slavery" refers as easily to Iphigenia's relationship to Diana as to her relationship to Thoas. Both hold her in bondage, and she desires her freedom from both: "O with what shame it is that I acknowledge / That I serve thee, Goddess, with a mute reluctance" (35–36). She may be reluctant to admit her recalcitrance toward authority, but it is there, and it is concrete proof of her spiritual heritage of rebellion.

The final nineteen lines of the monologue constitute a prayer to Diana, entreating the goddess once again to save Iphigenia and bring her back to her own family. The form of this final rhetorical unit is that of a classical tripartite Greek prayer, beginning with an invocation and a recounting of deeds performed in the past, continuing with an "if . . . then . . ." clause (e.g., "if ever I sacrificed to you, then hear me now"), and culminating in the actual request directed to the deity. Despite its classical form, however, this prayer is hardly classical in its content or effect, and this is so primarily because at every moment that the smooth-flowing rhetoric attempts to persuade us to one attitude or assumption, we are at the same time invited to see behind that rhetoric and to question it. The invocation to the prayer contains the proper appellations—"Goddess," "Savior," "Diana"— but begins somewhat less than auspiciously as Iphigenia states that her service to the goddess is one of quiet resistance rather than a free acceptance of duty. To begin a prayer by questioning one relationship to the deity invoked is certainly a radical departure from our expectations of what a classical prayer should be and separates this prayer decisively from any Greek model. The discrepancy between classical form and modern content could hardly be more obvious than in this very unusual invocation. Iphigenia then appropriately recounts a past deed of the goddess that has direct bearing on the specific request which will be made at the end of the prayer:

I have, moreover, trusted in thee ever
And now trust in thee still, Diana, who
Didst take me in thy holy, gentle arm,
The outcast daughter of the mightiest king

(39–42)

Diana saved her from her father's sword on the altar at Aulis. What Iphigenia does not mention, but what we already know, and what she will mention directly, is that it was Diana herself who in fact demanded her life in the first place. Diana has been responsible for both Iphigenia's life *and* death, and this knowledge must color our reading of this prayer. The parallelism of the lines "In solemn, sacred bonds of slavery" (34) and "In thy holy, gentle arm" (42) suggests that the chains of bondage and the soft arms of rescue are not so different. Why has Diana acted in this contradictory and incomprehensible way? We cannot know, and the play offers no answers, but it does offer a response, perhaps the only response. At the end of the "Song of the Fates" in the fourth act, the utter indifference of the gods to men is made explicit in these lines:

These rulers avert
The eyes of their blessing
From whole generations. . . .

(1754–56)

Old Tantalus, imprisoned in Hades, has heard the song Iphigenia is quoting; he thinks of the sad plight of his descendants "and shakes his head." He shakes his head over the incomprehensible actions of the gods; it is a response born of his great experience and suffering, and it is profound. Given that gods are characterized by such arbitrary and incomprehensible behavior, it is no wonder the humans in the play turn away from them. But, in a world where transpersonal ethical models are absent, where are humans to turn for standards of judgment? The Archimedean point of reference, so conspicuously missing in the world of Faust, cannot be said to be present in the world of Iphigenia either.

We as readers are no less uneasy than Iphigenia or her ancestor over the gods' inconsistent behavior, and the uneasiness we feel is not alleviated by the second part of the prayer, the section traditionally expressed in an "if . . . then . . ." construction:

Yes, Zeus' daughter, if thou didst conduct
That lofty man whom thou didst plunge in anguish

> Demanding his own daughter so that he,
> The godlike Agamemnon, brought his dearest
> Possession to thy altar, if thou didst
> Guide him with fame from Troy's walls overthrown
> Back to his fatherland, preserving for him
> His spouse and treasures, Electra and his son:—
> Then bring me too back to my own at last. . . .
>
> (43–51)

Iphigenia's hopes are based on the belief that, if Diana can bring her father home safely from the war to his wife and family, who have been well protected in his absence, then she also has the power to return Iphigenia to that happy family. Of course, Diana has done none of these things—Agamemnon returns home to be murdered by a wife who has become mistress of another; Orestes has in turn murdered his mother Klytemnestra; Electra seems to have gone berserk; and Orestes is driven across the earth by the avenging Furies. Iphigenia's basis for hope, then, expressed in these lines of exquisite rhetoric, is so patently groundless that the entire prayer seems a beautiful bridge of illusions built over the abyss of reality. Seldom in the Greek literature on which *Iphigenia* is based do we find such a prayer as this, where a bitter irony assures us that the suppliant's wishes are in vain. Goethe has taken the classical form of the prayer and subverted it into its very opposite, so that when Iphigenia reaches the culmination of her prayer at the end of her monologue— "And save me, whom thou once didst save from death, / From this life here as well, a second death!" (52–53)—we have no reason whatever to believe that the desperate hopes of Iphigenia are of any concern at all to the goddess.

At the opening of *Iphigenia*, then, we are confronted by a situation which, despite the very different language which conjures it up, is not so very different from the opening of *Faust*. Oskar Seidlin has noted:

> At the beginning there was the atmosphere of the prison: man caught by a merciless fate, banished to the deadly island where no messenger ever appears.[13]

As in *Faust*, an important aspect of this carceral atmosphere is the real and obvious absence of a transcendental dimension. Iphigenia is not yet consciously aware of this absence, but her prayer, which is clearly grounded in an illusory faith, reveals to *us* this disturbing truth: The gods may not be relied upon, and even worse, their arbitrary and inconsistent behavior is not to be understood by mortals. The best we can conclude is that the gods, in their benign manifestation, exist only as projections of human hopes and values, and these projections only occasionally coincide with reality. The actual doors to heaven seem as closed to man here as they are at the end of the Prologue in *Faust*. Iphigenia, faced with the decision whether to deceive King Thoas and thus to escape with her brother back to Greece, or to remain faithful to the kindness her host has shown to her and to reveal to him the planned escape, must ground her action in some ethical principle if she is to find a satisfactory answer to her dilemma. But the gods, representatives of the transcendental realm, have been shown in the very first monologue of the play to be unreliable, perhaps whimsical beings (if existing at all), and so cannot provide that answer. When they do speak (as in the oracle of Apollo), they speak ambiguously, and the burden of interpretation is cast upon the mortals. And so Iphigenia, like Faust, is thrown in upon herself. The scene of her imprisonment in the self looks less like a prison than does Faust's study because of the classical surface of the play which encourages us to see the landscape as one of Mediterranean beauty, but in truth it is no less confining. And, just as Faust's study still bore traces in the vaulted ceiling and the stained glass windows of a belief now vanished, so Iphigenia's world is still caught in the grasp of a primitive faith which even as the play opens is being revealed as empty.

Iphigenia's dilemma is a very real one; on either side there are pressing ethical commitments. On the one hand, there is her brother, to whom she owes familial allegiance; through saving him and returning with him to Greece, she hopes to institute a new age in the house of Tantalus, an era in which the age-old curse will at last be put to rest. On the other hand, there is Thoas, to whom she owes a great deal for his kindness and generosity. Her moral commitment to him is strong, for it is here that she has had the greatest moral triumph of her life in persuading the Taurians to abandon their age-old custom of slaughtering the foreigners who land on their shores. She has effected the abolition of one curse; in Greece she hopes to be able to abolish another. Yet, by her recalcitrance to remain with Thoas and to become his wife, she has jeopardized her earlier achievement, and Thoas threatens to reinstate the murderous practice. For her to argue that the gods do not desire sacrifices like this is meaningless, for her very presence in Tauris is itself testimony to the gods' demand for sacrifice. Where is Iphigenia to find answers to her ethical dilemma?

Iphigenia puts her trust in her own heart; she trusts her own feelings, and because she is fortunate and because this play is not a tragedy (Goethe simply called it a "Schauspiel"—a "play"), she is able both to have her cake and eat it too. She escapes with her brother and his friend Pylades while at the same time maintaining the purity of her heart by making an open confession of the deceptive escape plans to Thoas. Iphigenia gets off the horns of her dilemma very easily. (In speaking of the "humaneness" of the play, could Goethe have been referring, not to the virtues of Iphigenia, but to his own humane treatment of his fictive characters?) Many critics have seen in Iphigenia's good fortune the triumph of an ethics grounded in the purely human. This view is expressed most succinctly by Seidlin in a perceptive essay on the play:

> The image of man which Goethe has created in his Iphigenia is the "beautiful soul," a concept so dear to his heart because here and here alone the dichotomy of an animalistic and a spiritual part of man is resolved. The law which Iphigenia lives and which triumphs through her is neither the natural law "Thou must," nor the ethical law "Thou shalt," but a miraculous reconciliation in which the "must" and "shall" are one and the same.[14]

Seidlin goes on to say that the "beautiful soul" can in fact be beautiful because it is in the aesthetic realm—that is, in the work of art—that such a resolution between the two laws can take place, and I must add to this that it is *only* in the aesthetic realm that such resolution is possible. If this is then true, and such a reconciliation between natural and ethical demands is possible only in a work of art, then we must conclude that art and life must be very different indeed. The recognition of this resolution within art would not necessarily be cause for rejoicing, for this would only underline the discrepancy between art and life—"Ernst ist das Leben, heiter ist die Kunst" ("Life is serious while art is joyous") as Schiller will express it in the prologue to his *Wallenstein*, a drama more indebted to Goethe's *Iphigenia* than is usually recognized. The "beautiful soul" exists only in literature, and the very text of Goethe's *Iphigenia* reveals Goethe's own awareness of the fragility and artificiality of the concept. In a work of art, an ethics may be grounded in the purely human, but not in real life, and for this reason the play presents a beautiful and confident surface while at the same time it cautiously reveals the author's own deep uneasiness with the fact that it *is* only an aesthetic creation. Goethe would have good reason to be suspicious of this aesthetic realm which he had created as a form for this optimistic view of human ethics; a work of art need not, perhaps cannot, portray life as it actually is, and is capable of presenting human destiny from the most artificial perspective. Hardy's improbable unravelings of a hostile fate are no less defensible artistically than Goethe's more optimistic destiny laid out for Iphigenia. A comparison of Iphigenia's fate with that of Margarete will show just how arbitrary the consequences of the same ethical imperative can be within the aesthetic context. Margarete does exactly what Iphigenia does, that is, she puts her complete trust in her feelings, and yet she, unlike Iphigenia, comes to a dreadful end. The very words of Iphigenia could well be placed in the mouth of Margarete: "I do not analyze; I merely feel" (1650). But, unlike Iphigenia, Margarete's dependence on her feelings leads to catastrophe. To use the terms suggested by Seidlin, we could describe Margarete's case as a complete conflict of natural and ethical demands where no healing reconciliation is possible. But why should Margarete's trust in her feelings bring her to destruction while Iphigenia's trust brings her all she desires? Who is in a position to judge which heart is pure and which is not? Or, to put the question in Margarete's language, who has the right to interpret? Goethe was fully aware of the fragility of the aesthetic enterprise in *Iphigenia:* if such a world as would admit of the beneficence of fate and the reconciliation of one law to another as we see it in *Iphigenia* can only be an aesthetic one, then the aesthetic quality of that world must be flawless. This is why Goethe polished for nearly seven years on the surface of the play; he knew he must create "more harmony" in the style of the play precisely because it is *only* in the style, the rhetoric, and dramatic structure of the play, that the harmony can exist at all. When we look beyond the style, we discover the great discomfort of the author with the project, for it is, as he says, "verteufelt human."

If we consider for a moment the role played by Orestes, we see here even more clearly the sense of uneasiness within the drama. He enters in the second act and promptly reveals himself to be more anti-classical in his personality than even Iphigenia. In fact, he is in love with death—"It is the path of death that we are treading; / With every step my soul becomes more silent. . . ." (561–63)—and in the image of himself and Pylades as flower and butterfly there is a conceit that could easily have come from Novalis:

> . . . you, an ever blithe companion, like
> A light and many-colored butterfly
> Around a sombre flower, every day
> Would dart in new and playful life about me. . . .
>
> (647–50)

Like Iphigenia (and like Faust), he cannot live in the present; filled with remorse over murdering his mother, he cannot forget the horrors of the past. His is a state of spiritual paralysis, and while his friend Pylades continually encourages him to leave off his brooding and join him in the quest for "great deeds," Orestes cannot shake himself free of the Furies who plague him. It is important that we never actually see the Furies, for they are, like the gods of the play, shadowy creatures who require men's interpretation to give them their existence. Like Satan in the Walpurgisnight of *Faust*, they exert a kind of power that is enhanced by their very invisibility. Pylades, Orestes' bosom companion, and therefore the person most likely to have shared the experience of the Furies, hardly acknowledges their existence at all, and consistently treats Orestes' affliction as one generated from within himself rather than as one coming from the outside:

> Raise up your soul out of this gloominess;
> By doubting, you bring danger on.
>
> (608–10)

"Let the dead bury the dead" is Pylades' attitude toward the spirits who torment Orestes. To Pylades, the presence of such spirits is entirely dependent on their being *allowed* to exist:

> O, let hellish spirits
> Converse nocturnally about that hour! [Agamemnon's death]
>
> (628–29)

For Pylades, only the present matters, and in this respect, he is perhaps the most "classical" of all the characters in the drama. For him, the Furies are as unreal as the past; since neither can be used as impetus and aid to present action, they are simply to be forgotten.

The past, as well as any transcendental realm he may believe in, is for Pylades only to be used pragmatically:

> May recollections of fair times give us
> New strength for fresh careers of heroism.
> The gods have need of many a good man
> To do their service on this earth.
>
> (630–33)

And who is to determine just what that service is to be? There is no doubt in Pylades' mind: What he wants to do—accomplish deeds of heroism—is just what the gods want him to do. The gods are for him the rubber stamp of his own will. Orestes echoes the suspicion of Thoas and restates the major theme of the play when he says to Pylades: "With rare skill you entwine the gods' devices / And your own wishes neatly into one" (740–41).

Much has been written about the miraculous healing Orestes experiences in the presence of his sister, but it should not be forgotten that Iphigenia also undergoes a process of healing in the presence of her brother, for it is he who brings Iphigenia out of what she has called her "life here, a second death." Each needs the other for the fulfillment of the personality. Iphigenia gains through Orestes the opportunity to renew her commitment to her family, and through Iphigenia Orestes gains freedom from the curse which has kept him from being truly human. Now, he says:

> The curse is lifting; my heart tells me so.
> To Tartarus pass the Euminides,
> I hear their going and they close behind them
> The doors of bronze with far-receding thunder.
> The earth exhales refreshing fragrance and
> Invites me to its plains for full pursuit
> Of life's delights and high accomplishment.
>
> (1358–64)

The bronze doors have shut on the supernatural beings who seemed to exist until this point, and in a sense we might say that with these closing doors, all transcendental forces are shut out of the drama, for from this point on, the gods play no role at all. This is not to say, however, that they were ever to have been given unquestioned credibility. But, however ambiguous their existence in the earlier part of the play, they now become at best simply the projections of the humans in the drama. No deity comes forth to help Iphigenia in her dilemma at the beginning of the fourth act; Apollo does not appear to sanctify the daring interpretation given to his oracular pronouncement. When the heavens close in *Faust I*, divine authentication is withdrawn from man's interpretation of religious pronouncement; Faust may translate the Bible very much as he likes. Here, with the closing of the bronze doors of Hades, a similar freedom of interpretation becomes possible. The statue of Diana can now, with no second thoughts, be left behind in Tauris in the hands of barbarians, for Iphigenia, a human being, has literally and figuratively replaced the goddess, and this act of substitution, human for divine, is at the heart of the play.[15]

In terms of dramatic representation, the action could not be more obvious: Orestes and his friend have begun a search for the lifeless image of a deity; they return with an actual living human being. No deity has brought Iphigenia redemption out of her living death in Tauris; it is rather an act of human interpretation that makes her free:

> This [the oracle] we construed to mean Apollo's sister,
> While he had *you* in mind! Your harsh bonds are
> Now stricken off, and you, O holy one,
> Are now restored to your own people.
>
> (2116–19)

It is an act of human interpretation that has put her in a position to participate in the "great deeds" dreamed of by Pylades and Orestes. It is not just rhetoric that prompts Orestes to refer to his sister as "you holy one"; his phrase demonstrates that he clearly sees Iphigenia as the surrogate for the deity. This act of substitution is strongly supported by the rhetoric of the first three acts, the primary focus of which is the revelation of Iphigenia's identity. It is this act of revelation, accompanied by the rhetorical crescendos which culminate in the actual name "Iphigenia," that constitutes the complement to the healing of Orestes. Just as he must free himself from the Furies of remorse and guilt, so too must Iphigenia leave the dark realm of anonymity and openly announce to the world who she is and the history of the family which has brought her to the existence she now leads. The knowledge of her own hidden identity has been festering in Iphigenia, much as the knowledge of his crime has sickened the mind of Orestes, and the image of the festering wound which Orestes evokes when he says to Iphigenia:

> Yes, wield your knife, do not hold back at all,
> Slash wide this breast and open a path
> For all the rivers that seethe here within
>
> (1252–54)

could easily apply to Iphigenia's own state of paralysis; the streams unleashed by the healing of Orestes' mind are reflected in the streams of words in which Iphigenia releases the long withheld secret of her identity: "Hear! I am of the race of Tantalus" (306). Thus Iphigenia begins, and some one hundred and thirty lines later she reaches the culmination of her revelation speech: "I am that very same Iphigenia, / Grandchild of Atreus, Agamemnon's daughter" (430–31). The rhetoric of the first act as well as the course of the plot leads up to this: the revelation of Iphigenia's identity is the major action of the first part of the play and is the thematic counterpart to the healing of Orestes.

   In the second act, the rhetoric of the plot once again places Iphigenia in the full light of history. Pylades has recounted to her the portion of her family's history which up to that point has remained unknown to her—the murder of her father by Klytemnestra. Iphigenia asks what was the reason for the murder, and once again the long narrative of the house of Tantalus culminates in the naming of her own name:

> To Aulis he enticed her, and since some
> Divinity denied the Greeks their sailing
> By violence of winds, he brought his daughter,
> His eldest-born, Iphigenia, up
> Before Diana's altar, and she died.
>
> (908–12)

Thus Iphigenia learns that she is not only the victim of the curse on her house, but also the cause of the further workings of that curse. Angered at the sacrifice of her daughter, Klytemnestra accepted the love of another man and eventually murdered Agamemnon on his return from Troy. With the revelation of the identity of Iphigenia comes the recognition of her personal implication in the history of Tantalus and his heirs.

   The rhetorical climax of both acts one and two has been the naming of Iphigenia, and yet once more in the third act Iphigenia must reveal her identity, this time to her brother. Orestes asks:

> Who are you, you whose voice so hideously
> Turns back my inmost being on its depths?
> (1170–71)

to which Iphigenia replies:

> Your inmost being tells you who I am.
> Orestes, it is I! Iphigenia!
> I am alive!
> (1172–74)

By the end of the first three acts, all the relevant facts of the past have been recounted and revealed, and at the end of each narrative segment the name of Iphigenia has stood as rhetorical culmination. By the end of these three acts, Iphigenia has acknowledged her identity and accepted the historical circumstances which have determined that identity and given it its meaning. It should be emphasized here that Iphigenia's identity as it is revealed in these three sections is strictly historical, not religious. Until this point, her identity has been that of an anonymous priestess of Diana; now, with the full historical revelation of who she is, the religious identity is replaced by her own historical existence. Nietzsche once wrote, "Nothing is definable unless it has no history,"[16] and the insight has direct bearing here, for on learning and accepting her historical existence, Iphigenia casts off the definition of her identity which until then had seemed valid. "Not priestess! only Agamemnon's daughter" (1822), she cries in a moment of self-recognition. In the course of these three acts, the lines of the ethical dilemma facing Iphigenia have also been established, so that by the beginning of the fourth act we are ready to see the focus of the play shift from the past to the future as we see how Iphigenia will resolve the dilemma set before her and her loved ones.

The structure of the first three acts has been so designed that Iphigenia is gradually revealed as the focus of the historical events leading up to the point at which the drama begins. But she has become more than the perspective through which the events of the past are to be seen, for in the course of these three acts there has been a second revelation: Iphigenia emerges as the ethical focus of the play. Of all the characters in the play, it is above all Iphigenia who is in touch with her own heart, and it is from this source of strength that she draws courage to make the ethical decisions before her. Yet is the heart sufficient? By what criteria are we to judge the rectitude of the heart's decisions? When Iphigenia refuses the king's offer of marriage, she ascribes her decision to the gods who speak through her heart. But Thoas does not share her confidence that what she intends has divine sanction: "No god speaks; it is your own heart that speaks" (493). Iphigenia replies, "Through our hearts only do they speak to us" (494), a statement which destroys and validates the gods at the same time. For Iphigenia, the human heart has become the interpreter of the gods' will, but where is the external confirmation that the heart has interpreted correctly? Thoas' question, "Do I not have the right to hear them too?" (495), must not be passsed over lightly and there is surely a cynical irony in Thoas' reminder to Iphigenia that her "right to the table of Zeus" is an inherited one (499–501). The thought that she is descended from Tantalus, the greatest of the misinterpreters of the gods' will, must be sobering to Iphigenia. Tantalus committed his horrible crime in the belief that he was pleasing the gods with his sacrificed son. Could Iphigenia be equally mistaken in her interpretation of what the gods desire? Thoas reminds us once more of Margarete's question—who has the right to interpret?

It is the question of the sufficiency of the human heart which is one of the most important themes, if not *the* most important, in Weimar classicism. It is not a coincidence that Schiller was rereading *Iphigenia* at the time of Wallenstein's composition, since that trilogy is above all an exploration of the human heart as an adequate interpreter of human history and ethics. And it is at this point that Weimar classicism shows most clearly its debt to the assumptions and attitudes of the earlier period out of which it grew; the great heroes of Goethe's and Schiller's Sturm und Drang—Götz, Faust, Räuber Moor, Prometheus—are all children of the race of the Titans, and their chief inheritance from their forefathers is their confidence in the human heart as a guiding star to great deeds. And this firm emphasis placed on the human heart must find its corollary in the rejection of external criteria of judgment, whether that external realm be religious or social. In every one of the works of the Sturm und Drang, as we have seen exemplified in *Faust*, there is that emphatic rejection. The rejection of the external in *Iphigenia* is more subtle, but it is there, and as always in Goethe, this rejection is accompanied by uneasiness.

Nowhere in *Iphigenia* do we find any external confirmation that the reading given to the divine intent by Iphigenia's heart is the correct one. Indeed, nature itself seems to encourage the escape plans conceived by Pylades. Returning to the temple to hasten Iphigenia in carrying out her part of the plans, he tells her:

> Each hand is eager to lay hold of oars,
> And from the land a light breeze even spread
> Its lovely pinions, as we all observed.
> So let us hurry!
>
> (1557–60)

A fresh wind has risen to speed the escape, and every sailor is straining for the oars, but Iphigenia alone holds back because her heart prompts her to do so—to jeopardize the planned escape and the lives of Orestes, Pylades, and all the Greeks with them so that she may reconcile herself with Thoas. Certainly, behind this desire there is a noble motive, yet there is also something undeniably egotistical in her willingness to endanger the lives of all so that her own heart will remain pure. Pylades tries to persuade her that her clandestine escape will be judged proper by all who matter, but Iphigenia remains recalcitrant:

> *Iphigenia:* My own heart is not satisfied, however.
> *Pylades:* Excess of scruple is a mask for pride.
> *Iphigenia:* I do not analyze, I merely feel.
> *Pylades:* If you feel rightly, you must revere your action.
> *Iphigenia:* Unstained alone the heart approves itself.
>
> (1648–52)

In her reluctance to follow the practical wisdom of Pylades, Iphigenia shows most clearly her inheritance from the Titans. Rather than compromise her own independence and sense of integrity, she will assume enormous risks and take upon herself responsibility for the lives Thoas would kill. For ten years—the years between the sacrifice at Aulis and the fall of Troy—Iphigenia has accepted a static definition of herself as priestess, and now, with her hard-won acceptance of herself as a historically determined human, she can no longer remain passive in this religious definition, but must now accept an active role in the great deeds, the future history, which now lie before her. To do otherwise would be to reject that personal and historical identity. With the acceptance of her new identity, there has also been an implicit rejection of the realm of the gods. Lip service is still paid to the realm of the divine, but from the end of the third act, Iphigenia is acting on her own. Her world is no longer circumscribed by the temple's boundaries; her horizons have opened up to the entire world, and the dangers which she now must face are greater to the same degree that her scope for action is wider. In the fourth act, Iphigenia comes to a full realization of her own freedom and the dangers which come with it.

The course of the act is bounded by two lyrical passages—the first a song of the gods' benevolence, and the second a song of their indifference, even of their hostility. Between these two diametrically opposed songs, Iphigenia's dilemma is brought to the point of crisis. The opening song is one of thanks to the gods for having provided so helpful a friend as Pylades:

> Once the immortals destine
> Mainfold confusions
> For one of the dwellers of earth,
> Once they ready for him
> Utterly shattering changes
> Over from joy to sorrow
> And then from sorrow to joy,
> Then, be it close by his city
> Or on a distant shore,
> They undertake to provide
> Him with a tranquil friend,
> So that in hours of need
> There may be help at hand.
>
> (1369–81)

In its childlike belief that the gods will provide help in time of the affliction caused by the gods themselves, the poem approaches the desperate piety of Hölderlin's

> Wo aber Gefahr ist, wächst
> Das Rettende auch
>
> ("Patmos," 3–4)
>
> (But where danger is, builds
> Salvation also).

But the entire point of the song is drastically undercut when, within twenty lines, Iphigenia comes to the realization that she cannot follow the advice of the friend whose presence she has attributed to the gods' benevolence. The gods, it seems, not only inflict upon man great tribulation, but they also offer false remedies and methods of escape. Iphigenia recognizes that the way devised by Pylades, an escape effected through craft and deception, runs counter to her own human feelings; she insists that her own nature is utterly antithetical to such measures. Thus, the childlike trust in the gods suggested by the opening of the song is very quickly clouded by Iphigenia's perception that she simply cannot follow Pylades. The gift of the gods has proven unacceptable.

When Arkas, the king's messenger, appears to ask the reason for the delay in the sacrifice of the two Greeks, he only reinforces in Iphigenia the knowledge that whatever action she may take must be her own. King Thoas, angered at Iphigenia's refusal to marry him, has ordered the sacrifice of these men, but Arkas himself, delivering his master's message, hopes that Iphigenia will intervene and prevent the king from resuming the old barbaric practice. Iphigenia halfheartedly uses the gods as an excuse for her delay, but Arkas, unconvinced by this subterfuge, clearly states that it is not the gods who are at issue here, but Iphigenia herself and her own decision:

> *Iphigenia:* I have laid it in the hands of the gods.
> *Arkas:* They tend toward human means to rescue humans.
> *Iphigenia:* All things depend upon their slightest hint.
> *Arkas:* And I tell you it lies within *your* hands.
> (1462–25; emphasis added)

The short exchange of words with Arkas reveals more clearly to Iphigenia the delusion under which she had begun to act and brings her to the realization that her ethical commitment lies not with the gods, but with the world of humans:

> Now the voice
> Of this true man has reawakened me,
> Reminding me that here too I abandon
> Human beings.
> (1522–25)

In her own heart she replaces the commitment to carry out the imperative of Apollo with the strictly human imperative. Now, having recognized the unreliability of the gods and having chosen to obey the prompting of her own heart rather than blindly follow the demand of Apollo that his sister's statue be brought out of Tauris, she is still faced with conflicting ethical commitments. The oracle cannot be accepted without some act of human interpretation. The act ends with Iphigenia confronting the ethical conflict with only her heart to guide her, and it is no coincidence that at this point she remembers the Titans and the tragic consequences of their having acted as though they were the masters of their own fate. The independence of their action was expressed in the rebellion against the Olympian deities. Iphigenia is fully aware that in acting on the imperative of her own heart rather than on the words of Apollo she is walking in the footsteps of her ancestor the Titan, and is running the risk of sharing the fate of him and his race. She hopes that, by maintaining an independent course of action and holding to a reverent attitude toward the gods whom she is in fact ignoring, she will avoid the punishment suffered by those who go against the conventions of belief:

> And may the hatred
> That those primeval gods, the Titans, feel
> Toward you Olympians, not rend my tender
> Bosom also with its vulture claws.
>
> (1713–16)

Consciously, Iphigenia is praying that she may transform the hate of the Titans into gentle acquiescence, but the image that emerges in her speech, that of the vulture's claws, is a strong reminder of the monumental punishment meted out to Prometheus. Having offended Zeus by coming to the aid of the race of man, Prometheus is chained to a rock where daily a vulture tears into his entrails and eats them. The claws of the vulture as an image applies not just to the hate of the Titans, but to the injustice of the Olympians as well. The image appears in the speech of Iphigenia as involuntarily as the image of Tantalus appears in her opening monologue. At the very moment Iphigenia pleads for a benign interpretation of the gods, her language betrays her and reveals her own deep roots in the destiny of the Titans. Then, as though prompted by the involuntary memory of Prometheus' fate, Iphigenia consciously remembers the old song of the Parcae, which she heard as a child and which is a genuine expression of condemnation for the Olympians.

The song begins with a forthright description of the arbitrariness of the gods' actions:

> Dominion they hold
> In hands everlasting,

> With power to use it
> As they may see fit.
>
> (1728–31)

Hans Wolff, who sees the song as the turning point of the drama, describes the theme of the song as "the complete incomprehensibility of the gods."[17] Wolff, who reads the drama as an unambiguous victory of the ethical, interprets the vision of the divine offered in the song as comparable to a Christian notion of God:

> The gods described by the Song of the Parcae resemble the *deus absconditus* of Protestantism, the incomprehensible god of anger and predestination, whom mortals must fear because they do not understand him.[18]

It is on the basis of this reading of the song that Wolff justifies his ethical interpretation of the play, arguing that Iphigenia realizes as she sings that God's ways are not to be understood in human terms; she realizes that she must not expect human payment from God for a truly moral act, and furthermore, that such a god demands silent submission to his will. All this, Wolff argues, takes from her heart the inner rebellion she knew earlier and makes her capable of right action.

As appealing as this interpretation is—and it is by no means an isolated interpretation in the history of *Iphigenia* criticism—the grounds upon which it rests are not as sure a foundation as one could want. If the gods portrayed in the Song of the Parcae are truly only a veiled description of a Christian notion of God, then Iphigenia's act of submission could be read as a triumph of the ethical, but there are simply too many points of difference for the conversion to be convincing, and it is not at all clear that Iphigenia's attitude at the end of this act *is* one of submission. To begin with, the song speaks of gods, not God, and it cannot be assumed that these gods within the context of the drama speak with a unity of will. Have the actions of Apollo and Diana, for example, been seen to issue from one source? Certainly the actions of the gods in the history of the Trojan war and in the legends of the Titans, both of which form important backgrounds for this play, are anything but unified. Moreover, even the most dire Calvinistic concept of God sees him as not only unified, but as having a divine plan operative within the world. And even if men cannot fully know that plan, there are at least broad hints as to its meaning given in the Bible, a document which secures for even the bleakest of Christian predestination a measure of comprehensibility. No Christian view of God, Calvinistic or Catholic, sees God as totally absent from the world he created. But the gods spoken of here give no evidence of action within the world, apart from their occasional appearance in legend and in the projected imagination of humans. Far from being active in the world, they seem to be sublimely indifferent to it, walking above it, not through it:

> Those others, however,
> Sit endlessly feasting
> At tables of gold,
> And striding from mountain
> Across to mountain.
>
> (1744–48)

Their indifference is without compassion, and to them the sufferings of the Titans come as sweet incense:

> They scent from the chasms
> The smoking breath
> Of the stifling Titans
> Like a thin cloud of odor
> Up-wafting from sacrifice.
>
> (1749–53)

Finally, a Christian god of predestination depends for the very nature of his existence on the belief in a life beyond the grave for mortals, and of course there is nothing of the kind in *Iphigenia*. The only immortality granted to beings other than gods seems to be the deathless sufferings of the Titans, and old Tantalus, bound in Hades for eternity, symbolizes not so much unending life but rather is an undying symbol of the opposition to the gods and their incomprehensibility. Tantalus stands as an eternal symbol of the disharmony in the universe:

> The old one, the exile,
> He harkens in hollows
> Of night to these songs,
> Thinks of children and grand children
> And shakes his head.
>
> (1762–66)

This is not a Christian notion of God cloaked in classical disguise; surely these gods are closer to the Epicurean gods whose complete indifference to the world encourages in men a skeptical spirit and thus gives to them a definite degree of freedom. Like the Lord in *Faust*, these gods are far removed from the world of humans and do not provide for men ethical models, and so Iphigenia's response is not so much one of pious submission as of "benign neglect" of the gods. The strength Iphigenia draws from the song gives her the power to act independently of them, to reject her identity as their representative, and to obey the sense of her own identity—"Not priestess! Only Agamemnon's daughter!" Whatever ethical action Iphigenia will prove capable of, she will perform that action despite, not because of, the gods. Whatever principles of ethics are implied in Iphigenia's actions will have to be grounded in the purely human, and the question which is asked so insistently at the end of the play has already been formulated: Is the purely human adequate grounding for ethical action? In a sense, Iphigenia has no choice, for in the two opposing views expressed about the gods at the beginning and the end of the fourth act, there is abundant reason for complete skepticism regarding what we can know about the transcendental dimension of the universe, if indeed there is one. If the will or wills of the gods are unknowable, then they can have no effect from the human point of view in determining human action. Their possible existence here is as irrelevant to Iphigenia, who must make a practical decision in this world, as is the Lord in *Faust*, whose assurances of the ultimate victory for the forces of good do nothing whatever to alleviate Faust's sufferings or to bring him out of his self-imprisonment. Iphigenia will repay the gods' indifference with indifference, although it will be reverent indifference, and she will act as if they did not exist. The fact that Iphigenia and her brother escape with the vision of great deeds before them gives the illusion that her action has been the right one, but, strictly within the context of the play, there is nothing to confirm this and so to give it status as more than illusion.

Schiller's comment that the play is "remarkably modern" is perhaps more appropriate than he knew, for the play depicts the growth of man out of the age of religious dependence on gods into an age of self-reliance, and so documents the sense of the secularization of life which predominated at the end of the eighteenth century. Looking back from our own century, we may even describe the world into which Iphigenia emerges as an existential one since the play posits a positive substitution of man for god and recognizes that man's identity is historical, not universal. The universalizing rhetoric of the first act was, as we have seen, only camouflage for the depiction of a particular, unique set of circumstances. The classical form proves to be a means to achieve a very unclassical aim, for finally, it is Iphigenia's own historical identity, not any external law, which determines the ethical choice between Greece and Tauris. There is by the end of the play no question as to where her primary allegiance lies. Once she knows the historical facts of her family, and, what is more important, once she has admitted her real identity to King Thoas and to herself, the only true course open to her is an attempt to bring reconciliation to her family, that is, to adopt the duty laid on her by her historical identity. The ethical commitment to Tauris, a commitment derived from a far more universal ethical principle— to repay kindness with kindness—pales completely in the face of the personal commitment Iphigenia feels to fulfill her own destiny, a commitment derived not from an abstract ethical principle, but from an assessment of her own historical circumstances. To remain in Tauris would be to continue in a paralysis and would mean a denial of her own self. Whether or not Iphigenia can succeed in bringing her family together once more we cannot know, but what matters here is that Iphigenia, waking out of ten years of passivity and imprisonment, refutes the charge made in the opening monologue that only men are fit to perform great deeds, and the great deed she sets for herself is the enormously difficult task of reconciling her family:

> Do men alone, then, have the right to do
> Unheard-of feats? Can only men clasp things
> Impossible to their heroic bosoms?
>
> (1982–84)

That Goethe saw the task as truly impossible is confirmed by the plans he made for a sequel to the drama, to be called *Iphigenia in Delphi*. There, Orestes, Iphigenia, and Pylades were to encounter the mad Electra in Delphi. Only by a "fortunate turn of events" is the murder of Iphigenia avoided. Goethe saw the impossibility of the dramatic situation reflected in the impossibility of his own creativity:

> If this scene succeeds, there is hardly anything greater or more moving to be seen on the stage. But where is one to find the means and time to create it, even if the spirit is willing![19]

The task Iphigenia sets herself is as impossible as is the dramatic representation of it on stage.

The words "unheard-of feats" echo a thematic motif which runs through the play and has largely been neglected by critics, who have tended to concentrate their attention on the thematic words "pure" and "human." However, the great deeds to which Iphigenia now prepares to devote herself play as great a role as the concepts of heart and humanity. They may even form a kind of opposition to the theme of the heart, for the question is apparent: can one perform great deeds and retain the purity of heart so longed for by Iphigenia? The failure of Goethe to take up the task of *Iphigenia in Delphi* implies an answer. The theme of the "great deeds" is first touched upon in Iphigenia's opening monologue in the contrast between man and woman. It is clear here that she sees man alone as the doer of great deeds. The theme then recurs when Pylades enters and attempts to rouse Orestes from his morbid passivity and on to great deeds:

> Am I not full of joy and spirit still?
> And joyousness and love are wings that soar
> To mighty deeds.
>
> (664–66)

Throughout his lines Pylades speaks of great deeds of the past and of the great deeds of the future which he and Orestes will undertake together if only Orestes will throw off his delusions of the avenging Furies. When Orestes does recover from the spiritual paralysis laid on him by his sense of guilt and remorse, his thoughts too turn to those same great deeds. It is significant that the motif of the great deeds appears in his speech directly after he has described the closing of the doors of Tartarus on the avenging Furies:

> To Tartarus pass the Eumenides,
> I hear their going, and they close behind them
> The doors of bronze with far-receding thunder.
> The earth exhales refreshing fragrance and
> Invites me to its plains for full pursuit
> Of life's delights and high accomplishment.
>
> (1359–64)

The ability to perform great deeds seems here to be the concomittant of the disappearance of the representatives of the transcendental. Finally, Iphigenia's own resolve to act is closely linked to her memory of the old song that tells of the indifference of the gods, and this indifference closes the gods off from Iphigenia's world as securely as the bronze doors of Tartarus seal off the Eumenides from the world of Orestes. Iphigenia finds that she too is capable of great deeds only after she has freed herself from an identity which derived from a naive belief in a transcendental realm. The paralysis she has suffered as priestess of Diana has been broken, and she has found her way to action.

Finally, we must return to the initial question—can there be an ethics grounded in the purely human? Is in fact Iphigenia's action to be regarded as ethical at all? Seidlin puts the case for the ethical interpretation most succinctly:

> The moral consciousness in Iphigenia has so completely become immediate feeling that she needs no ethical law; for this ethical law does not exist over her, but has grown into her, has become a part of her being.[20]

Can there be such a thing as an internal moral law which needs no external moral law from which it derives? If such an internal moral law does exist, it, like the reconciliation between natural and ethical imperatives, can do so only within the aesthetic realm, within the work of art, for in the real world the belief in exclusively internal moral laws makes it difficult to distinguish a Saint Francis from a Hitler. The contradictions in the belief have become the hallmarks of our own age, and evidence of the decline in the belief in external moral laws is abundant everywhere; every dropout from society who accepted one of the many "one's own" philosophies of the 1960s was following the star of his own internal law, and we may remember that Charles Manson, who orchestrated a mass murder, felt that he was merely following his own *daimon*. The difference between Iphigenia and these extreme examples of internalization of law is that Iphigenia exists only in the aesthetic realm where the consequences of following her own heart can be safely controlled by the author. But even if Goethe has proved to be more "remarkably modern" than Schiller could have guessed, and has anticipated in his *Iphigenia* a spiritual condition of man similar to that elaborated by later existentialists, particularly Nietzsche, still Goethe does not give his wholehearted assent to the freedom Iphigenia displays, for over against the "great deeds" envisioned by all three Greeks, there is the constant and haunting reminder of Tantalus, warning that the eventual outcome of the enterprise might well be catastrophe. Seidlin's description of Iphigenia's internal law is acceptable only if we recognize at the same time that Goethe shows every sign of uneasiness with it.

Without recourse to external principles according to which we may judge actions, we cannot know whether a single action is good or bad; we can only feel, and of course the entire drama is constructed to make us *feel* that Iphigenia's decision to return to Greece is right and noble, and that her decision to be honest with Thoas is the proper one. The act of seduction which Faust performs on Margarete—"simply trust your feelings"—is here reenacted by the author on his audience. Whether or not King Thoas is convinced that Iphigenia's decision is the right one is impossible to tell. His short response to her eloquent and impassioned plea for his blessing on their enterprise, his laconic "Farewell," is certainly inadequate if we are to see in him an external confirmation of the "ethical" actions of Iphigenia. To my mind, a better intepretation of the final scene would recognize Thoas as representative of an older order—he is after all left with the statue of Diana, the symbol of the older religious perspective—and to see in his reluctant "Farewell" not a blessing, but a passive recognition that he cannot be an obstruction to the emerging new world of internal imperatives. Like the worlds of Margarete and Götz, the world of Tauris exists as a historical epoch left behind by the new types which are emerging: Faust, Weislingen, and Iphigenia. Thoas reluctantly watches the Greeks leave for their "brave new world," a Greece no longer dominated by the curse of the gods and of the human past. Whether or not the goals of Iphigenia and her band will be accomplished cannot be foretold, but the king's simple and enigmatic response holds out as much skepticism and doubt as encouragement. Iphigenia herself has described the "unheard-of deeds" which lie before her as "impossibilities" (1983), and her word may prove prophetic.

The interpretation I am suggesting is in accord with that of Daniel Wilson's recent reading of *Iphigenia* in the light of contemporary "abduction operas" of the late eighteenth century. Wilson sees the plot of *Iphigenia* as similar to those of the conventional stories of the Christians rescued out of the hands of the Turks:

> Significant elements of the action in *Iphigenia*—the couple who strive with cleverness and tricks to flee from "slavery," the discovery of the enterprise and the threatened punishment, the magnanimous forgiveness, the king's renunciation of his

own feelings of love and the release of the prisoners, finally the . . . fact that the "noble deed" of the supposed barbarian shows his moral superiority over the "civilized" Europeans—these are not just secondary themes, but are the very heart of the "abduction opera."[21]

Reading Goethe's *Iphigenia* in the context of its contemporary literary atmosphere leads Wilson to see the resolution in the drama in a far less optimistic light than earlier critics have done, even to suggest that Orestes' healing at the hands of Iphigenia is no healing at all, but that in fact Orestes simply "implicates himself once more in the violent destiny of the Greeks and of the descendants of Atreus."[22] Seeing Goethe's work in this larger context reveals not only the darker implications of the work, but also the fact that Goethe was taking advantage of a theme that was already very familiar to educated Germans of the time and was very popular. Robert Heitner has pointed out that between 1697 and 1779 there were at least eighteen versions of the Iphigenia legend published in Europe.[23] The successful escape Goethe writes into his work resonates with the successful escapes typical and even expected in a whole genre of drama; this only underscores the "literary" and artificial nature of the optimistic reading. The plot, conventional and familiar, tells one thing; the text's awareness of itself, revealed through the faulty rhetoric and the "unconscious" presence of Tantalus and Prometheus, tells another.

It is above all the classically formed rhetoric and the successful outcome of the action which persuade us that the prospective world of man's independence will be achieved once the Greeks are back at home and that the human displacement of the divine will create a new order better than the old. A similar optimistic vision of a better world occurs in fact at the very center of the drama, in the third act, where Orestes, now seemingly cured of madness, sees a vision of the Elysian Fields, in which all the members of his family are walking in peace with one another:

> They walk in peace, the old and young, and husbands
> With wives; how godlike and how like each other
> They seem to move, these forms. Yes, it is they,
> The forebears of my house.
>
> (1271–74)

The rhapsodic passage continues as Orestes recognizes Thyestes, Atreus, Agamemnon, and Klytemnestra, each reconciled with the others and each welcoming Orestes into their peaceful world. The harmony and beauty are almost complete; it is only when Orestes asks to see Tantalus, "that beloved man and much revered who used to sit in the councils of the gods" (1303), that he learns that Tantalus is still unreconciled to the rest and suffers still his horrible punishment:

> You seem to shudder? You turn away?
> What is it? The peer of the gods is in pain?
> Alas! The all-too-powerful ones
> Have riveted horrible torments
> To that hero's breast with iron chains.
>
> (1305–9)

And so the vision of the reconciliation and harmony ends with a chilling note as Tantalus appears once again, the symbol of the eternal discord of the universe. The dream of Orestes, like the vision of Aeneas in the underworld, which also ends on a frightening note of deep pessimism, may be regarded as an ecphrastic paradigm for the entire work of art. Just as the dream vision finds its order and beauty deeply disturbed by this final image of Tantalus, so too the entire world of *Iphigenia in Tauris*, with its plastic and harmonious vision of confidence in the human heart, finds itself rendered problematic by the deep currents of pessimism which course inevitably beneath the calm and glistening surface.

The paradox of human autonomy which runs through the drama reaches its culmination at the end of the play: Iphigenia, as representative of the human, emerges as the victorious replacement of the divine, yet this exaltation of the human is undermined even as it is proclaimed, and the ascendancy of the human heart as sole arbiter of the ethical is called into question at the very time it is given this status. The closing speech of Orestes is a rhetorical construct built on the two sides of the paradox. First, the credibility of the gods is called into question:

> We now perceive the error which a god
> Cast like a veil about our heads when he
> Bade us set out upon our journey here.
>
> (2108–10)

Like Iphigenia in her opening monologue, Orestes seems to be saying more than he realizes. Ostensibly, he is extolling the sly ways of the god, who through ambiguity has brought the Greeks to the proper place for Orestes' healing, but the imagery—"error," "veil"—gives a disturbing moral dimension to the actions of the god. The contrast is clear: against the deceptive ways of the divine we see the scrupulous honesty and clarity of Iphigenia. And in this contrast there is repeated the Promethean accusation of the gods.

At the end of his speech, Orestes praises Iphigenia for being the very antithesis to the deception and violence which have characterized the actions of the gods:

> Men's highest glory, violence and cunning,
> Are by the truth of this exalted soul
> Now put to shame. . . .
>
> (2142–44)

The negative qualities listed by Orestes are the attributes of men, but, according to the opening words of his speech, we may extend these characteristics of violence and deceit to the gods as well. Their violence is manifest in the sacrifice demanded of Iphigenia's life and in the torture of Orestes by the Furies. Their deception is obvious in the ambiguous oracle of Apollo, a pronouncement which becomes effective only after it has been interpreted by human intelligence. Yet this interpretation of the divine words is not given the confirmation it receives in the original Greek play by the appearance of a *deus ex machina*, and receives only the grudging and skeptical assent of Thoas, whose "Farewell" seems to contain as much doubt as enthusiasm.

The drama ends with the paradox unresolved—are humans truly autonomous, or are their actions determined by willful and irrational gods? Won't Iphigenia's claim to autonomy be forever troubled by dreams of Tantalus and his terrifying punishment? The glorious assertion of human independence is made against a dark background of uncertainty and is an assertion which can only be made with encouragement in the aesthetic realm where art can give the impossible plausibility:

A poet seeks to set free that destiny which,
Undulating and horribly formless, knows
Neither measure, nor aim, nor firm direction,
But instead blows fiercely and destroys with loud violence.
There art takes a hand, with loving illumination,
Upon the chaotic mass, and unfolds at once
With the help of inspiration, song and speech,
All working simultaneously and together with judicious motion.[24]

4
Roman Elegies: Surrogates of Life

The problem is not that we attach value to aesthetic semblance (we do not attach nearly enough), but that we have not yet taken it all the way to pure semblance, that we have not yet sufficiently separated existence from appearance, and thereby established forever the limits of each.
—Schiller, On the Aesthetic Education of Man

IF *Iphigenia in Tauris* presents a covert Promethean figure whose struggles for autonomy run counter to the placid classical form which embodies them, the Roman Elegies show us a poet whose appropriation of a classical voice is no less problematic, for here too the form of the poetry stands in a kind of opposition to its contents. As with *Iphigenia,* an understanding of the agonistic relationship of modern content to classical form is crucial to any interpretation of the works. Where in *Iphigenia* an oracle demanding interpretation is at the center of the work, in the Roman Elegies it is the poet's own secret, to which the poet calls attention again and again, that summons the reader's interpretative faculties. And, where *Iphigenia* treats thematically the problem of morality and the independent human heart, the Roman Elegies have raised the problem of morality and the poet's heart by their very existence; in earlier criticism, appreciation of these splendid poems was intimately tied to the question of Goethe's intent. Was it defensible or not?

In the middle of the nineteenth century, a scholarly debate was published in the *Jahrbuch für Philologie und Paedagogik* which centered on the morality and nature of poetic creation found in the Elegies. Both opponents were academics, Professor H. J. Heller of Berlin and Professor H. Düntzer of Cologne, and both enter the debate in the firm belief, often stated explicitly, that the Elegies must be defended against the charge of amorality (at best) and even lasciviousness (at worst). Yet despite their common goal of rescuing Goethe, each is completely at odds with the other in the correct approach to the avowed mission, and each expresses antipathy to the other in language whose intensity would be shocking in a contemporary journal of literary criticism. Both are conscientious scholars, and within the body of the debate there is a large amount of information relevant to the Elegies, but the controversy is also instructive to review in itself, for it gives us a very good picture of the tone of academic discourse in nineteenth-century Germany where the morality of literature was an issue of utmost importance. Because it provides a good sampling of the modes of intelligent reading given Goethe in the century before our own, it is a valuable piece of evidence for anyone concerned with the history of Goethe's reception and the formation of the poet's reputation. For my purpose, however, the debate is important primarily because it raises questions concerning the relationship between imitation and originality which are of direct importance to the understanding of Weimar classicism in general and to the understanding of the Roman Elegies in particular. Because of this, I propose to recount the issue of the debate in some detail.

Heller began the debate by publishing in the *Jahrbuch* of 1863 a long article on the ancient sources of Goethe's elegiac poetry.[1] The essay comprises more than one hundred pages of close reading and discussion of the Roman Elegies (and the Venetian Epigrams), in which Heller directs the reader's attention to every imaginable parallel citation that could be drawn from the Latin elegiac poets. It is this close comparison with the Roman tradition that is the heart of Heller's argument, and he is firmly convinced that all the parallel passages brought to bear are immediately relevant and were definitely known to Goethe at the time the Elegies were created. However, a close examination of the citations presented by Heller and the related passages in Goethe reveals a varying degree of congruency or relevance. Some parallel passages present an almost word-for-word similarity, while others are so far-fetched that they hardly seem comparable in any way. Because of this relative lack of discrimination, Heller's work is a wide-ranging assortment of texts and is of limited scholarly use. It must be admitted, however, that scholarship here is intended only as a means to a greater end—that of salvaging Goethe's moral reputation. It is crucial to Heller's purpose to document a Latin model for almost every line of Goethe's text, because the redemptive plan he envisions for the Elegies is to argue that it was not Goethe who was lacking in defensible moral constitution, but rather the Latin elegists whom Goethe was imitating. (Heller avoids the obvious question of the morality of imitating immoral literature.) To this end, he must reduce to the greatest possible degree the "personal" experience in the Elegies and is forced to see the poems rather as a pastiche of Latin conventions, rhetorical strategies, and stylized sentiment.

Heller's article drew an angry response in the *Jarhbuch* of the following year from Düntzer in Cologne.[2] He reads the Elegies in a totally different manner from Heller and sees in them, not so much an imitation or translation of a Latin tradition into German, but rather a thinly veiled expression of the poet's own personal experience. This experience, however, is not simply the events in Rome through which the poet had lived (a love affair in a foreign land would be too frivolous to ascribe to Goethe), but is instead the poet's later experience in Weimar, transferred poetically back into those days the poet spent in Italy. Specifically, the experience which stands behind the Roman Elegies is, as Düntzer puts it more succinctly some eleven years later in his influential commentary on the poems of Goethe, the poet's comfortable domestic life with Christiane Vulpius: "the happy relationship of love with Christiane allowed our poet to achieve in the spring of 1789 our Elegies which are tied to the memories of the blissful stay in Rome."[3] (Düntzer's frequent use of the possessive—"our" poet, "our" Elegies—is a clue to his proprietary relationship to Goethe and shows the kind of personal investment made by these critics in the reputation of "their" poet.) For Düntzer, the happy love for Christiane led Goethe to "relive" his Roman experiences in the light of that love and to see in them a poetic context for a description of his present relationship to the woman he loved. For Düntzer, the Elegies are saved, then, because the amorality of Goethe's relationship to the Roman girl of the poems is really only a transparent classical façade imposed upon an affectionate and monogamous relationship which actually existed in the poet's life in Weimar. It would have been impossible, Düntzer reasons, for Goethe to express his erotic feelings for Christiane in poetry directly, since he was not yet married to her, but the use of classical meter and rhetorical forms as a subterfuge enabled the poet to articulate those feelings in a socially acceptable way. Because this is the only mode of salvation he envisions for the Elegies, Düntzer is relentless in chipping away the classical surface so carefully illuminated (perhaps, half created) by his colleague in Berlin.

Düntzer wants to see in Goethe a poet whose values conform in essential aspects to those of the critic and his contemporaries, and so he reads the poet against a background of matrimonial probity; for him, Goethe's relationship to his wife-to-be is suffused with a moral purity which is almost holy. Consequently, for Düntzer, Heller's readings become immoral because of the inherent comparison between this pure and unassailable love of the poet and the frivolous, highly sexual love lyrics of the ancient world, and he is merciless in pointing out the inappropriateness of Heller's more far-fetched parallel citations.[4]

Moral outrage and shock are the major weapons in these critics' arsenal of rhetorical devices, and Heller has the parting shot. In a rebuttal to Düntzer, Heller responds to the assumption that the Elegies (and the Epigrams) are the direct expression of the poet's own experience:

> The direct conclusion which one must draw when considering the 102nd and 103rd Epigrams under the above mentioned assumptions of Mr. Düntzer . . . and which will reveal itself when one shells the kernel of the matter out of the whitewashing way these critics have of expressing it, would be that the poet abandoned his presumed beloved in Venice with an unborn child. What? Goethe could have sought out an adventure of love in Venice after he was already as good as married to Christiane Vulpius? What? The poet would have been so heartless as to have abandoned a child in Venice, and that after he had been blessed with such domestic bliss in Weimar? What? And not only does the poet proclaim himself guilty of this action, but in fact throws the whole affair openly into the face of the entire German public![5]

Neither plan for salvation can cover all the details of the elegiac poetry, and the degree to which both critics will misconstrue passages to bring the poet into the fold of morality is often amusing (especially in the light of the explicitly erotic Priapic elegies written by Goethe at the time of the Roman Elegies, but withheld from publication until 1914),[6] and it is remarkable that the impetus to save the Roman Elegies morally does not hinder, but in fact encourages these critics to label one another as reprobates. The possibility that the situation is just the reverse—that "their" poet deserves moral condemnation and that compared to him both critics are far more acceptable in terms of public morality—never occurs to either of these men, each of whom is too eager to prove the moral acceptability of literature and the depravity of his colleagues. The debate laid out by the two scholars continues through the remainder of the century with critics taking one side or the other, finding more questionable parallels in the Latin elegists, or seeking out more evidence that Faustine, the woman of the Elegies, is really Christiane Vulpius. The final contribution to the debate is the dissertation written and published in Bonn in 1913 by Elisabeth Eggerking.[7] Convinced of Düntzer's position, she nevertheless gives a useful summary of Latin elegiac conventions and their echoes in the Roman Elegies. However, her primary purpose is to read Christiane into Faustine, and she goes so far as to claim that, just as Catullus' Lesbia is metrically the equivalent of his "lover" Clodia, Tibullus' Delia that of his "lover" Plania, and Propertius' Cynthia the metrical equivalent of Hostia (the latter in each case the "real" woman behind the poetry), so too Faustine is the metrical equivalent of Christiane. It is perhaps possible that these two names could be pronounced as metrically equivalent, but this would mean pronouncing Christiane as three rather than four syllables, and eliding the second *i* into the following *a*. This runs counter to Goethe's metrics in the poems, where such diphthongs are always pronounced as two syllables. It seems highly unlikely that Goethe was consciously reading "Christiane" into "Faustine," and Eggerking's equivalency is probably the consequence of her own overriding desire to see behind every aspect of Goethe's poetic-erotic adventures in Rome the figure of his beloved in Weimar and so once again to save Goethe from the accusations of immorality.

What dominates almost all the nineteenth-century discussion of the Elegies is a concern for the moral rehabilitation of a text which on the surface runs counter to the prevailing notions of acceptable social behavior, or, to be more precise, counter to what was considered acceptable public admission. It is revealing that Heller finds it inconceivable, not so much that Goethe would have had an extramarital love affair, but that he would publicly display the details of such an affair in his poetry: "when even the most wanton person would be careful to conceal such affairs, and to share them, if at all, only with the most trusted of friends under the seal of the deepest secrecy."[8] The question underlying all this moral concern is whether or not a reading of Goethe's Elegies can give us a direct insight into the reality of the poet's experiences in the world outside himself. Scholarship has gone so far as to search out all the actual Faustines living in Rome in the 1780s and to offer to Goethe's readers one or two plausible candidates for the honor of being *the* Faustine of the poems. It is then into the features of this Faustine that the person of Christiane is to be read. If, however, we are unable to make the leap of faith and believe that the Roman girl was in fact only a literary surrogate for the one true love in Weimar, then the only other mode of rehabilitation is to see the Elegies as so *completely* divorced from the personal experience of the poet that the poems become no more than a beautifully constructed series of imitations of elegiac tropes and sentiments. Such a polarization of possible readings is the result of a drastic simplification of the complex relationship between the poet, his literary antecedents, his personal experience, the fictive persona of the poem, and the poet's own perhaps parodistic attitude toward the literary enterprise on which he is embarking. Not only is this complex relationship composed of many elements, but the actual balance between the elements may vary considerably from poem to poem, and may not even remain stable within the context of any one poem. It is in fact this very variability between the elements within the Elegies which gives the poems their characteristic tone. In such a tortuous interweaving of rhetoric, personality, and irony, the truth behind the poems may well be inaccessible. Possibly the only truth is the elegy itself.

A close reading of one Elegy can serve to demonstrate this complexity within the text. All of the Elegies are playful in style, but perhaps none so playful as Elegy XV, and it is this whimsicality which makes the poem a good place to begin a discussion of the entire cycle. The opening lines of the Elegy are an allusion to a famous story told by Spartianus, the biographer of the emperor Hadrian. According to the legend, the poet Florus wrote a little poem directed at the emperor:

> Ego nolo Caesar esse,
> ambulare per Britannos,
> scythias pati pruinas
> (I don't want to be Caesar
> and march through the ranks of Britains
> and suffer Scythian frosts.)

Hadrian, learning of the poem, responded with one of his own:

> Ego nolo Florus esse,
> ambulare per tabernas,
> latitare per popinas,
> culcices pati rotundos[9]

(I don't want to be Florus,
parading through the taverns,
hiding in the cook-shops,
suffering the circling gnats.)

Goethe uses the two little poems to construct a situation at the beginning of his own elegy in which a choice must be made (a classic priamel). Not surprisingly, he chooses to side with the poet Florus:

Caesar would hardly have got me to travel to faraway Britain;
    Florus's taverns in Rome would have been more to my taste.
If one must choose between the mists of the dismal north and a
    host of
Hard-working southern fleas, give me the fleas any day![10]

                                                                    (299–302)

The modern poet sides with his earlier fellow-poet, not only because he prefers the south to the north, but also because he, like his predecessor, prefers to play with words rather than participate in national political affairs. And this poem is, above all, a play with words. The "taverns" of line 300, taken directly from the Latin poem, quickly becomes the "inns," the "Osterie" of the modern Italian city:

And I have now even greater cause to salute and to praise you,
    Osterie—as inns here are so fittingly called . . .

                                                                    (303–4)

These three words which refer to the same thing are given in a casual and off-hand manner which makes them seem quite unimportant, yet in this rhetorical play with language which calls attention to itself, there is a clue to the nature of the poet as creates his role in the poems. The playfulness of using these three words to refer to the same unassuming object reveals a relationship that will characterize the Elegies: the multiplicity of language against the singularity of experience. In calling attention to this relationship between language and experience, the poet reveals himself to possess a nature very much like that of Mephistopheles, whose cynicism is often at work to deflate the rhetoric of Faust and to reveal experience in all its baseness. The Romans called this place a "popina," Germans call it a "Schenke," and in modern Italian it is "osteria," but all this verbal variety can be reduced to the same thing: a place in which the poet can meet his beloved. Similarly, in Elegy XII, the poet describes in detail the complex system of rites and practices of the Eleusinian mysteries, all of which are conceived as elaborate subterfuge for the one sexual act which is the basis of all the highly ramified and ornamental language of ritual:

> . . . Have you now caught the hint, my beloved?
> A sacred spot is shaded by this myrtle bush!
> Our pleasure will bring to the world no real threat!
>
> (238–40).

Buried under the weight of elaborate ritual and mystifying language there is the simple fact: here is a place to make love. This persistent interplay between the reductiveness of desire and the elaborate ramifications of language is at the heart of the Elegies. The tone of these poems is of course nowhere so cynical as that of Mephistopheles, but in both we find the same erotic grounding for the multiplicity of the world and of language. Sitting in the place of Faust in his study, Mephistopheles lectures the student on a proper profession:

> In particular, learn how to control women.
> Their eternal oh's and ah's
> So manifold,
> Can be cured at *one* single point,
> And if you do a half decent job,
> You'll have them all under your thumb.
>
> (2023–28)

A thousand words can be stilled by the one sexual act, for the language these women speak is nothing but the language of desire; for them, language simply marks the contours of an absence of sexual gratification and can be quieted only when that absence is filled. So, too, the Roman Elegies speak a language of desire, for nowhere in the poems is the poet satisfied, but is instead everywhere converting his sexual desire into the complexities of language. The irony here is that the poet *knows* his language to be the surrogate for experience, but, like Faust in Margarete's little room, he prefers the displacement of language to the plenitude of actual experience.

In his commentary, Heller, is disturbed by the use of the plural ("osterie") in the sixth line of this Elegy, especially as the thought continues: "You showed me today my beloved, out with her uncle" (305). Heller writes:

It must seem strange that Goethe continues in the plural. Surely the beloved went with Goethe or the fictive lover into only *one* such inn. It would simply be too disgusting if the two of them had gone wandering from bar to bar. The plural cannot be used in German, as so often happens in Latin poetry, as a substitute for the singular.[11]

Heller concludes that the use of the plural for the singular is an awkward imitation of Latin style and draws attention to the striking similarity between Goethe's elegy and Ovid's *Amores* I, 4. Heller may be correct in believing that the substitution of plural for singular is an awkward importation of Latin syntax (although Goethe nowhere else in the Elegies does something like this), but the use of the plural is also much more than a mere Latinization, for it is another example of the poet's conversion of the oneness of sexual desire into the multiplicity of the poetically created world. Just as the woman's one unfulfilled desire becomes a thousand "oh's" and "ah's," so too the poet's sexual desire is projected onto a countless number of "osterie." Düntzer, undisturbed by this seemingly unimportant grammatical point, and always delighted to find historical reality behind the language of the poem, is certain that the "osteria" meant is the Osteria Campanella next to the ruins of the Marcellus Theater (a favorite gathering place for Germans in Rome at that time), but surely the use of the plural here renders such specification pointless.

At the end of the second quatrain there is a curious inversion. The girl appears, accompanied by her uncle, a man she has often deceived (or so the poet assures us), so that she may be with the poet in the local wine-shop. The actual words, however, present an unexpected twist:

> . . . together with her uncle,
> Whom the sweet girl has so often deceived, so she might possess
> me . . .
>
> (305–6)

It is not the poet who possesses the girl, but the girl who possesses the poet. In a more conventional elegy, we would have expected the phrase to be something like "in order to please me" or "in order to visit me," but here we find the unusual situation in which it is the girl who is in control; "to possess me" leaves no doubt where the control lies. The poet's helplessness in the face of this Faustine is an integral part of the poem, and is already prefigured in the second line where the poet shows the easy control Florus would have exercised over him. Like the poet of the "Dedication" to *Faust*, the poet here too plays a passive role of observation and recording. Where in the "Dedication" the poet is seduced by the wavering, insubstantial forms, here it is Faustine who performs her act of seduction, and this time the act is performed in script. Goethe is careful to show that the contrast between the poet and the girl is not simply the contrast between passivity and action, but also between northern and southern temperaments:

Here was our table, with its familiar circle of Germans;
   And at a table near by, next to her mother, she sat.
Clever girl! she shifted the bench and so rearranged things
   That I could see half her face, and her whole neck was in view.
                                                            (307–10)

Like a Romantic landscape, the situation here is both natural and symbolic at once. The Germans seem characterized by the wooden table around which they are clumped. The adverb which describes them, "vertraulich," could hardly be more German. Not only does the word imply a close kind of camaraderie, but it almost suggests a conspiracy of silence. The word is one which, like "gemütlich," describes a particularly German relationship, and it is almost untranslatable. This northern closedness is in sharp contrast to the openness of the south: the girl is clearly flirting unabashedly with the poet, arranging herself carefully on the bench so that what the poet sees is her neck and the profile of her face, a pose designed to arouse the interest of any classical sculptor. Against the quiet reserve of the Germans, the Italian girl is all language:

Raising her voice rather high for a Roman girl, she did the
   honours,
Gave me a sidelong look, poured the wine, missing her glass.
                                                            (311–12)

It is this lively volubility combined with the graceful classical pose that attracts the poet and possesses him entirely.

At first glance, then, the poet's attraction to the girl seems to be an attraction of opposites, and yet the two may also be, on a deeper level, more similar than opposite, may in fact be kindred spirits, as the name of the girl—Faustine—suggests. Perhaps the spilled wine may be seen as a symbol of this similarity: the material of shared experience, wine, becomes material for writing. Instead of drinking the wine, Faustine *writes* with it, and the writing produced is both provocation for the poet and substitution for the girl herself, for it is to the writing and not to the girl that the poet directs his attention. After only a brief observation of the girl's physical charm, the poet is quickly drawn to the cryptic message traced in the wine. Once again the situation is both natural and symbolic:

Over the table it spilled, and with dainty finger she doodled—
   There, on the wet wooden page, circles of moisture she traced.
My name she mingled with hers; I eagerly followed her finger,
   Watching its every stroke, and she well knew what I did.
Quickly at last she inscribed a Roman "five" with an upright
   "One" in front of it—then, when I had seen this, at once
With arabesque-like lines she effaced the letters and numbers,
   But left stamped on my mind's eye the delectable "IV."

(313–20)

The sequence is clear and is paradigmatic for the entire cycle: from silence to language to writing. And yet the writing which is produced at the end of the sequence is itself as enigmatic as silence, a kind of secret which must be interpreted by its reader. This theme will be expressed in greater fullness in the last elegy of the cycle where the poet is compared with Midas, whose secret was revealed to all by the whispering reeds. Here, the secret of the poet is reflected by the secret of the girl within the poem, and the sharing of the secret in writing draws the threads of similarity between the poet and his creation as surely as the threads between Goethe and his Faust.

The writing of secrets in wine is a frequent topos in the Latin elegies which serve as models for Goethe's poems. It appears, among other places, in Tibullus I.6, 19, in Ovid's *Amores* II.5, 15, in his *Heroides* I.33, and in the *Ars amatoria* I.569, but it is the fourth poem of the first book of the *Amores* that provides the closest parallel to Goethe's elegy:

   me specta nutusque meos vultumque loquacem;
      excipe furtivas et refer ipsa notas.
   verba superciliis sine voce loquentia dicam;
      verba leges digitis, verba notata mero

(17–20)

(Keep your eyes on me, to get my nods and the language of my eyes; and catch my stealthy signs, and yourself return them. With my brows I shall say to you words that speak without sound; you will read words from my fingers, you will read words traced in wine.)

The circumstances of Ovid's poem are similar to those of Goethe's elegy: the beloved and her husband attend a banquet where the poet is among the invited guests; amid the general sociability of the banquet, the beloved and the poet exchange covert signs of their love. It is generally acknowledged that Goethe had the Latin poem in mind, but the similarities do not go much beyond what has been pointed out. In fact, the comparison is more interesting for the differences it presents. In Ovid, the poet, far from being the passive observer, actually orchestrates the evening's exchange of secrets. It is *he* who instructs the girl in what she is to do to deceive her husband—*quae tibi sint facienda tamen cognosce* . . . ("yet learn what your task must be . . . ," 11). In Ovid, the poet is dominant, not only because of the commands he issues to his beloved, but also because within those very commands he reveals a confusion of emotions which gives us a clear insight into his own personality:

> ante veni, quam vir—nec quid, si veneris ante,
>   possit agi video; sed tamen ante veni
>
> (13–14)
>
> (Arrive before your husband—and yet I do not see what can be done even if you do arrive before him; and yet, do arrive before him.)

If there is helplessness here on the part of the poet, it comes from seeing the futility of his efforts. In Goethe, the poet makes no effort whatever, and where the Ovidian elegy gives a detailed depiction of the poet's complex and passionate personality (and it is this personality which dominates the tone of the poem), in Goethe's poem, we get very little sense of a distinct personality:

> I had sat speechless, biting my burning lip till it bled; half
>   Mischievous pleasure I felt, half was aflame with desire.
> Still so long until nightfall, and four more hours then of
>   waiting!
>
> (321–23)

Where in Ovid the poet's passionate emotions lead him to comic, hopeless activity, in Goethe, the poet remains silent, biting his lip, his emotions locked within himself. However, if there is little that is comparable to the Ovidian personality here, there is on the other hand a great deal which reminds us of other lovers in Goethe's works—especially of Eduard in the *Elective Affinities*. Like Eduard, the poet here is intrigued less by the actual sight of his beloved than by certain scriptive clues (or secrets) that seem to point to a *future* happiness. For Eduard, the great source of fascination is the mysterious "E" and "O" which are entwined on an old goblet in his possession. Forgetting that the initials are simply his own (his full name is Otto Eduard), he sees in the conjunction of the two letters the promise that he and Ottilie are destined for one another. Eduard also forgets that glass is a very fragile symbol of permanence and when the glass shatters, his life too is broken. Eduard's fascination for Ottilie often centers on her own writing, as, for example, when he observes that her handwriting is taking on the characteristics of his own. Similarly, the poet in the elegy sees in the evanescent, impermanent writing in the wine a promise of his future happiness, and when we remember that the name of the beloved is Faustine, we wonder if the poet is not making the same mistake as Eduard; it is not another person the poet is in love with, but with himself.

Of course, the poet is only half serious in the description of his frustration and boredom, yet the picture of him sitting, biting into his lip until it bleeds, is the image of a man trapped in passivity. The product of all this passivity is poetry; as it is for Faust, language here is a fascinating but unsatisfying substitute for the immediate contact with the world, for direct knowledge and activity. Faust's desire for real experience could well be the desire of the poet in the elegy:

> That I may learn
> The fabric of the world, see all the seeds,
> Watch the wheels run,
> And stop rummaging around with words.
>
> (382–85)

And so, when the poet of the elegy has nothing else to do, he proceeds, without so much as a line of transition, into what becomes the next section of the poem, a grand encomium to the city of Rome. This hymnic section begins precisely at the midpoint of the poem (line 26), and it is almost as though the poem were beginning afresh.

Like the opening two lines of the elegy, the first two lines of the
second half are directly dependent on an earlier poem from the Latin
for their existence, and this time the poet acknowledges his consciousness of the fact that he is paraphrasing earlier poetry:

> High sun, pausing to gaze down at your city of Rome,
> Nothing you ever have seen has been greater, and nothing you
>   will see
> This was the truth that your priest, Horace, in rapture foretold.
>   (324–26)

The lines are an allusion to Horace's *Carmen saeculare:*

> Alme sol, curru nitido diem qui
> promis et celas, aliusque et idem
> nasceris: possis nihil urbe Roma
> visere maius

(Dear sun, you who with your shining chariot bring forth day and
conceal it again, you return each day different and yet the same: you
will never see anything greater than this city of Rome).

And probably the next lines of Goethe's are a paraphrase of Propertius III. 20, 11–12:

> Only today do not linger, consent to be brief in your survey,
>   Sooner than usual to take leave of the fair Seven Hills!
>   (327–28)

> Tu quoque qui aestivos exigis ignes,
>   Phoebe, moraturae contrahe lucis iter

(And you, Phoebus, can lengthen the ray of summer
sun, abridge the hour of lingering light.)

The obvious citational aspect of the poetry at this juncture of the
elegy is brilliant and achieves a number of effects simultaneously.
First, this consciously imitative mode of creation casts the poet into
the category of the epigone and dilettante, a pose which accords well
with his present detached attitude toward the poetry he is creating
and which is consistent with his general posture of passivity in the
poem. At this point in the poem, the poet is ostensibly marking time
until he can go to visit his beloved; language literally becomes the

surrogate for activity; seldom in Goethe is language so clearly acknowledged as the expression of simple unfulfilled desire. This brings us to the second effect created by the passage, that of a very specific kind of irony. Since the poetry being spun out is nothing more than the pastime of the poet, the importance of the piece lies not so much in its content or its style as in its simple existence as an artifact to prove that the poet had time to kill. In this regard, the second half of the poem is palpable evidence of the mediatory nature of poetry; no poetry can be the very experience it purports to relate, but is rather a recreation of that experience, and this poetry goes even further in announcing that it is written precisely *as* a substitute for the original experience. Time and again, Goethe reveals his fear that in recreating an experience in language the experience itself will be lost. This fear is the reason for the often repeated doubts about language and writing which are found throughout Goethe's works:

> ... how difficult it is not to put the sign in the place of the thing, to keep the being always living before one and not to kill it through the word.[12]

That such fears about language must be expressed in language itself is highly ironic; and the recognition of this irony leads Goethe to use the ambiguous and dubious nature of poetry as a theme in his poetic work. Goethe's poetry shows itself as a force which both creates and destroys at the same time. Or to use somewhat different terms, poetry (especially poetry like this second half of the elegy) will reveal and conceal simultaneously. In this case, what is revealed is an educated, urbane poet whose ability to weave the poetry of earlier ages into a creation of his own is astonishing and highly entertaining. What is concealed is a man with strong and unfulfilled sexual impulses. The discrepancy between the two personae gives us the particular irony we find in the elegy. The very choice of topics, the glory and history of Rome, is especially comic in the light of this discrepancy. A man waiting to consummate his sexual desires might whet his appetite by indulging his sexual fantasy and so anticipate the actual satisfaction in kind. But Goethe's poet here represses his desire thoroughly under the heavy weight of Roman history recounted in an appropriately heavy, rhetorical style. Is the sexual desire so great that only such a heavy topic can suppress it and keep it concealed? The amusing irony here is that the poet has substituted the history of Rome for his own sexual desires, and it is this act of substitution which is the most consistent movement within the cycle of the elegies and may be traced back to the ancient linguistic play Roma-Amor which amused the ancient Latin poets and which lies at the heart of this cycle of modern poems.

Perhaps nowhere is this substitution of Roma for Amor more succinctly expressed than in the final lines of Elegy III:

> So Mars engendered sons for himself!—the twins were nursed
> By a she-wolf and Rome becomes the queen of the world.
>
> (59–60)

No sooner has the act of love been consummated but Rome has already been founded, grown into a metropolis, and become ruler of the world. All this between the hexameter and the pentameter of an elegiac distich. In Elegy XV, the substitution of Roma for Amor is accompanied by the substitution of other poets' voices for Goethe's own persona in the poem. The result is that, even though it may in fact be the poet's own desire that time pass quickly, the borrowed words and hyperbolic imperatives (requesting the sun to end his day earlier than usual) which express that desire render the authenticity of will somewhat doubtful. The effect is something like that of using a mass-produced greeting card to convey to another the sender's deep sentiment. Such mediation of sentiment through an alien voice may not entirely destroy or invalidate the feeling expressed, but it does vitiate the intensity of the original impulse. The appropriation of another's voice to intone one's own desires violates the ethic of sincerity and must result, consciously or unconsciously, in irony.

In his commentary on the elegy, Heller argues that the section from line 335 to 345 is entirely derived from Latin models and he cites as sources Ovid, *Fasti* VI, 400–414 and V, 637; Tibullus II.5, 25–33; Ovid, *Ars amatoria* III, 19; and Propertius IV.1, 1–4. Goethe's lines virtually drown in this sea of inspiration, but the large number of Latin lines brought to bear as parallel citations should be a clue to the inexactitude of any one. A close examination of these "sources" reveals that none are close enough to Goethe's poem to be called with any certainty the model used by Goethe, while at the same time it must be admitted that most of the material is close enough thematically or stylistically for us to assume that it was in some way formative. If nothing else, the passages cited serve to establish as a topos in Latin elegy the "tunc . . . nunc" method of describing the Roman city. Goethe is obviously aware of this convention, and while he probably does not have any specific occurrence of the topos in mind as an exact model, he nevertheless has his poetic persona create out of these many poetic voices of the past, almost like the work of a ventriloquist, an authentic reconstruction of the topos as he whiles away his time.

The argument over the exact nature of the Latinization of Goethe's elegies is the focus of the early criticism which surrounds them. The parallels just cited are typical of all which have been discovered by critics for the entire cycle; they are related but hardly exact. They serve to convince us that Goethe knew the Latin elegiac poets well, but they do not convince us that the Roman Elegies are merely a pastiche of Roman elegiac conventions, nor do they persuade us that they are strict imitations of an ancient model. In a more recent essay, Georg Luck has reconsidered the arguments and concluded, very persuasively, that in the Roman Elegies there are actually very few passages that can with certainty be traced back to definite passages in the Latin poets.[13] Instead of characterizing the Elegies as a mélange of ancient topoi and phrases, he finds the ancient element of the Elegies more like a "patina" spread over the whole.[14] This patina, however, becomes more than a mere coating and is a persuasive rhetorical mode; the synthetic language Goethe has created for his Elegies consciously calls attention to its glittering surface qualities much more than it directs readers' attention to depths below. Luck says:

> If one disregards the direct echoes of the Augustan elegiac poets, what remains as an essential element is the language and style of those poets—not the language of Tibullus or Ovid, but a kind of koiné in which Propertian elements are predominant.[15]

Both patina and koiné seem to me excellent ways of characterizing the specific nature of the language Goethe has constructed in the Elegies, and both point to the surface of the language, to the superficial aspect of the poetic idiom. A patina is a surface covering, an incrustation which conceals the texture beneath it, while a koiné is an artificial, learned language which enables a speaker to share his thoughts in a medium not his own with a group of similarly educated persons. And it is to the surface quality of its own existence that the language of the Roman Elegies, like the language of *Iphigenia in Tauris,* constantly calls attention. His language reveals at all times a consciousness of its own artificiality, but it never allows that artificiality to be precisely determined. The result is that through the Elegies we are given a full and persuasive representation of life while at the same time we are consciously deprived of any certainty that what we are beholding is authentic or anything more than a mere literary fabrication. The question of the "real" Faustine becomes a paradigmatic problem for the critic: the poems themselves raise the question and it can never be answered. Revelation and concealment are so bound to one another in the Elegies that any reference to outside reality must be seen as irrelevant.

Goethe describes this process of conscious creation in an essay published around the time of the composition of the Elegies (1789). The essay is entitled "Simple Imitation of Nature, Manner, Style"; in speaking of the artist, he writes:

> He sees a harmony between objects which he can only intro-duce into a single image by sacrificing the particular: he finds it tedious to spell out what is in front of him according to the letter; he invents his own method, makes his own language to express what his spirit has grasped in its own way, to give an object which he has repeated often its own characteristic form, without having nature before him every time he repeats it, or without even recollecting it very vividly.[16]

The poet's language becomes abstracted from the object that language is to represent; the language becomes a system in itself, capable of bringing together elements that could not have been united outside that system of artifice. Thus, in order to bring to-gether otherwise irreconcilable elements, Goethe adopts the koiné of the Latin elegists, but this adoption is not a simple one, for Goethe's koiné is an imitation, a translation, and a resuscitation all at once. And the poet's awareness of the artificiality of his language gives this poetry, like the poetry of Iphigenia in Tauris, the implied message that the harmony of elements found here could exist only here, in the aesthetic realm. The self-acknowledged artificiality of the language underscores the separation, if not the very hostility, of life and literature.

The Latin elegists provided the raw material for the koiné which Goethe adopted, and the process of appropriation was a complex one. After his thorough and insightful investigation of the Roman Elegies, Luck concludes: "In order to understand Goethe, one does not need to know the ancient models."[17] And, certainly the Elegies may be read and appreciated by readers at various levels of discern-ment, but a full understanding surely must take into account at least the fact that there *does* exist a body of ancient poetry which the poet in his own highly unusual way is appropriating, even if, as readers, we do not need to know these ancient models in any great detail. Perhaps such an insistence reveals too strong a hermeneutical bias towards historical understanding, but it is difficult to believe that, in the case of the Roman Elegies or of any literature so firmly grounded in the literature of the past, one can read and simply understand. To appreciate Goethe's Roman poetry, and especially to gain a sense of the secrets which lie embedded in the text, it is necessary to have some understanding of the koiné as it was used before Goethe took it up as his own.

To begin with, if we accept the theory that Goethe is here adopting for his own uses a poetic syntax over two thousand years old, we must ask ourselves, if we are to understand its modern use, not only which specific elements were appropriated, but which were left out. It is this problem of selectivity in art that Goethe himself raises in the course of the essay on imitation already mentioned:

> It is natural that someone who paints roses will soon learn to recognize and distinguish the freshest and most beautiful specimens, and will pick them out from among the many thousands offered to him by the summer. Thus there is already a choice, even if the artist does not have a clear general concept of the beauty of the rose. He is concerned with tangible forms: everything depends on defining the difference in texture, and the colors of the surface.[18]

What Goethe says about the selected object of artistic representation holds true for the selected style of representation. Faced with a complete grammar of love, seduction, and frustration in the Latin elegists, Goethe carefully chose what he could use and what he would omit. It has long been noted by scholarship that what is most conspicuously lacking from Goethe's elegies is the frank and open description of physical sensuality. The poems appear to be about sensuality and sexuality, but manage to skirt the subject every time it begins to appear. In discussing the final lines of the Ninth Elegy, Heller compares Goethe's description of the pleasures of love—

For above all else, Love gave to the flatterer the gift
    Of awakening joys which scarcely to quiet ashes had sunk—

to a passage from Ovid's semi-pornographic *Amores* III, 7—

Et mihi blanditias dixit . . .
Sed non blanda, puto, non optima perdidit in me
Oscula: non omni sollicitavit ope . . .

(And she spoke to me flatteringly . . .
But I reckon it was not just enticing kisses of the
most upright sort that she lost on me; she did not
employ every resource to arouse me, but . . .)

In making his comparison, the critic feels compelled to apologize for having lifted the "veil" which lies over Goethe's text:

I am sorry that, since I have undertaken to explain
the Elegies by a comparison with the ancient models,
I must now make clear by drawing on the Ovidian elegy
what Goethe left in discrete disguise.[19]

While for Ovid, the frank and even obscene language of *Amores* III, 7 is perfectly consistent with the register of emotions and rhetorical conventions appropriate to the elegiac form, for Goethe such an inclusion was not possible. Although he wrote a few elegies much closer in tone to the Ovidian model cited here, these elegies were not included among those published in the poet's own lifetime,[20] and this absence of the explicitly erotic is evident even in the title of the published poetic cycle. Originally titled *Erotica Romana*, Goethe soon changed this to *Elegien. Rom 1788*. In the edition of 1806, the title became simply *Römische Elegien*. Whatever sexual experiences Goethe may have had in Rome, the poet in the Elegies suppresses far more eroticism than he reveals, and the object of interest in the poems is less the actual sex-life of the poet in 1786 or 1787 than the verbal exchange the poet makes for that real experience. It is actually the absence of the poet's sexual experience that interests us in the Elegies.

The theme of sexual absence is, in fact, perfectly explicit in the Elegies. Just as the Latin elegists will substitute the obstacle to the beloved (a door, a crowd, etc.) for the beloved herself as the object of the poet's concentration, so too does Goethe's poet find surrogates for his attention. In Elegy XV, for example, it is the Roman numeral "IV" which remains in the eye of the poet's mind long after the girl has disappeared. What true-to-life lover would wait for his beloved with a vision of a numeral impressed on his imagination? Only a poetic persona which is itself a composite of other poetic voices would so easily substitute the sign for the person, and it is just such a poet who, in Elegy XI, makes the absence of sexuality itself the subject of the poem:

These few leaves are a poet's oblation, oh Graces: on your pure
    Altar he lays them, and these rosebuds he offers as well,
And he does this boldly. An artist is proud of his workshop
    When he looks round it and sees such an assembly of gods.
Jupiter bows his majestic head, and Juno holds hers high;
    Phoebus Apollo strides forth, shaking the locks from his brow;
And Minerva looks sternly down—and here's light-footed Hermes
    Casting a sidelong glance, roguish, yet tender as well.
But on soft Bacchus, the dreamer, the gaze of the lovely Cythere
    Falls with sweet longing; her eyes even in marble are moist.
She remembers his ardent embrace, and seems to be asking:
    "Where is our glorious son? Here at our side he should stand!"
                                   (195–206)

This elegy has never raised much critical attention. Heller finds it less interesting than the others because it has little in it to connect it overtly to the Latin elegies; he calls it simply a "reflection of Goethe's studies in the plastic arts."[22] For scholars following Heller's lead, the major critical point in the poem has been the attempt to identify the actual statues Goethe had in mind in describing the sculptor's workshop. Düntzer's commentary is interesting only for its persistent and hopeless attempt to rehabilitate Goethe's moral reputation:

> The connection with Bacchus and the desire of the goddess of love are roguish inventions of the poet, who thus presents this pair of gods as a model of the love which binds the poet to his girl friend. Here naturally he is not thinking of any Roman beloved, but of his Christiane.[23]

The obsession to read Christiane into every female of the poems is extraordinary, but at least here Düntzer admits Goethe shows a modicum of whimsy (a rare occurrence in the critic's attempt to read these poems as serious, if camouflaged, love poems to his wife-to-be). Yet perhaps the poem is even more whimsical and roguish than Düntzer imagines. If we recall that the son of Bacchus and Aphrodite is Priapus, and that the usual sculptural representation of the god was as a large phallus, or as a "phallus provided with a grotesque body,"[24] we see that there is more to the absence of the god than a simple maternal thought on the part of the goddess of love. Only one critic, Ferdinand Bronner, has given any importance to the Priapic background of the poem:

> Elegy XI is devoted to the plastic arts; here too *experience and learning* are brought together into close relationship. The inspiration came from the Priapea, where it is a consistent motif to enumerate the gods, giving each his attribute or other means of identification in a few lines.[25]

While Bronner is probably correct in seeing the short characterizations of the gods as an imitation of the Priapic genre, it is in fact the very absence of Priapus in the poetic form devoted to him that is the main interest in the poem.

The poem opens as the poet dedicates his verses to the Graces, the lovely, if somewhat passionless, goddesses of poetry and the arts. They preside over an altar whose purity is given concrete representation in the second gift the poet presents—rosebuds, the universal symbol of the virginal and sexually inexperienced. (Are the poet's verses themselves somewhat jejune—"these *few* leaves"—because of their acknowledged abstraction from the earthly and sexual?) The poet is then implicitly compared with the sculptor whose workshop seems (but *only* seems) to be a pantheon. Now, a pantheon is precisely what the word suggests in its etymology—*all* the gods. But in this sculptor's studio there is only the semblance of a pantheon because at least one god, Priapus, is missing. This elemental absence casts over the rest of the pantheon a pale and disturbing light. The scene reminds one of the fading of the gods in Wagner's *Rheingold* once Freia, goddess of youth and love, has been taken from their midst. In the Elegy, the eviscerated gods are all appearance. In the description of the gods who *are* present, there is emphasis on the word "seems": Jupiter seems to nod his monumental head while Juno seems to raise hers. The others "seem" equally animated, and Aphrodite seems to ask about the absence of her son Priapus. If the sculptor's workshop only seems to be a pantheon, and if, by implication, there is also an element of "seems" in the work of the poet, then we are tempted to ask what lies behind this superficial appearance.

The poem is light and whimsical, but if we allow ourselves to see beyond the Anacreontic patina of the language, we may see that the piece has a deeper side and presents a serious comment on the nature of classical representation. The insight is almost Nietzschean: the calm perfection of this art, represented by the Olympian statues in the sculptor's workshop, is pale and anemic because it is purchased at the price of passion and genuine sexuality. The serenity of the Olympian deities is an illusion, a dream whose function it is to displace the unaesthetic realities—that is, Priapus with his oversized erection. This is the point of Aphrodite's question: Should not the pantheon be complete? But it remains (as the body of the Elegies remains) a truncated corpus, for the god of erotic love is missing from this gathering of the gods as surely as true eroticism is missing from the poems. What separates this poem from the Anacreontic lyrics of Goethe's youth is the inherent realization of the poet here that the light, highly aesthetic work he is crafting has been made possible only by exacting a high price, and that price is life itself. Thus, the poet comes like a priest to the pure altar of art bringing symbols of his continence—his poetry and his rosebuds. And thus, the sculptor takes delight, not in his relationship to life, but in his workshop which is a house of illusion. Just how seductive this illusion can be becomes apparent in the middle section of the poem where the statues are described as if their actions were those of a living creature. But we are not allowed to forget for long that this world is only an artistic creation, for the poem ends with the reminder that Aphrodite's pose only *seems* to ask about the presence of her son. If Bacchus and Aphrodite had really made love, should there not be evidence of that union? But the evidence remains undisclosed and Aphrodite only seems to ask. The absence of Priapus is recompensed by the presence of these multiple images; and once more Roma, the realm of art, has been substituted for Amor.

The theme of the exchange of Roma for Amor is the consistent motif throughout the Elegies, and it is perhaps for this reason that Elegy XI stands at the midpoint of the series.[26] Elegy XI expresses in relatively unambiguous symbolic language the absence of sexual passion from the sculptor's studio, and, by implication, from the work of the poet. This central elegy is prefaced by a shorter poem which also treats the theme of the exchange of Roma and Amor:

Alexander and Caesar, Great Henry and Great Frederick
    Gladly would yield up to me, each of them, half of his fame,
If in return even one brief night in this bed I could grant them;
    But, poor souls, they are dead; Hades imprisons them all.
Therefore rejoice, living man, in the place that is warm with your
      loving:
    Cold on your shuddering foot Lethe's dread waters will lap.
                        (189–94)

The sentiment of the poem is most likely a poetic rendering of a statement made by Frederick the Great in a letter to Voltaire (October 9, 1757): "Un instant de bonheur vaut mille ans dans l'histoire." It is reported by Varnhagen von Ense that Goethe was struck by this comment and it is known that Goethe read the posthumously published works of Frederick shortly after his return from Italy.[27] This has led critics justifiably to assume that the Frederick of the poem is Frederick the Great, and Erich Trunz, with no explanation, identifies the Henry of the poem as Henry IV of France.[28] It seems to me more likely, however, that the Henry referred to would be one of the Holy Roman emperors, either Henry II or Henry IV, both of whom waged campaigns to win Rome, and were, like Caesar, emperors of the Roman empire, though in their case the empire had taken on the additional name "Holy." I would venture further that the Frederick of the poem is not Frederick the Great, despite the adoption of his sentiment as a thematic leitmotif for the piece, but rather Frederick Barbarossa, the Holy Roman emperor crowned in Rome in 1155. It seems unlikely that Goethe would treat in such a whimsical fashion the great king who had just died and for whom he had the greatest respect. Frederick's dispassionate nature and his dislike for women were generally known facts, and for Goethe to have used him in the poem in this way would either be ironic in a pointless way or simply tasteless. The Holy Roman emperors seem to me a more likely reference since they shared with Caesar a strong connection with Rome and because by the late eighteenth century they had achieved a legendary status far beyond that of the more recent Henry of France or Frederick of Prussia. We also know from *Poetry and Truth* that Goethe was from his earliest youth fascinated by the history of the Holy Roman Empire, living as he did in the city where the emperors were elected. But, no matter to whom the names refer, the point of the poem is clear: these men, whose existence is now preserved only in the literature that depicts their past glory, would gladly give up that glory for one night of love. This welcome exchange—Gloria for Amor—is a variation of the exchange of Roma for Amor and reveals once more the unhappiness inherent in the transformation of life into art.

A similar variation occurs in Elegy XIX where Amor and Fama are set in opposition to each other:

Our good name is in danger, I fear; between Love who commands me

And the goddess Repute there is, I know, bitter strife.

(389–90)

To explain this opposition, the poet recounts a mythic story of the trick played on Fama by Amor. Fama, a mighty goddess who always had to have the last word, never tired of telling how Hercules was devoted entirely and solely to her. Since "Fama" is derived etymologically from the verb *fari* ("to speak"), it is not surprising that the goddess is closely associated with voluble language:

> . . . too talkative, rasping away
> With her clangorous voice—and each time the gods were
>   assembled,
> All of them, great and small, heartily hated its sound.

(394–96)

Only to Fama does the poem give an extended and rhetorically elaborate speech, following which, the poet makes clear, there was no response: "All were silent, for none of them felt like provoking the loudmouth" (411). Amor, mischievous god of love, does not compete with Fama in words, which are her favored weapons, but creates rather a visual *tableau vivant* to represent his triumph over her power: Hercules, the darling of Fama, is brought together with Aphrodite in a scene of sensual splendor. Amor orchestrates the display:

> Then he transvested the pair, laboriously laying the lion's
> Pelt across Omphale's back, putting the club by her side.
> Next, with flowers he decked the resisting hair of the hero—
> But with a distaff in hand, Hercules joined in the joke.
> Thus the Love-god completed this teasing pose . . .

(415–19)

The tableau is intended to represent in a nonverbal way the power of Amor—not just love, but sexual passion—yet the scene is so artificial as to be hardly sexual at all. And, of course, this nonverbal art is no less an artifice than is poetry itself. And, to distance the scene even further from the sexuality it is supposed to represent, the tableau must be conveyed to us through language, the realm of Fama, and so gives once more an implicit triumph to her. By reporting the victory of Amor in words, the poet in fact gives Fama what is most dear to her—the last word.

Later in the poem, the poet describes the blind demonic urge that Amor is capable of exciting:

All who would flee from him fare the worst with the maker of
  mischief:
Girls he would offer them—if these they imprudently scorn,
Then indeed he will pierce their pride with his angriest arrows:
Male he inflames for male, makes a man dote on a beast.
                                                    (445–48)

Homosexual passion and bestiality are among the many forms of
sexual attraction Amor can excite, so we are told, yet when Amor
designs a scene to represent this awesome power, the tableau is as
devoid of sexual urgency and genuine lust as the workshop of the
sculptor in Elegy XI. In fact, the scene of Aphrodite and Hercules
under Amor's sway is downright silly; it seems that Amor himself,
when representing his power, falls into the same difficulty as the poet
in which the immediacy of the emotion or power to be represented
becomes transformed into stasis by its transformation through the
aesthetic act. And so Elegy XIX presents a paradox: while the poem
consciously asserts the primacy of Amor over Fama, that victory is
undermined by the very fact that it must be constituted in language,
which is the native realm of Fama. The implicit victory of Fama over
Amor is confirmed by the bloodless tableau arranged by Amor to
demonstrate his own power. By converting his power into art, Amor
emasculates himself in the same way as the chaste poet of Elegy XI
who has taken on the posture of a priest. Even though it is common
knowledge that Amor can excite a person to blind passion, it seems
that when that power to arouse is to be represented aesthetically, the
syntax of representation takes over and the actual fact to be represented becomes lost. Amor's anemic representation of his own power
seems once more to substantiate Goethe's fear that the sign will
replace the thing and the essence will be killed by representation.[29]
    It is this dichotomy between word and thing that provides the
poet with the ending for his elegy. In a tone of irony, the poet compares himself with Hercules:

I too am learning this now, and the jealous goddess already
  Plagues me a little: she spies out my most secret delights.
So the old rule holds good—I revere it in silence: for "when their
  Mad kings quarreled, the Greeks paid for it"; so too with me.
                                                    (455–58)

Torn between the demands of Fama and Amor, the poet ultimately
gives the victory to Fama by making his secrets public (this will be

the theme of the following and final elegy). In Elegy XIX, the assertion of the poet's silence is of course negated by the very existence of the poem he has just written and the publication of the Elegies as poetic language will be the complete conversion of the poet's Amor into his personal Fama.

What is this secret the poet mentions so often? The simplest answer is on the personal level: the poet has made love to some woman in Rome. This seems to be the experience that provides the basis for the opening for Elegy III: "Do not regret, my darling, the promptness of your surrender! / I think no less of you now, nor did you lose my respect" (43–44). Speed is the theme of this elegy; the rapidity with which the beloved has fulfilled the poet's desires is matched by the speed of legendary lovers of the past, but the speed of love's fulfillment is also matched by the speed with which love is converted into its surrogate—the speed, that is, with which Amor becomes Roma. As in Elegy X, the variation of the Roma-Amor exchange present here is a temporal one: one moment of love over against a thousand years of glorious history. The speed with which gods and heroes made love is illustrated by four episodes from classical mythology. The first three are almost comic as they present an accelerando of lovemaking moments:

In the heroic age, when a god fell in love with a goddess,
  Passion was born at a glance, and in a trice was appeased.
Do you suppose that Venus herself, when she fancied Anchises
  In the Idaean grove, pondered for long what to do?
Did the moon-goddess think twice when she kissed the fair
    sleeping Endymion?
  No! for the envious dawn would soon have waked him instead.
At the loud festival Hero set eyes on Leander; and that same
  Night, all aflame with desire, into dark waters he plunged.
                                                      (49–56).

The two goddesses racing for Endymion is a humorous image, and with a comical use of prolepsis, the poet has Leander plunging into the Hellespont before Hero has even had time to return home. The speed of lovers to satisfy their desires is thus accelerated to an impossible pitch, and in the concluding quatrain, this speed is transferred to the exchange of Roma for Amor:

Rhea Silvia, the royal virgin, went down to the Tiber
  Fetching water, and Mars snatched her up into his arms;

So Mars engendered sons for himself!—The twins were nursed
By a she-wolf and Rome becomes the queen of the world.

(57–60)

No sooner has Mars raped the girl but a she-wolf is already suckling
the offspring of that union, and within the space of one poetic line,
Rome has been built and is already ruler of the world. Almost instan-
taneously, Rome has occupied the site of Mars' lovemaking; Amor
has yielded to Roma and Rome is the city of literature and history. Is
this, then, the secret? that personal experience—the poet's love—
becomes within the twinkling of an eye an aesthetic artifact abstracted from the life that gave birth to it?

From the very opening lines of the cycle, Rome has been characterized as the city of language:

Speak to me, stones, o speak to me you lofty palaces,
Streets, give me a word . . . .

(1–2)

Rome is Fama, the city of language and literature, dominated by its
"Triumvirs," the elegiac poets, and this is the Rome for which the
poet is searching. Perhaps this, more than any love affair, is the
poet's secret: that the displacement of life with literature is almost
instantaneous and that the love the poet pursues is not for any
Italian girl (nor for Christiane Vulpius), but for *his own literary
fame*. Propertius, Catullus, and Tibullus are not called the Roman
Triumvirs (the literary equivalent of the political greats in Roman
history) because they loved, but because they wrote, and the modern
poet does not pursue Faustine because she is a beautiful Italian girl,
or because she is Christiane in disguise, but because, as her name
tells us, she is Faust, the poet's major bid for future literary fame. It
is appropriate here to recall the image of the poet looking at his own
name intertwined with that of Faustine in Elegy XV and to remember that it is the poet's desires, more than the satisfaction of those
desires, which his poetry perpetuates. Just as the love of Mars and
Rhea Silvia became in a moment the city of Rome (no sooner done
than said), so the poet's love for Faustine will become poetry in as
short a space of time. The potential for displacement between art
and life is a disturbing reality for the artist and one that he will try to
conceal from his public, but of course he will be unable to keep this
secret to himself because the very essence of his art is its revelation.

The "secret revealed" is the other theme of the Elegies; for revelation and concealment go hand in hand in this set of poems. In "Selige Sehnsucht," perhaps the greatest of his later lyrics, Goethe once more expresses this poetic concomitance of revelation and concealment:

> Tell no one, tell only the wise,
> For the crowd would only jeer;
> The living are the things I praise—
> Those that long for death by fire.[30]

The paradox of the living who seek for death is matched by the paradox of the secret which is established and revealed at the same time. The speed of transformation from secret to publication is the equivalent of the speed of transformation of Amor into Roma. Secrets abound in the Elegies; in Elegy XII, for example, where the poet initiates his beloved into the secret rituals of the devoted:

> Filled with wonder, the initiates understood the story,
>   Motioned to their lovers—have you now caught the hint, my
>   beloved?
> A sacred spot is shaded by this myrtle bush.
>
> (237–39)

Any spot in Rome may be the scene of lovemaking, a spot holy to those devoted to Amor, for all Rome is a *locus amoenus*; but with equal speed the sexual desire represented by that spot may become reified into literary expression. In this elegy, the poet reveals half the secret to his beloved and leaves the other half concealed. It may not be tactful to tell the beloved that her submission to the poet will soon be transformed into an expression of the poet's art.

Perhaps then the poet's secret in the Elegies is that the true love affair he writes of is between the poet and his art. It is this solipsistic view of art that informs one of the earliest but most important of Goethe's essays on art, the review of J. G. Sulzer's *Die schönen Künste in ihrem Ursprung, ihrer wahrer Natur und besten Anwendung* which Goethe published in the *Frankfurter Gelehrte Anzeigen* in 1772:

> For the artist, the only concern is that he feels no joy in life except in his art, and that, submerged in his artistic talent, he exists there with all his sensitivity and creative powers. As far as the gaping public is concerned, whether they have been

justified after all their gaping is done, or not, what difference does that make?[31]

It is this self-reflexive world of his own creation that is the artist's true joy. Earlier in the essay, Goethe compares this art to a glass palace where reality and fiction become one. The artist must strive, he writes,

> . . . until he finally succeeds in locking up the entire system of all his real and imagined needs into one palace; to confine, as far as possible, all the scattered beauty and rapture in his crystalline walls, where he will become weaker and weaker, substituting the joys of the soul for the joys of the flesh.[32]

Between 1772 and the writing of the Roman Elegies (1788–90), Goethe's view of his own art seems not to have undergone any essential change despite the patina of classicism cultivated in Weimar and perfected in Italy; if anything, the accretion of the classical style has refined the artistic walls and made them even glassier and the act of substitution mentioned in the essay has become the thematic content and preoccupation of the works of art themselves. The Rome of the Elegies is that vast literary edifice whose crystalline surface Goethe shares with the poets of the past. It is a construct born out of desire and its nature is to arouse further desire which will in its turn be transformed once more into art: "O who will whisper to me? which the window where I will first glimpse / The lovely creature who'll bring me to life with fire?" (5–6). But Rome, or the literary tradition which it symbolizes (Fama), can never satisfy desires and so the poet will depict himself as a priest (Elegy XI) or as a man trapped in his own inert self (Elegy XV), or as a man so given to his art that he composes poetry even as he lies in the arms of his lover:

Often I even compose my verse while lying in her arms,
    And have counted hexameters, gently tapping them on her back
With a metrical hand. . . .

(107–9)

The immediate conversion of sexual desire into poetry could hardly be given a more concrete image.

It is interesting here to recall the original title of the work, "Erotica Romana." The shift in title to Roman Elegies occurred as Goethe was completing the cycle of poems and possibly reflects the growing sense of distance between the poet and whatever the Roman experience which led the poet to the creation of the poems. The elegiac genre at the end of the eighteenth century already had a long history behind it which encompassed many an attempt to bring into German not only the tone of the ancient genre but the metrical form in which it was embodied.[33] By the time Goethe took up the form, an established canon of expectations was associated with the elegy: a poem in this form was normally expected to be a melancholy (or mock-melancholy) meditation on the loss of a person or thing loved by the poet. Goethe's only poem before 1788 to bear the title "Elegie" shows in its superscript the serious side of the gnere: "on the death of my friend's brother,"[34] while a contemporary poem of Anna Luisa Karschin, "On the Death of a Canarybird," captures the potential for mock-seriousness in the form. Whether whimsical or serious, the elegy depended on the sense of loss for its meaning, and just such a sense of loss permeates the entire Roman Elegies. Dominik Jost, in a recent book on the cycle, describes Goethe's feeling of loss after the return to Weimar and the conflict created within the poet whose heart was still in Rome:

> Here the conflict is clearly visible in which Goethe found himself cast soon after his return to Thuringia in the summer of 1788. The Roman experience, as it is depicted in the Roman Elegies, must forfeit its wholeness, its universality, and fell into two parts. On the one hand, Goethe's situation in the everyday human world . . . and on the other, the culture and learning of the ancient world, represented by the city he had just left. The two fragments were in no way to be brought together again into a complete whole. The period of unbroken existence was past; Goethe celebrated it in retrospect in his first completed lyrical cycle . . .[35]

It could perhaps be argued that Goethe had never in his life, not even in Rome, experienced a period of "unbroken existence," but whether or not such a period actually existed, the absence of it as an ideal is an essential part of the experience of the Elegies and the creation or re-creation of such an idyllic period was possible only within the realm of art. But even as his art proclaims the wholeness of "unbroken existence," it also reveals its own cognizance of its artificiality and its own awareness of the absence which lies beneath the plenitude of the enticing plastic surface. In the Elegies, this absence becomes concretized in the absence of the Priapic, or sexual element, and while the pantheon of Elegy XI seems to present a harmonious whole, in fact, that very Apollonian vision serves as camouflage and substitute for the Priapic element and the sexual reality which it represents.

The "few pages of poetry" which the poet lays on the altar as a pristine offering to the Graces is perhaps Goethe's reference to his own slim volume of poetry. This act of self-referentiality reveals a fact about the process of production of these poems, for in fact the cycle of twenty poems is small partly because it is a truncated corpus, lacking the four explicitly erotic poems which were written at the same time as the other twenty, but published for the first time in 1914.[36] In what order the elegies were written is not known, but it is likely that, whenever he composed the four more Priapic poems, Goethe was well aware that they could not be published with the other, tamer twenty. The absence of Priapus—the concrete absence of the four poems directly devoted to him—in the text as it was printed is a loss which represents the poet's personal sense of loss on returning from Rome and is as important a constitutive factor in the composition of the Elegies as the Roman experience which is elaborated more intricately in the poetry. The cycle of poems treats thematically its own status as a truncated corpus, or as emasculated sexuality; the four omitted poems are very different.

In the fourth of the unpublished elegies, Goethe speaks in the actual voice of Priapus, and complains that time has left him behind: "Here at the corner of the garden I stand, the last of the gods, / Crudely formed, and time has injured me still further" (91–92). Unlike the gods of Elegy XI whose forms are captured in permanent marble, Priapus has been carved in a living material, wood, and has not been carved very well at that. He is, in other words, not the object of any great aesthetic refinement, and he suffers from a fate of decomposition. Nevertheless, despite the fact that the little god is rapidly deteriorating into a formless mass of rotten wood, he still attracts to himself a rich fertility and life: "Vines hung with gourds nestled around and ascended the aging trunk, / And soon my penis was creaking beneath the load of fruit" (93–94). The fertility which surrounds the little god stands in marked contrast to the cold lifeless statues who only seem to exist and who wonder why there is no evidence of their lovemaking around them. Nowhere in the published elegies is the connection between sex and fertility so explicit as here; here there is no transformation of desire into art but only the simple conjunction of fertile abundance and sex—this is Priapus speaking, not the poet. The little god, befouled by ravens in winter and mischievous boys in summer—"Filth above and below!"—turns to the poet to restore his state: "Now through your efforts, o artist sincere, will I be able to gain / Among the gods the place rightly due me and to others" (101–2). And, in return for the poet's services, the god of sex promises him vastly enhanced powers of sexual performance:

In return, your magnificent rod will swell out from your middle
A good half foot, when your lover orders you to it.
And may your tool not tire out until it has gone through the
twelve
Figures of love as Philainis artfully set them out.[37]

This contract offered to the poet by Priapus can only be ironic, for this poet is a man of the modern world, not of the ancient. What good are the promises of such sexual prowess to a man frightened by the possibility of venereal disease (Elegies XVII and XXII)? The poet sees venereal contagion as the curse of the modern world; it prevents the poet and his contemporaries from the magnificent and promiscuous lovemaking of the ancients and their gods: "And when Cynthia startled you in those other embraces, / She found you faithless, to be sure, but she found you healthy" (unpublished Elegy II, 53–54). Because of the altered circumstances of the world, the poet of the Elegies will certainly be unable to restore Priapus to the place he holds to be rightly his, and the hopes the little god has placed in the poet can only be in vain. A world in which love is innocent and free from the worry of disease can only be created in art and the poet of the Elegies has done all a modern poet can do in the service of Amor by creating through scholarship and literary artifice a crystal palace which may *seem* to be the beautiful world of the past. But this poetic world is conscious of its own artificiality and so at every point undercuts the reality of the fictive world with self-recognition.

In his defense of the poems, Schiller in his "Naive and Sentimental Poetry," calls the Roman Elegies "poetic, human and naive,"[38] the last term referring to the unreflective, unmediated nature of the poetry as Schiller conceived of it. Perhaps a truly naive poet would be able to restore Priapus to his former place of honor, but neither in Goethe nor in the poetic persona of the Elegies do we have anything like such a poet. Rather than enjoying a direct connection with life, the poet in the majority of the poems seems more interested in his own desires than in their gratification, more interested in the arabesques of his own mind than in the companionship of another who would draw him out of his crystal palace and into the world. In the loveliest poem of the cycle, we see the poet closing his doors to the world in order to be alone with his desires:

> Light the lamp for me, boy!—"But it's daylight still! you are
>   wasting
> Oil and wick, sir, in vain. Why close the shutters just yet?
> See, the sun is not under the hill, only under the housetops!
>   There is another half-hour yet until the angelus rings."—
> Wretch! Obey me at once! My beloved is coming!—and
>   meanwhile
> Till she is here, little lamp, comfort me, herald of night!
>   (293–98)

Here the poet looks very much like Faust, happier to be alone in the "prison" of Margarete's room with his own fantasies of her than to share her actual company. Jost has pointed out the importance of just such small, darkened rooms for the Elegies: "The sheltered room, hidden in the midst of the city like a cave in the landscape, remains the most prominent setting in the Roman Elegies."[39] Much the same may be said of *Faust*, and just as the experiences of Faust are bound by the books which define the contours of his study, so here the poet's experience is circumscribed by the literary anteced-ents to whom he pays homage.

The final elegy of the published cycle brings the poems to a point of closure by focusing intensely on the image of the secret revealed. At the center of the poem is a tale taken from Ovid, the story of Midas and his donkey's ears.[40] Punished for having preferred the music of Pan to that of Apollo, Midas is given donkey's ears which he tries to conceal beneath a Phrygian cap. His barber discovers the secret and is bursting to tell it abroad, but is restrained by the knowl-edge that such publication would mean his certain death. Since his life depends on absolute silence, he digs a hole in the ground and tells his secret into the empty space which he then covers up. But reeds sprout above the spot and as they rustle in the wind, they whisper the secret to the world:

> Reeds spring up, and when the wind blows they rustle and
>   murmur:
> Midas, Midas the king, Midas has long pointed ears!
>   (471–72)

A reed is not only a grass, but was also the Roman pen, and so the secret of Midas, like that of the poet, is disseminated abroad through the instruments of writing. The poet in the course of the elegy discusses the means of publication appropriate to his secret and expressly dismisses mere verbal means of publication; he also rejects the possibility of telling only close associates of his secret:

> Which of my friends can I tell? Not a woman, for she might be
>   angry;
> Nor a man either, for he might be a rival to fear.
>
> (475–76)

Nor is nature the place to tell his secret:

> And to confide my joy to the grove, to the rocks and their
>   echoes—
> That is for lonely youths, that will not do at my age.
>
> (477–78)

No; it is to writing that the poet commits his secret—"Listen, hexameter, listen, pentameter! you then shall hear it" (479)—for it is above all in writing that the poet may both reveal and conceal himself at the same time. It is in writing that the poet may create the artificial edifice which can bury his secret beneath a burden of literary allusion and convention. And now, at the end of his poetic cycle, the poet elevates writing to the preferred position as vehicle for the revelation of his secret, and, indeed, no sooner has this priority been established but the poet immediately gives in to the impulse toward revelation. He re-creates a nocturnal visit of the beloved:

> Many men seek her favors and try to ensnare her, the bold ones
>   Crudely, the cunning ones more subtly; but all she outwits.
> Prudently, gracefully, she slips by, for she knows where surely her
>   lover
>   Ardently listens and waits, knows hidden ways to his arms.
> Moonlight, o hesitate now—she is coming; no neighbor must see
>   her!
>   Rustle the leaves, little breezes; no one must hear her approach!
> And you, o my beloved songs, may you blossom and flourish,
>   Swaying in love's warm winds, rocked by their gentlest
>   breath. . . .
>
> (481–88)

Is this the memory of a real experience or only a poetic reformulation of those nocturnal visits which have been an integral part of the elegiac convention since the Latin poets first used it? Is this little piece of narrated memory stimulated by the mention of the act of writing? The fact that the entire passage is constructed in the present gives the section an air of unreality and leaves the impression that what the poet is describing are his own fantasies and desires of the moment rather than a narrative of past experience. The passage is in a kind of optative mode and it is curious that the entire point of the passage is to emphasize that no one but the poet must see the girl as she comes to pay her visit. Almost every line refers to the frustrated attempts of others to see or hear her. (Does she really exist? Doesn't the "surely" of line 484 give the passage the sense of what the poet would want rather than giving it the sense of a narrative certainty?) And the direction of the passage is not toward a culmination of the poet's love, but rather passes on quickly to an invocation to the moon, then to the breezes, and finally concludes with an address to the poet's own poetry, his "beloved songs." The poet's poems literally replace the girl as the poet's beloved. As the image of the girl hastening to the poet fades, the vision of the poet's songs growing and blossoming strengthens, so that at the end of the elegy we see yet once more the rapid transformation of desire into art.

The final couplet of the poem is a witty continuation of the "secret" thematic and concludes the elegy with a false sense of resolution and revelation which leaves the poet's secret intact: "Chatter as those reeds did, and at last tell Rome all about us: Tell of two lovers whose glad secret is secret no more" (489–90). The conclusion of the poem is another game of "hide and seek"[41] in which more questions are raised than answered. First of all, to whom is the secret revealed?—to the "Quiriten," citizens of ancient Rome. But these are the people who are already familiar with the secrets of lovers, and to the extent that Rome is the symbol of literature, especially the literature of love and of the elegy, the poet's revelations of his secret to the Romans is only adding one more name—the poet's own—to the list of those Roman poets who have already sung of their love. By revealing himself as one of them, the poet joins the ranks of the "Triumvirs" who established the genre he now perpetuates. As far as those people are concerned who would most like to know the poet's secret—the friends in Weimar and the modern reader in general—the poet has explicitly excluded these from the circle to whom he will give his revelation (475–76). Second, the "secret" of the poet's love has in fact already been revealed from the very first elegy, so what can this secret be that is revealed "at last"? It is not the secret of a lover (which has been no secret at all, since it has been the theme of virtually every one of the poems) which interests us, but the poet's "own" secret which may not be the same at all. By substituting one secret for another, the poet deflects investigation away from the deeper question of literary expression and of experience articulated in conventional inherited forms, and so concludes the poem with a pretty image and a false sense of closure. The poet remains hidden behind his mask and reveals what he does reveal only to the already initiated—the "Romans," the citizens of another world.

The Roman Elegies prove in the end to be anything but the naive products of a poet who is at one with nature, who lives in the moment, and who enjoys only the here and now. They prove rather to be the highly self-conscious works of a thoroughly modern sensibility which is so supremely capable of resurrecting a style and a poetic idiom of the past that his own modernity seems to be eclipsed by the very language he employs. But this modernity and the poet's self-absorption in his own works are not entirely hidden by the pretended naivete and outward-directedness. On the contrary, the very problematic personality of the poet and his obsessions are all the more provocative for the attempt the poet makes to disguise them in classical dress.

5

Hermann and Dorothea: Aesthetic Stasis in a Political World

We are convinced that no German author would consider himself to be classical . . . We do not wish to have the revolutions which classical works would introduce in Germany. . . .
—Goethe, "Literary Sansculottism"

NO other work of Goethe has achieved the broad popular appeal of *Hermann and Dorothea*. *Werther* caused far greater excitement at publication, but it also aroused a vigorous and negative response from many who recognized the destructive potential the work possesses. *Wilhelm Meister's Apprenticeship* was greeted enthusiastically by readers who had long awaited a second novel from Goethe, but was soon subjected to harsh criticism from the younger generation of Romantics. *Hermann and Dorothea* reaped only accolades, from every quarter of the reading public and for generations to come. The tribute paid to the work continued, and the adulation lavished on the work in the nineteenth century became so great that many critics in our own day have felt the need to preface their discussion of the work with disclaimers or apologies:

> To speak on Goethe's *Herman and Dorothea* is, it seems, to embark on an unfashionable enterprise. For the fame and glory of the poem, in which our forefathers flatteringly and self-complacently saw themselves reflected, are vanished.[1]

> I would like to say from the very outset that I intend to speak on Goethe's *Hermann and Dorothea* more out of enthusiasm than with the intent of presenting something new to scholars.

I do not find it, as Karl Vietor does, faded, or, as many others, trivial, limited, boring, or old-fashioned.[2]

To our eyes, the nineteenth century has come to represent too often a period of comfortable self-satisfaction, whose values—home and family, church and country, stability and conservatism—have been eroded by the rapid development, the anxieties and political horrors committed in our own century. It seems that for our age to read with approval a poem like *Hermann and Dorothea*, a poem apparently intended to be a tribute to that vanished comfortable middle-class life, is to identify too closely with the perishables of the past century and so to assume a pose either quaint or nostalgic. Neither is particularly congenial to the contemporary critic, and so we find the defensiveness of those who, fighting the tide of their own age, still wish to regard the poem as readable and worthy of serious critical attention.

Perhaps the response of critics in the nineteenth century to *Hermann and Dorothea* was as overwhelmingly positive as it was because in this poem they found a work which could be held up as proof positive that the Goethe of the Roman Elegies was not the whole Goethe, possibly not even the real Goethe. Here was the completion of the trajectory implied by Düntzer's criticism of the Elegies: after commemorating the passion for his (lawful) beloved, the poet now sings the praises of hearth and home. A decade of domestic bliss had so tamed the poet that his poetic mission had become patriotic duty; he therefore casts in eternal form those ideals recognized and subscribed to by his society. The touching sincerity apparent in the gentle story which forms the narrative nucleus of *Hermann and Dorothea* must have seemed even to the most literal-minded and skeptical of critics convincing evidence that the Roman Elegies were no more than the product of the poet's misplaced whimsy. If sincerity is the touchstone of the poet's true feelings, here was the true Goethe and the poet of the Roman Elegies could be forgiven his lapse in taste. *Hermann and Dorothea* was the corrective needed to preserve the national poet from charges of amorality and social subversion.

In their unanimously positive evaluation of the poem, critics of the nineteenth century were only continuing a line of opinion already firm in the poet's own time. In the creation of no other work did Goethe enjoy so much help and support from friends. The writing of the little epic went remarkably fast for Goethe; conceived in the summer of 1796, it was published in October of 1797.[3] Before publication, Goethe gave several private readings and sent out manuscript copies of the work to friends; the response was uniformly enthusiastic. Karl Ludwig Knebel, to whom Goethe had shown his work in progress and to whom the poet had sent a copy of the elegy "Hermann and Dorothea" (which would later preface the longer work), wrote Goethe in December of 1796: "Thank you, dear friend, for the precious gift of your Muse. It is thoroughly delightful. How pleasing are the tones which come straight from the heart! I say Yea and Amen to everything. . . ."[4] No less extravagant than such praise from his friends (certainly the Roman Elegies never garnered anything like this) was the sum of money given to the poet in compensation for the rights to publication. The publisher Vieweg in Berlin contracted with Goethe to pay one thousand Talers in gold for the rights. This was the first real honorarium the poet had ever received, and it was remarkably generous for the day.[5] When the poem appeared in print, it was available in several formats, among them a deluxe edition bound in silk, and with a little knife *and* a pair of scissors attached to the binding as a convenience for the cutting of the pages. The poem itself was thus sent into the world as one of the lovely amenities of the middle-class life it ostensibly praised. Goethe had one of these fine editions sent to Schiller, who, in a rare moment of humor, reported to a friend:

> One hardly knows what to say when one receives poems of this kind and quality in connection with a knife and a pair of scissors and so sees the highest as well as the lowest needs of mortality satisfied at once.[6]

Schiller's amusement is certainly justified; there is a curious redundancy of cutting instruments packaged along with the poem. It is as though the publisher, in his enthusiasm to ornament the poem appropriately, somehow went beyond the mark and fell into parodistic exaggeration. Does this format suggest a hidden or unintentional insult to the work? A visual cutting remark? Surely Vieweg did not consciously mean it thus (the many unlicensed reprintings of the poem which so annoyed Goethe tell us that the publisher truly loved the little epic *and* the profits it brought him), and yet the very format of the poem as it first appeared is emblematic of the work itself: a surface so beautiful and polished that it delights and mesmerizes the eye, and only later does the observer behind the eye begin to ask questions, which ultimately are directed at the surface itself. Because these questions never seem to find a satisfactory answer, the surface itself begins to appear in the role of a façade rather than an integral element of style. The surface literally demands the tools that came packaged with the book, for a radical incision is required to get to the heart of the work.

Yet, despite this suggestive conjunction of poem and cutting tools, the very fineness of presentation which the book received at its appearance does reveal to us the high regard which the work was accorded and which was to continue through the following century. How different was this widely directed publication from that of the Roman Elegics which appeared in Schiller's *Horen*, a journal read only by a very small intellectual community. The Elegies came out after much hesitancy and prevarication only to be greeted with coolness and disdain; *Hermann and Dorothea* came out with a flourish and went straight to the hearts of its readers.

From its very inception, *Hermann and Dorothea* was conceived as a work which would appeal to the large middle class whose tastes had been largely formed by the aesthetics of the late Enlightenment and the subsequent cultivation of sentiment and sensibility. This was an audience who had cried in its youth over the sad destiny of Werther and who now, middle-aged and well established, was still capable of tears when touched by a gentle, human story. In a sense, *Hermann and Dorothea* is addressed to the Alberts and Charlottes who, seeing the comfortable world they had defended against Werther's emotional turmoil once more cast into turbulence—this time the political upheaval of the Napoleonic Wars—would cling all the more resolutely to the order and values they knew were threatened. The tears shed over *Hermann and Dorothea* were shed in part because the audience to whom the work was addressed knew that the world depicted in the poem was under siege and was very fragile. Goethe himself was the first to cry over the work; Caroline von Wolzogen recounts an evening when Goethe read from his manuscript:

> I remember with emotion how Goethe read to us in deep affection of the heart and with tears bursting forth the canto which contains the conversation between Hermann and his mother beneath the pear tree shortly after it had been composed. "This is how one can melt on his own embers," he said as he dried his eyes.[7]

What are these tears and where do they come from? Why was Goethe so affected by his own work? He never failed to respond to the poem and declared to Eckermann in 1825 that his love for the little epic had never diminished: "*Hermann and Dorothea* is almost the only one of my longer poems that still pleases me; I can never read it without heartfelt sympathy."[8] But as genuine as Goethe's love for the work was, the continuation of this famous conversation with Eckermann brings that love into a strange light: "It is especially dear to me in the Latin translation; it seems to me more elegant there, as if, in its form, it had been returned to the original."[9] Can Goethe be saying this without irony? What poet would prefer to read his own work in another's translation, and in a dead language at that? The comment is even more perplexing when we recall that at the time of its composition Goethe was striving to give the poem's contents a completely contemporary character; this is why he transferred the story as he found it from the time of the expulsion of the Austrian Protestants (1731) to the poet's own time. In December of 1796, he had written of the poem to a friend: "The time of the action is roughly this past August."[10] Why should he then prefer to see the modernity of the story compromised by rendering it into a language whose major literary documents lay almost two thousand years in the past? The love the poet professes for the work begins to seem a very strange sort of affection.

Some light is thrown on this affection for the Latin by a letter Goethe wrote to Christoph L. F. Schultz in 1823 on receipt of the Latin translation:

> I was given the Latin translation of *Hermann and Dorothea* and was put into a very peculiar mood: I had not read this favorite poem of mine for many years, and now I saw it as if it were in a mirror which, as we know from experience and more recently from studies in entoptic colors, has the ability to exercise its own magic power. Here I saw my thoughts and poetry in a much more refined language, the same and yet transformed, whereby it occurred to me that, above all, the Roman strives for the concept, and what in German often remains innocently veiled becomes in the Latin a kind of maxim, which even if it is removed from the emotion, still is salutary to the intelligence. But I do not want to think more on that subject for such a comparison leads too deep into the text.[11]

I have quoted this letter at length because it reveals an important point: Goethe's fascination for the Latin translation was a fascination for the process of "wiederholte Spiegelungen" ("repeated reflections") which so preoccupied the poet as he grew older. The process is a historical one, and one by which the original aesthetic perception may become reified into a monument whose existence is as open to future interpretation and artistic transformation as any object from the "natural" world. Goethe saw this happen to his *Werther*, just as he saw himself transform the idiom of the Latin elegies into new yet kindred works of art. Goethe perceived that in the course of time, feelings and perceptions which have been caught in works of art become hardened and lose much of their original immediacy. The poetic effect which exists because something in the work has remained "innocently veiled" becomes clarified in the translation—that is, some of the ambiguity has been removed by the choice of the translator—and the original effect loses thereby much of its evocative power while it gains through the new clarity. The style of the Latin is salutary even if, or perhaps even because, it removes us from the original sentiment. The new life given to the older work through the translation is a further, if distorted reflection of the original: ". . . here there arises in this relatively desolate situation the possibility to re-establish something true, to create from the wreckage of existence and tradition a second presence."[12] In this process, the effect of the translation is similar to that of the poetic work itself in that it transforms an original impulse (in the case of the translation, this "original impulse" is itself already an older work of art) into something new and so recreates a distance between the formative, aesthetic product and what that art represents. The process of "repeated reflections" is a process of ever-further distancing. So, with a kind of perversity, but with an unflagging adherence to his conviction that art must announce its separation from life, Goethe claims to prefer the translation over the original.

But was the original text of *Hermann and Dorothea* truly an original in the first place? In fact, it was already a kind of translation. Just as *Faust* is in some sense a redaction of the older Faust texts, *Iphigenia in Tauris* a "revision" of the Euripidean drama, and the Roman Elegies a resurrection of the ancient elegiac poetry, so too does *Hermann and Dorothea* lean heavily on literary texts of the past to constitute its own existence. The historical web of text which lies just beneath the surface of Goethe's poem stretches back to Homer and the Old Testament, but the most immediate predecessor for the epic, and by far the most important, is Heinrich von Voss's *Luisa*. In the elegy which eventually came to preface the epic, Goethe pays homage to this earlier work:

I present you to Germans themselves, in the quieter home
Where man, near to nature, still learns to be human.
And may the poet's spirit guide us, who united his Luisa
Quickly to the worthy friend, all for our pleasure.

(33–36)

The ingenious juxtaposition of nature and education in the second line of the passage is a summary articulation of the process we have described: Germans may be close to nature, yet the education they strive to achieve is "human"—the gap which exists between nature and culture is reaffirmed while at the same time it "seems" to be bridged because the Germans are "near" to nature. Especially when we remember that these lines follow an assessment of the poet's relationship to Homer ("Yet to be a Homerid, even only as the last, is good"), we may safely guess that the education the poet refers to here is an artistic one. Art and nature in the poet's own day are irreparably separated, but in the world of Homer, they were united; for the Homerid of the eighteenth century (himself only a pale reflection of Homer), a union of art and nature is only possible as an artifice achieved through art and a humane education. A modern German may be *near* to nature, but a true union with nature such as Homer enjoyed, may only be approximated, self-consciously, through art and education, that is, only through the very antithesis of nature. Such an education must be humane (or humanistic); by placing himself through study and artistic endeavor in the long line of literary texts which lead from the poet's own unhappy time back to the original text where nature, the poet, and his subject were all one, the modern poet may reconstruct that original union within his own aesthetic confines, but because such a reconstruction will inevitably be a self-conscious one, the work cannot avoid an integral element of irony. Goethe's *Hermann and Dorothea* is just such an endeavor of reconstruction, and in the elegy which precedes the longer work, the poet makes clear that his attitude toward his own time is indeed far from optimistic: "But the sad images of the times I will pass by . . ." (37). In beginning the journey back to the original text, the first step is the most important; for Goethe, the journey begins with Voss's *Luisa*.

In a conversation with Böttiger in December of 1796, the period of most intense work on his own poem, Goethe spoke of his debt to Voss. Speaking of the class of people Voss was able to represent successfully in his idyll, Böttiger reports, "They are the so-called people of standing in a small town, how they are and how they live";

to this Goethe replies, "This is to the credit of Voss, without whose *Luisa* this poem could not have come into being."[13] The year before, Goethe had written to Voss, whose work had just appeared in book form:

> For what you have recently done for Luisa, I thank you, as if you had set up one of my oldest friends and were taking care of her. I have read and recited the third idyll, especially since it appeared in the *Merkur*, so many times that I have learned it quite by heart.[14]

Even if Goethe is politely exaggerating here and in fact did not quite know the poem by heart, it is still crucial to an understanding of Goethe's poem that we remember his own deep familiarity with *Luisa* was intimate and of long standing. Voss's poem is the true middle-class idyll; here the epic form serves as genuine glorification of the ordinary and everyday. This is the "credit" Goethe refers to: the transference of epic meter and dictional conventions to the sphere of the decidedly unheroic. *Luisa* launched an entire genre in German literature which extended through the nineteenth century into the twentieth and which, besides *Hermann and Dorothea*, includes such minor masterpieces as Mörike's *Idyll of the Bodensee*. Goethe recognized the powerful potential for his own art which lay in the ironic juxtaposition of classical form and nonclassical content and in *Hermann and Dorothea* he includes much that would inform the wary reader of the poet's dependence on the earlier text for the formation of his own.

To begin with, both poems open in a very similar vein: the solid, well-nourished, typically small-town *pater familias* is holding forth within his own domain. In *Luisa*, the father is a pastor and is surrounded by all the beauty which a quiet, bourgeois life can afford:

> Outside in the airy coolness of two broad-leafed lindens
> Which, adorned by yellow flowers, full of the hum of bees,
> Rustled above the mossy roof and shaded the midday room,
> The honest pastor of Grünau, patriarchically resplendent
> In housecoat, delighted his Luisa with a joyous banquet.[15]
>
> (I, 1–5)

Like the father in *Hermann and Dorothea*, the father here is "digni- fied," and like the mother in Goethe's poem, the mother here is "the good, understanding housewife." Both mothers are calm, efficient managers of household economy, but Goethe uses Voss as a point of departure, for the mother in his story has depths of intuitive empathy with her son unknown to Luisa's mother. In *Luisa*, the atmosphere is often satiric rather than ironic and the mother is often the stock character, admonishing her children for their lack of good breeding:

Dear Papa, since today is my birthday I have the right
To be downright unmannered, and yet you'll drink my health!
But Mother, wicked mother, you forgot to bring me the wine!
   Thereupon answered the good, understanding housewife,
Mischievous girl! You think that it means something to be
Born today, you eighteen-year-old chicken!

(I, 585–90)

This dependence and deviation between texts and characters is demonstrated by Goethe's use of the Vossian epithets. The first time he describes the mother, he uses the epithet just as he found it in Voss, but in the course of the poem "housewife" becomes "mother." In Goethe, the housewife proves to be a remarkably understanding mother, while in *Luisa*, the housewife remains only a housewife to the end.

If in the depiction of the mothers there is an intertextual dependence followed by independence, the character of the fathers reveals even closer affinities and greater deviation. Above all, it is the link of the housecoat which first calls our attention to the relationship between the two. In *Luisa* we see the father for the first time "patriarchically resplendent in housecoat"; it is as though all the privilege, comfort, and leisure inherent in class and familial position were embodied in that housecoat—the man is literally as resplendent in this symbol of middle class contentment as we might expect Patroclus to be in the borrowed armor of Achilles. For the pastor of Grünau, the housecoat is the most conspicuous symbol, but in *Hermann and Dorothea* this very housecoat has been thrown into the rag bag; when the mother gathers up used and unwanted articles of clothing to give to the passing refugees, the housecoat is among the first to go:

Will you forgive me? Your chest too has been plundered.
And especially the housecoat with the Indian flowers,
Of the finest cotton, with the finest lining of flannel,

Was given away. It was old and thin and out of fashion.

(I, 28–31)

Is this elimination of the symbol a comment on the parent text from which the housecoat has already once been plundered? Or a comment on the social class so well represented by the piece of clothing? This housecoat, positioned similarly at the opening of each story, is a reminder that Goethe's text is indeed built on the earlier and that Goethe's father will be in some respects the same father with which the reading public was already familiar, but something essential has been rejected from the later text, and this absence casts its shadow from the very beginning of the work. Later in the poem, we learn that Hermann took to his fists to defend the image his father cut in the old housecoat (IV, 159–72), again an indication that this garment has outlived its time. The emphasis on the old-fashionedness of the housecoat underscores the anagogical relationship of Goethe's text to that of Voss: the same symbol appears, but in Goethe's text the symbol is imbued with far greater meaning than it possesses in the parent text. We might even say that so much is revealed by the new scrutiny given to the old symbol that the symbol itself must be discarded and new symbols found; the old law of the parent text must be replaced by the new law of the younger. We find this sense of "replacement" throughout the text of *Hermann and Dorothea*, and similar comparison with *Luisa* is invited in a large number of instances. For example, while we learn very early in each work that both fathers are "comfortable" and at ease in life, we also learn very quickly that this attitude is not so appropriate to the world of *Hermann and Dorothea* as it was to the world of *Luisa*. Grünau is a small German town at peace with itself and with the world, a community well looked after by a benevolent aristocracy whose kindness is symbolized by the beautiful tea service given to the pastor and his family by the local countess. In *Hermann and Dorothea*, this idyllic middle-class life has been called into question by the streams of refugees fleeing through the countryside. In this world there is no well-intentioned nobility looking after the welfare of the middle class; there is no mention of any higher authority than the burghers themselves, and this autonomy of the characters sets Goethe's work distinctly apart from that of Voss. Perhaps this is why the old housecoat is now out of date and must go: in this world there is no place for self-satisfaction and complacency.

The change which has taken place in the world is most clearly represented in the contrast between the comfortable burghers and the hardships suffered by the refugees from the west bank of the Rhine. Nowhere is this contrast greater than in the first canto. The pharmacist has gone out to the roadside where the refugees are passing and he describes what he has just seen; in a long passage he recounts one disaster after another, each told in the most concrete terms:

> But, the creaking wheel, forced from the ruts to the edge
> Of the causeway, slipped and the wagon plunged into the ditch,
> Capsized, and in the fall people were thrown into the field
> With horrifying screams. . . .
> And so the wagon lay smashed and helpless the people,
> For the others came and passed hurriedly by,
> Each only thinking of himself and carried on by the stream.
> We hurried to the scene and found the sick and old
> Who at home and in bed could hardly bear their sufferings,
> But here on the ground, were wounded, moaning and groaning,
> Burnt by the sun and choked by the waves of dust.
>
> (I, 137–40; 144–50)

It is difficult to recall any passage in Goethe's works where human suffering is so graphically portrayed. Then, only fifteen lines later, we are given this luxurious description of the wine served by the mother to her guests:

> Carefully the mother brought the clear, excellent wine
> In its bottle of cut glass on a tray of polished pewter,
> Along with the green Römer, true vessels for the Rhine wine.
> And so sat the three around the gloriously polished,
> Brown, round table which stood on mighty legs.
> Joyfully the innkeeper and the pastor touched their glasses.
>
> (I, 166–71)

Certainly this contrast is no accident; the family drinking wine from such glorious vessels at this mighty table while the flood of refugees passes by strikes us as a very Epicurean image: safe above the turbulence, the fortunate enjoy their feast. But of course the scene is filled with the irony that comes from placing ordinary middle-class mortals into this expansive, Homeric form, and the irony brings us back to a hard reality: the world of Hermann's family is *not* the indestructible world of Epicurean divinities, but is just as fragile as that left behind by the refugees, and the contrast between the horrible experiences of the refugees and the family's easy enjoyment of a summer afternoon shows us a world where, as Goethe would describe it later in *Elective Affinities*, "indifference and antipathy are in fact right at home."[16]

Is this then why the old housecoat is entirely out of fashion? Because the world of Grünau is no longer the real world, having been replaced by a world of turmoil and revolution where complacent bourgeois life is simply no longer possible? I put this very strongly because the contrast in the opening canto is very pronounced and because I wish to show that opposed to the conventional nineteenth century reading of the work as a glorification of middle-class life there is another possible reading which sees the work as a strong criticism of that life. It would be going too far, however, to suggest that the work is nothing but such a defamation of the middle class, just as it is going too far to see the work in an entirely positive light. Both extreme readings are inadequate primarily because they fail to take into account the pervasive irony of the work. In a recent discussion of *Hermann and Dorothea*, Frank Ryder and Benjamin Bennett give a brilliant analysis of the irony of the work and show how this irony serves to hold in suspension opposing interpretations and values:

> . . . irony not as the means to a specific communicative end, but rather as a total expressive attitude, with no end that is not already embraced by its own nature . . . we shall argue . . . that Goethe's "opinion," insofar as such a thing exists, is composed of entirely unreconciled opposites.[17]

Taking their definition from Kierkegaard's *Concept of Irony*, Ryder and Bennett argue that the irony of *Hermann and Dorothea* is one which always leads back to actuality, not away from it:

> The actuality intended by irony . . . is always something like the grossly imperfect bourgeois actuality apparently affirmed in *Hermann and Dorothea*. An irony that in any way idealizes actuality thereby also makes a display of itself and so ceases to be irony.[18]

In other words, the poetic rhetoric of *Hermann and Dorothea* leads not to an idealization of middle-class life but to the reality of that life which has its positive and its negative sides. In the opening canto, for example, the striking contrast between the sufferings of the refugees and the comfortable life of the burghers is countered by the open generosity of the mother in giving to the refugees what she can spare. Because Goethe leaves such opposing actions—generosity and complacency—unresolved, the actuality of the story, and the class of people who enact it, is enhanced.

Voss, on the other hand, has created a true idealization of the world he describes. A simple comparison of the opening lines of *Luisa* and *Hermann and Dorothea* makes this difference apparent. Voss's line presents a lovely setting for the idealized types which are to appear within it. Like a camera panning a scene before focusing on details, the line presents a landscape which is commensurate with the actions about to take place within it. Goethe's opening is remarkably abrupt, beginning as no epic ever has, in the middle of a conversation: "But I've never seen the market and the streets so empty!" At once, within the space of this opening line, the classical form is announced and subverted, and the irony of poetic usage is immediately established which points to the actuality of the situation while at the same time creating a distance between the reader and the world portrayed: "the hexameter awakens, as prose would not, a complex of associations which invites the reader to adopt a critical perspective upon the limitedness of this narrated world."[19] It is this "silent irony" which separates Goethe's work from that of Voss. In *Luisa* the irony is always apparent as Voss again and again calls attention to what he is doing; in the father's admonitions to his son there is a direct reference to the act of writing dactylic hexameters:

A thousand times, son, I've warned you of these bad manners!
Don't toast with your glass as if it were a cracked pot,
Or one of the new swarm of poets' unrefined hexameters
Which thump down without rhythm or music, for heaven's sake!
(I, 636–39)

Presumably, Voss would exempt himself from those whose hexameters were awkward and ill-formed, and that is precisely the purpose of these lines, for the reminder to the son to toast elegantly is completely gratuitous; the author simply wants to let his readers know that he considers the job he is doing to be a good one. Further, Voss is at pains to let the reader know that he is among the modern liberal thinkers whose creed is tolerance and the unity of mankind:

... we rejoice with all
Who have done good according to their power and noble insight,
And who showed the way to a higher power, with Peter,
Moses, Confucius, and Homer the loving poet, with Zoroaster,

And Socrates who died for truth, and also with the noble
Mendelssohn! He would never have crucified the son of God!

(I, 411–16)

Mendelssohn, who died two years after the publication of *Luisa*,
must have been pleased to hear of his special dispensation from the
guilt of the Jews for having crucified Christ.

Voss also calls attention to the specifically Homeric models
which he is using to create his own brand of classicism:

There they now held conference, how to rebuild the gardens
At Seldorf, now desolate, to be like the fertile gardens of
     Alkinoos . . .

(III, First Idyll, 114–15)

Voss clearly wants his work to be seen as an example of the bourgeois classicism characteristic of so much of the art in his own day;
in describing Luisa's hair, he points directly to the self-conscious
classical movement of which he considers himself to be a part:

. . . and she smoothed down the locks
With a wide-toothed comb of tortoise shell, delighting in the
     curls,
And arranged the hair with braids like those of Hellenic virgins:
Thus once Praxiteles and Phidias formed the maidens
Of heaven, or Angelika, the Muse, will paint herself like this.

(III, First Idyll, 187–89)

Like Angelika Kauffmann, Voss uses the classical form to idealize
his subject matter, and as he idealizes himself as a narrator, so he
idealizes the world he is depicting. It is this that makes the occasional lapses into the satiric mode so jarring and vulgar. It is not
that, as in Goethe's poem, there are here unresolved oppositions
forming the narrative. Such lack of resolution would preclude any
unambiguous viewpoint from which an interpretation could be
drawn. On the contrary, Voss is unreflectingly smug about the class
he depicts and to which he holds membership; interpretation of
Luisa from this standpoint is all too obvious. What we have in *Luisa*
is rather a work which is simply at times satirical and at times
idealizing and sentimental. The two modes are absolutely distinct
and seem hardly to have anything to do with each other. To say that
the two modes are unresolved in the work is to imply an artistic

connection between them, but none in fact exists. Voss has simply inherited the two major trends of late eighteenth-century literature, the satirical and the sentimental, without understanding the possible connection between them. Voss was quick to see the difference between his work and Goethe's, and he was not enthusiastic about the later poem. In September of 1797 he wrote to his friend, the poet Gleim, ". . . let Dorothea please whom she will, she is not Luisa."[20] Fortunately, Voss was right, and his dislike of the poem stands alone in the general chorus of approval the poem received at the time of its publication.

Not once in the course of his story does Goethe call attention directly to his art and this sets *Hermann and Dorothea* apart not only from *Luisa*, but from his own Roman Elegies as well. In those earlier poems, the poet often links himself to the great names of the tradition in which he is working and discusses within the context of the poetry itself the kind of poetry he is creating (the reference to hexameters and pentameters, for example, in Elegies V and XX). It is an important part of the poet's strategy in the Elegies to play among the various modes of distinctions that can be drawn between experience and its aesthetic representation, and to this strategy the highly subjective narrator is essential. If Goethe's irony may generally be said to reside in the intertwining of unresolved opposites, those opposites within the context of the Elegies could be termed the poet's experience and its aesthetic representation while in *Hermann and Dorothea* the opposition could be located, as Ryder and Bennett argue, within Goethe's ambivalent attitude toward the middle class. The first type of irony is much closer to the Romantic irony defined by the Schlegels, in which the personality of the poet-creator is never allowed to disappear from view. Hence, the "subjective" narrator of the Elegies is a necessary part of the irony. The irony of *Hermann and Dorothea* returns us to the actuality of the middle-class existence, whose values and perspectives are at the heart of the idyll; thus a narrator whose personality remains obscured and whose narrative seems "objective" is crucial to the effect. The narrator of *Hermann and Dorothea* is much closer to the narrator of *Elective Affinities*, a work whose pervasive irony also depends on the fundamental ambiguity of the author's vision of society.

I believe it is possible to trace the ambivalence toward the middle class which lies behind the narrative of *Hermann and Dorothea* all the way back to the original conception of the project as Goethe described it in a letter written in December of 1796:

> I have tried to separate off the purely human in the life of a small German town from the dross in the epic crucible, and at the same time have attempted to reflect back the great movements and changes of the world-theater out of a small mirror.[21]

Is such a task really possible? How can we know what is the essence of the "human" and what is the dross? And can the great shifts of human history really be reflected in a small mirror? Would such a medium of reflection not be essentially a distortion which could only invalidate the accuracy of the depiction and compromise its historical truth? How can the "purely human" be distinguished from out of the great changes mankind undergoes? These questions are so fundamental to the undertaking Goethe proposes that it would be foolish to think he was oblivious to them, yet very little of the earlier criticism of *Hermann and Dorothea* takes these questions into account; generally, it operates as though the purely human were simply a given and as though the connection between historical movements and the individual were a simple matter of reciprocal reflection. This has led to the reading of the work as a glorification of the German middle class, where allegorical substitutions are easily made: the essentially or eternally human is equated with Dorothea and the classical, while the temporary and historical is equated with the contemporary German (Hermann). Other allegorical substitutions are of course possible, but this has been the one most frequently made.

At first glance, the allegorical interpretation is very attractive: Hermann, the contemporary German, bound by the narrow perspectives and mores of his class and historical circumstances, rises above these limitations to unite himself to a woman who embodies the classical heroic ideals. A marriage between Germany and Greece is thus prefigured in the marriage of the two young people. Yet, as satisfying as this interpretation is, and as well as it accords with the Hellenizing movement dominant in nineteenth-century Germany, it still represents the imposition of a very imprecise structure upon a very complex poem, and ultimately poses more questions than it answers, the most important of which is why the pervasive irony in the work? The irony, for example, of placing the classical heroic ideal in the figure of a woman while the male plays the role of unheroic passivity? The irony of giving the distinctly unheroic Hermann a name bound to evoke the most heroic associations in a poem of epic hexameters? The elevation of the German middle class through its amalgamation with the classical ideal is an essential component of this interpretation, yet the actual depiction of the middle class in the poem is far too realistic to admit as plausible this elevation into the ideal unless we are to believe that the coming generation who are to enjoy this elevation is to be radically different from the one just previous. But here there are difficulties as well, for Hermann is too much like his father for us to believe that any great change is to occur. After consideration of this allegorical reading and admitting its attractions and relevance to the narrative, ultimately it must be rejected. We find that the great potential offered by the poem for allegorical interpretation is only the beginning of irony, for finally the poem invites, but frustrates, all allegorical readings by subverting the easy equations. Allegory and irony are uneasy partners here; where the allegorical impulse points to a resolution of opposites in the marriage of Hermann and Dorothea, irony qualifies the nature of the resolution so drastically that in the end the opposites remain in their state of irresolution.

I have tried to show that precisely this kind of unresolved opposition is present already in the first canto of the work in the sharp and pointed contrast between the refugees and the burghers. Dorothea is fortunate enough to find her way out of the stream of refugees and into the warm circle of middle-class life, but this is in no way a resolution to the glaring contrast of wealth and hardship offered in the first canto, nor does her salvation vitiate the power of the pharmacist's description of the suffering of those fleeing the revolution. The refugees remain in their miserable condition, and it is by sheer chance that Dorothea is able to escape sharing their fate. Like Iphigenia, Dorothea very nearly misses her opportunity, and, just as in *Iphigenia*, the elaborate exposition of just how close failure comes to the heroine draws our attention to the artificial nature of the work of art. The resemblance between the two heroines of Greek name is brought out by Oskar Seidlin:

> In the time the pastor leaves free by refusing to say immediately the words which will bring a resolution, there takes place in the intimacy of a middle-class chamber in a small German town, no less than on the island of the Taurians, the apotheosis of a great heart. Dorothea's introduction into the household was to take place under false pretense, but what was even worse: Dorothea had made herself guilty of misrepresentation (to be sure, out of love, just as Iphigenia has done),

and has followed the deceptive suggestion because it seemed to bring her near to the fulfillment of her dearest dreams and hopes.[22]

Like the salvation of Iphigenia, the salvation of Dorothea is a near miss, but art celebrates the very improbability of such a rescue. "The mounted messengers of the king come very seldom," Peachum says as Mackie Messer is rescued from the gallows, and Goethe knew as well as Schiller that "life is serious while art is joyful." To make the improbable seem plausible requires considerable art, yet the very effort expended to make the flawless context falls back on itself and calls attention to the artificiality of the work. The salvation offered to either heroine against all odds would be unacceptable in an aesthetic context that was flawed; only aesthetic perfection, or near perfection, can distract a reader from the high improbability of the story. This is why Goethe could spend years polishing the metrics of *Iphigenia* and it is why he was so concerned with the metrical form of *Hermann and Dorothea*. The classical facade must be so luminous and serene that it discourages the reader from lifting the veil and looking into the seriousness of what really lies beneath.

And yet Goethe *did* want the reader to look beneath. Just like the "open secret" of the Elegies, the surface of *Hermann and Dorothea* reveals gaps that invite the reader to peer beneath. Ryder and Bennett have shown how a careful manipulation and distortion of the hexameter line "is intended to evoke a sense of pervasive and unresolved discrepancy between form and content."[23] And, just as careful analysis of the metrical form of *Hermann and Dorothea* reveals a conscious "assault on metrical orthodoxy,"[24] so too an examination of the relationship between form and content reveals a very unsettling discrepancy for critics wishing to interpret the work as a glorification of the middle class, of the "noble heart," or of the "purely human." A careful examination reveals that the form here, like the form of *Iphigenia in Tauris*, is intended to deceive and distract, but that it is also calculated to leave clues to its own deceptive nature. Goethe seldom discussed this secretive side of his art, but this is probably what the poet was referring to in a strange comment made to Heinrich Voss in 1805. At that time, Goethe had given to Heinrich Voss, the son of the author of *Luisa*, the job of correcting metrical mistakes in *Hermann and Dorothea* (a typically Goethean situation, and one that lends itself to some psychological probing). Voss declares in a letter that he found much there to correct[25] (as have Ryder and Bennett, with the exception that the later critics give Goethe more credit and find convincing reasons for the metrical liberties); later Voss reports how Goethe, when confronted with the seven-foot line, "Ungerecht bleiben die Männer, und die Zeiten der Liebe vergehen" (II, 186), decided to leave the line as it stood, declaring, "The seven-foot monster can just stay here as a sign!"[26] I suggest that Goethe here reveals his own secret—and gives to the future a clue to the ambiguity that is at the heart of the work. The line stands as a "symbol" or a sign of the poet's awareness that his own aesthetic creation is an imperfect appropriation of another's form (Homer) and content (Voss). And so we have a further irony: the poet has chosen that very form for his narrative which was most calculated to create distance between his audience and the content of the story; he has then chosen to tell in this distance-creating form a story so designed to arouse the strongest sympathies in the reader that few can resist its emotional appeal; the form itself is then polished and refined, but at the same time the poet leaves within the body of the text "mistakes" like the seven-foot line, mistakes so obvious as to invite the reader's skepticism as to the poet's metrical competence. Like the allegorical potential of the work which ultimately serves to frustrate rather than aid interpretation, the smooth epic meter turns against itself to frustrate the epic effect.

All this might seem at first designed to create the kind of irony associated with the Romantics, and with the irony found in Goethe's own Roman Elegies, that is, an irony that draws the reader's attention away from the content and from the form itself and to direct it instead to the character of the narrator or poet who is manipulating both. However, this is *not* the effect here, since the devices used by the poet to call attention to his presence within the text of *Hermann and Dorothea* are too indirect. Only when we look carefully at the metrical subtleties do we realize that there is here a self-conscious sabotage of the elected form, and only when we learn as a historical certainty that Goethe was indeed aware of the discrepancies in the form and that he actually preferred to leave them within the text (as he admits in the letter to Voss), and only when we compare the metrical problems of *Hermann and Dorothea* with the other works in epic hexameters (such as *Reineke the Fox*) where the metrics are handled with complete mastery, can we be sure that what we are confronting is a deep irony of inadequate form and not simple inaccuracy of meter.

If the pervasive irony of *Hermann and Dorothea* functions, as Ryder and Bennett (and I) believe it does, to limit the potential idealization of the world depicted and to bring the reader back to the actuality of the middle-class world with all the ambiguity present in a realistic, that is to say "real-life" situation, it also functions to create in the reader a state of mind far closer to the experience of tragedy than to the experience of idyllic pastoral we sense reading *Luisa*. This sense of the tragic is not generated from the events of the story which are so sentimental and touching that it is easy to see why more than a century of readers, including the poet himself, shed tears over them; nor is the tragic sense generated from the form of the work which, although epic in style, is nevertheless unobtrusive and at times gently humorous. The sense of the tragic is rather the result of a discrepancy between the harsh actuality of life and the idealization potential in the story; in other words, as in *Iphigenia*, the realization that such salvation as is achieved in the story is achieved precisely because the story is an artificial aesthetic construct prepares for the reader an anagnorisis akin to that prepared for the protagonist in classical tragedy. The salvations of Iphigenia and Dorothea are bright moments of aesthetic triumph set against a concept of life which is by no means so optimistic. We readers know that you cannot go home again in real life, but the characters in this body of literature manage to do it nevertheless. For the readers of these works, there is the painful realization that life is truly serious while art is cheerful and optimistic. This is why we read this work (and all the works of Weimar classicism) with a kind of nostalgia in its most original sense: with a pain of longing to go home again, a deep desire for the trip back. We see Iphigenia and Dorothea regain their past happiness and so we, like Goethe, cry tears because we are not like them. Whether this is classical or romantic matters little, but if Goethe is to be classified as a "classical" author, I would place him next to Pindar, whose vision of the small beatific moments which illuminate life was close to Goethe's own idea of art:

> Creatures of a day, what is any man?
> What is he not? Man is but the shadow of a dream;
> But when a gleam of sunshine comes as a gift of heaven,
> A radiant light rests on men, and a gentle life.
>
> (Pythia VIII)

This pessimistic kind of classicism provides a frame of mind in which the kind of irony we have been discussing is entirely at home. The irony of *Hermann and Dorothea* works simultaneously to direct the reader to the actuality of the real world with its unresolved oppositions and, at the same time, to posit a narrative sequence which hints at resolution—the marriage of Hermann and Dorothea (male and female, present and past, temporal and timeless, etc.). This discrepancy between actuality and ideal is perhaps the ultimate unresolved opposition and points to the status of the work as artifice, for only a work of art can have it both ways: to leave fundamental elements in an unresolved state of suspension while giving the impression of resolution.

One of the deepest ironies of the work results from the unresolved opposition which exists in the work between change and continuity (a theme which occupied Goethe all his life, but particularly at this time, as the poem "Permanence in Change," written in 1803, demonstrates). The most obvious symbols of these two terms within the text are the revolution taking place in France, whose violence has sent the flood of refugees into the peaceful valley across the Rhine, and the conservative small German town where Hermann and his family make their home. The two worlds are dramatically opposed, as Jane Brown has pointed out in a recent essay on *Hermann and Dorothea:* "The worlds of the poem make clear this polarity—the town walls protect the idyllic world from the epic world of war and history which rushes by on the highway. We are even told that the way from the town to the highway is in poor condition, which helps to preserve the isolation of the idyllic world."[27] The rapid change occurring in France is well documented by the long narrative given in the sixth canto by the old judge, while the stability and continuity of the middle-class life is the subject of the pastor's long encomium delivered at the opening of Canto V:

> . . . mankind should
> Always strive for improvement, and as we see, he also strives
> Always after what is higher, at least he seeks what is new.
> But don't go too far! For along with these inclinations
> Nature also gave us the desire to dwell in what is old
> And to take pleasure in what one is long accustomed to.
> . . . also dear to me is the calm and peaceful burgher
> Who treads his paternal land with quiet steps
> And who cares for the earth, each task in its appointed time.
> For him the earth does not change with every passing year.
>
> (V, 6–11; 19–22)

Hermann is the primary exemplification of the conservatism praised in this long passage. Not only is he instinctively opposed to wearing the latest fashion, he also defends his father when the other children call him old-fashioned. In his strong attachment to the land, Hermann looks very much like a peasant, so much so that his father admonishes him:

> . . . I've always told you, since you only show
> An inclination to horses and to farming the land,
> That what you are doing is the work of a hired hand, who works
> For a man of real substance. . . .
>
> (II, 246–49)

But it is as a literary character that Hermann shows his most conservative aspects: more than anyone else in the little epic, Hermann evokes Homeric memories. In his adroit handling of horses, Hermann is clearly an echo of Hector, whom Homer calls the tamer of horses:

> Hermann hurried to the stall at once where the spirited stallions
> Calmly stood and consumed with relish the clean oats
> And the dried hay, mown on the best of meadows.
> Hurriedly he laid on them the polished bridle-bit,
> Pulled at once the thongs through the lovely silvered clasps
> And fastened the long, broad reins . . .
>
> (V, 132–37)

This long description with its epic exactitude of detail and its abundance of epithets gives Hermann an aura of Homeric heroism, but just as this effect is achieved, the poet destroys the illusion by ironically concluding the passage with the object of all this Homeric activity: the comfortable middle-class coach, a vehicle which hardly needs such nobly harnessed steeds to draw it, and which, by its sheer comfort, acts as the very antithesis to the hard heroic work just expended. The contrast between what is epic and what is anti-epic is great and is left unresolved here, just as it is in another scene of Homeric resonance, the scene in which Hermann cries to his mother to intercede for him with his father (Canto IV, a scene which recalls the scene in Book I of the Iliad, where Achilles cries in the presence of his mother, Thetis). Because the contrast between the epic and idyllic aspects of Hermann's character is sustained, Hermann's essential identity remains undisclosed. Is he the true Homeric, heroic figure, and is it he, rather than Dorothea, who is the representative of the "purely human"? Or, is he the true child of the middle class whose world is anything but heroic and unaltering?

Similarly, in the character of Dorothea there are also paradoxical oppositions: is she the larger-than-life heroic figure who, like a modern Saint Ursula, defends her young virgins against the marauding invaders, or is she the typically sentimental young woman of popular eighteenth-century literature whose slipping foot always lands her in the arms of a waiting man (Canto VIII, 89–93), a young woman who is too diffident to admit her affection for the man rescuing her from life as a refugee? Artifice makes such conflicting attributes of a personality mesh and makes such an unlikely combination seem, if not probable, at least acceptable in this specific context.

Despite the complexities within each character, however, in the broad outline we may say that Hermann's situation in life does represent bourgeois stability, while Dorothea's condition as a refugee makes her a symbol of change and upheaval. But here too irony undercuts the easy dichotomy, and the irony is found on many levels. First of all, if we examine the conservative life of the middle class as it is portrayed in the work, we find that their "remaining with the old" (as the pastor euphemistically calls it) preserves precisely the kind of rigid social structure that will make change, when it comes, violent. The social organization of *Hermann and Dorothea* is given greater detail of delineation than any comparable social situation in Goethe's works; we see exactly where Hermann's family stands in the social fabric of the small community and we also see just what anxiety Hermann's father suffers when he thinks his son might be slipping back into a social level the father has risen above (II, 248–49). Hermann's father has achieved an enviable position in society, as the pastor easily acknowledges— "Hail to the citizen of the small / Town, who combines with his farming the business of a townsman" (V, 31–32)—for he stands somewhere between farmer and merchant and he hopes that his son will in fact achieve even more. For the father, the conservatism praised by the pastor as the best attribute of life in a small town seems to be accompanied by a strong element of social ambition, as well as the anxiety of retaining the status quo. In other words, there is a marked discrepancy between the society as depicted by the pastor and the actual life of the town which is supposed to typify the pastor's description. For example, the pastor praises the social position of Hermann's father and says:

He is not troubled by the cares of the avaricious city folk,
Who always are used to striving after what is richer and

What is higher, even if they have little themselves. . . .

(V, 34–36)

But what is the father doing but precisely this? He wants Hermann
to marry one of the daughters of the wealthy neighbors so that his
social position will be improved, and the father suffers all the anxieties mentioned by the pastor. The conservatism of middle-class life
in the small German town is a careful maintenance of the status
quo, yet there also seems to be room for a certain amount of social
mobility, and the father is eager to take advantage of the opportunity; he admonishes Hermann with the words every son born in an
upwardly oriented environment has heard:

If my father had cared for me, as I have cared for you,
Had sent me to school and provided me teachers,
Well, I would have been something more than an innkeeper.

(II, 256–58)

"Remaining with the old," when put to practical application, looks a
great deal like a kind of selfishness; the theoretical enlightened self-
interest, which had become a cliché of eighteenth-century social
philosophers, loses here, in actual practice, much of its idealistic
benevolence.

Second, the very reason the revolution burst forth in France was,
in the opinion of the old judge, to counter the indolence and selfishness of the old society:

. . . it seemed that the band
Which encircled so many lands would come unbound,
Which had been held in place by indolence and selfishness.

(VI, 11–13)

Here we have precisely those two attributes by which the negative
aspects of life in the small German town have been characterized.
This small town society seems, then, even more fragile than at first
glance: Threatened from without by the revolutionary wars, it is
also threatened from within by those same elements which brought
the revolution to France. But the revolution has provided no answer
to the vice of selfishness, for the very vice which it was intended to
eradicate becomes itself the bitter result of the revolution; the old
judge describes the effect of the movement on the German provinces
near France:

... the heavens soon clouded. For the place of leadership
A race of decadents began to fight, unworthy to create anything
  good.
They murdered each other and suppressed the new neighbors
And brothers; they sent out a self-seeking horde.

                                                    (VI, 40–43)

The course of the revolution in France proves to be a vicious circle;
from the selfishness of the old régime through a short period of
idealism to the selfishness of the new order.

  Revolution intensifies those social ills it was meant to correct,
while the stable society as yet untouched by revolution exhibits
the same ills that brought about the violent reaction elsewhere.
Seen in the light of this bleak depiction of human society, the
ending of the little epic takes on its full ironic import. Even critics
who have read the poem as an encomium to the small town
middle-class life have been somewhat embarrassed by Hermann's
enthusiastic defense of what is "his." Staiger, sensing the power of
the poem to lie in the tension between the idyllic life of the little
town and the threat to that life, locates the threat entirely in the
French Revolution:

  It [the small town life] is threatened by a much more dangerous enemy, the spirit of the French Revolution, which endan-
  gers all idyllic peace, threatens to destroy all worthwhile possessions, poisons spirits with deceptive hopes, and turns dear
  ones against one another.[28]

The passion of Hermann's final speech is justified for Staiger by the
enormity of the threat from without. But is the threat only from
without? After the heavy emphasis thrown on "selfishness" as cause
and result of the revolution in France, can we read Hermann's
speech without sensing in it a very pessimistic irony?

All the stronger let the bond be then, Dorothea, in the
General upheaval! We will hold close and fast, close
To one another and firmly to the possession of our goods.

                                                    (IX, 299–301)

"This is ours!" Let us say this and assert it!
For still those people are praised who were determined
And fought for God and law, for parents, wives and children,

Who stood together and laid the enemy low.
You are mine, and now what is mine seems more mine than
  ever.

(IX, 307–11)

Surely the triple repetition of "mine" in the last line above is no
accident. Above all, Hermann's emphatic pride of possession confirms our suspicion that he is not so different from his father after
all, and that the cycle rehearsed in France will be repeated on a
smaller scale by the lives of the middle-class Germans.

Throughout the work, the father has been portrayed with all the
negative aspects of middle-class life: uncurbed materialism, obses-
sive social ambition, complacency toward the suffering of those
whose lot in life is not so favorable, a narrowness of perspective on
life. The spiritual poverty of the life represented by the father has
earlier been recognized by Hermann, who is his father's most passionate critic:

But, ah! the simple act of saving, later to enjoy,
Does not make one happy, nor does piling goods on top of one
  another,
Nor one acre after the other, no matter how beautiful.

(IV, 181–83)

Such difference of opinion seems at first to place the two men in
opposing camps and to align Hermann with the humanitarian ideals represented by the initial phase of the French Revolution. In the
conflict of the son with the father, there is a pale reflection of one
of the most pervasive of Sturm und Drang themes. To a reader
familiar with the literature of that period, it would seem obvious
that the son should represent a moral ascendancy over the father.
(It is interesting that in most of Goethe's later major works, there
is this persistent carryover from the Sturm und Drang period of his
life, the conflict of generations—in *Wilhelm Meister* and *Iphigenia
in Tauris*, for example, and in *Elective Affinities*, where much of
the tragic outcome can be blamed on the fact that Eduard and
Charlotte did *not* rebel against their parents' wishes.) In establishing for Hermann a moral victory over his father, much could be
made of his attaching more importance to his heart in making his
choices; in his decision to marry Dorothea, as his mother says, "it
was his heart that made the choice" (V, 47). Where the father is
calculating and avaricious, Hermann seems innocent and generous.

Hermann is also capable of shedding tears (IV, 65–70), another characteristic of the Sturm und Drang hero which would surely be an embarrassment to his father.

Yet, despite all these differences, is Hermann in the final analysis really so unlike his father? Early on, we are given clues to their similarities. In Canto II, Hermann replies "with determination" to the pharmacist's speech in praise of bachelorhood; this is the phrase most often used to characterize the father's way of speaking. Also, the father is given to making judgments on first impressions—"One look at the house and you know what the owner is like, / Just as you know on entering a town what the council is like"(III, 12–13)—and, although we would expect the opposite from the slower, more thoughtful Hermann, in fact the son forms his judgment about Dorothea just as quickly. Fortunately, his initial judgment is confirmed by the investigations of the pastor and the pharmacist. Hermann has also inherited his father's pride; "my pride was wounded," he says in recounting his unhappy experience at the neighbor's party, and in fact Hermann was ridiculed at that party for the same reason the young folk have laughed at his father—both are stubbornly old-fashioned.

So it comes as no surprise that in the end Hermann begins to look very much like his father, but how are we to evaluate this maturation? Bennett and Ryder describe the natural cycle suggested here as a "vicious circle." Referring to the pastor's praise of the natural cycle of life in the small town—

Show the youth the value of nobly ripening years,
And show age the value of youth, so that both take delight
In the eternal cycle and so life may end in life!

(IX, 52–54)

—Bennett and Ryder say, "in reality this 'eternal circle' is a vicious circle, the eternal inescapability of bourgeois narrowmindedness repeating itself from generation to generation."[29] We have seen this very cycle complete itself within the nine cantos of the work, and it is difficult to reconcile the innocent young man who went out on an errand of mercy with the man who asserts, "You are mine, and now what is mine seems more mine than ever." Stripped of its optimistic veneer, this vision of eternal cycles endlessly repeating reminds us strongly of Werther's bleak vision of nature where successive generations end, not in life, but in death. In this endless and meaningless repetition of nature, Werther finds cause only for despair:

> It is as if a curtain had been lifted from before my soul and instead of the vision of unending life there lay before me the abyss of the eternally open grave . . . my heart is undermined by that destructive power which lies hidden in the totality of nature. Nature has not created anything which does not destroy itself and all around it. . . . I see nothing but an eternally devouring, eternally ravening monster.[29]

It is over this vision of nature, a vision which was always at the periphery of Goethe's creative consciousness, that the pastor places his euphemistic and classically optimistic facade. Yet it is curious that this man of religion does not place upon this blind movement from generation to generation any spiritual redemption nor teleological meaning; his entirely humanistic viewpoint only confirms the carceral nature of the vision. His is not a religion of sacramental salvation, but one of human understanding: ". . . Man has need of patience, also of the pure, / Even unchanging, peaceful thought and clear understanding" (V, 25–26). No matter how appealing this rationalistic religion may seem, especially in the context of a "classical" work, the severe limitation of this outlook is demonstrated in the last scene, where the pastor, instead of helping resolve a potential crisis, subjects the unhappy and embarrassed Dorothea to a cruel game of twenty questions:

Hermann was fearful and motioned to his spiritual friend
That he might put himself in the fray and clear up the
    misunderstanding.
The clever man stepped quickly up and saw the maiden's
Quiet displeasure and unexpressed pain and the tears in her eyes.
Then befell the pastor's spirit the desire not to clear the
    misunderstanding,
But rather to test the agitated spirit of the maiden.

(IX, 106–11)

But, surely Dorothea's character has long since been tested and approved. What is the point of the pastor's unfeeling sport? Perhaps Goethe is suggesting that in a world of suffering refugees, the pastor's clever rationality is as out of place as the father's comfortable complacency.

The conversion of Hermann into his father is a troubling one and renders the title of the last canto, "Outlook," ironic in the extreme. The outlook for the future seems to hold no potential for change. And no less disturbing than the revelation of the eternal natural cycle as a vicious circle is the vision of peace offered by Hermann in the last lines of the work:

> . . . And if now the enemies threaten us, or if
> In the future, I will gird myself and take up arms.
>
> (IX, 313–14)

> And if every man thought as I, so might would stand
> Against might, and we all would rejoice in peace.
>
> (IX, 317–18)

That the troubled peace that exists between two armed camps is not the brightest prospect is a truth too familiar to readers and critics of the twentieth century, but surely it was just as obvious two centuries ago. Hermann's arming himself is a reversal of the millenarian's vision of swords beaten into plowshares and as such is a perfect exemplification of what the old judge saw happening in his own home:

> Rapidly the peaceful implements of farming were transformed
> Into weapons; pitchfork and scythe now ran with blood.
>
> (VI, 72–73)

Again, the cycle proves far less benign than the pastor's gilded version of it.

Against this dark trajectory of Hermann's development is the sentimental and touching story of Dorothea who, like Ruth, finds a saviour and a home. Which of the two narratives is the more powerful? Certainly readers in Goethe's own time and for the next century and a half read the work for its most positive aspects; critics like Gundolf who found the apparent optimism uncongenial to their views of Goethe simply ignored the work. For me, the two sides of the work are almost equally weighted; each serves to undercut the other with irony. There is certainly affirmation of life here, but there is also a grim recognition of its terrible nature. Perhaps the best example of the covert and pessimistic undercurrent of the narrative, which runs the entire length of the story, lies in the descriptions given to the weather conditions as the story progresses. At the opening of the work, the weather has never seemed so beautiful; Hermann's father, like the bees in Keats's poem to autumn, thinks "warm days will never cease":

Such weather is not often to be seen with such a harvest,
And we will bring in the fruit, just as the hay has already been
   brought in,
Dry; the heavens are clear, not a cloud to be seen,
And from morn to night the wind blows with a gentle coolness.
Now that is steadfast weather for you! the corn is almost over-
   ripe.
Tomorrow we begin to cut the abundant harvest.

(I, 45–50)

But within the course of the day, the weather proves not to be con-stant at all, but has changed dramatically; the story reaches its con-clusion beneath gathering storm clouds, and by the end of the work the rain has already begun to fall. At the opening of Canto VIII, which is entitled with the name of the Muse of tragedy, Melpomene, we see Hermann and Dorothea against the background of this threat-ening sky:

And so the two walked into the setting sun, which
Hid itself deep in thick, storm-threatening clouds,
And from this veil sent here and there glowing rays
Of light, an ominous illumination, over the fields.
"May this threatening weather," said Hermann, "not bring
Us hail and violent rain."

(VIII, 1–6)

The conclusion of the story is very unsettling, not only because we have gone from clear weather to the beginning of a storm, but be-cause in the characters of both Hermann and Dorothea there is also a marked change; instead of the innocent young people they were when we first met them, we now find giants:

The door flew open and the glorious pair appeared and
The friends were astounded, the loving parents were astounded
To see the stature of the bride, like to that of the groom;
Indeed, it seemed the doors were too small to allow the large
   figures
To enter, who now together crossed the threshhold.

(IX, 55–59)

Where earlier Hermann looked like a small boy as he quietly left the room under his father's loud criticisms (II, 272–73), here the door flies open to reveal a person of mythic proportions.

What is the meaning of this change in proportion? Why do Hermann and Dorothea now threaten to burst the confines of the room by their very presence? Brown sees this change in stature as representing the intrusion of the epic world of war and history into that of the idyllic world and as marking the end of the isolation of the idyllic world from the rest of the world.[31] We may assume also that the answer lies partly in the rapid maturation of Hermann into a self-sufficient adult, and it is possible that the image presented here may be interpreted even more symbolically. Could Hermann and his bride represent, for example, a generation greater than its predecessors, a generation capable of bursting the narrow bounds of middle-class existence and values? Or, could the sudden growth of Hermann represent a surge of conservatism equal to the power of the French Revolution, so that the linear movement toward change represented by the Revolution will meet symbolically in this new German youth an equally powerful insistence on the structures and patterns of the past? And could this matching of power against power prefigure the actual historical wars which followed in the wake of the French Revolution? We cannot locate precisely the symbolic referent of the growth of Hermann into this larger-than-life image, but we sense intuitively that the "Outlook" sketched here is an ominous one, as full of ambiguous portent as the skies are full of hovering storms. Is this marriage the affirmation of a cyclical pattern in human destiny, or is this the marriage of wills, strong enough to effect a change in the course of history? The questions raised by the conclusion of the work leave unresolved all the oppositions that have been inherent in the text throughout the poem, and must remain unanswered. Like the portentous marriage at the end of the novella, "The Strange Neighbor Children" in the *Elective Affinities*, this marriage leaves the reader asking whether this is a blessing or a disaster.

Hermann and Dorothea juxtaposes two opposing perspectives on history—the linear and the cyclical. The linear is represented by the revolution in France and by Hermann's apparent growth away from his father and all that his father represents; the cyclical by the failure of the revolution through a return to age-old vices and by Hermann's appropriation, at the end, of his father's character. These two perspectives are never really brought into alignment, but remain in unresolved opposition: Revolution is shown to be a failure in changing human nature, and human nature is shown to stand in eternal need of change.

Conclusion: Anti-Pygmalion

Under sweet breezes, escaped from time, I dreamed
Of contest with the high songs of antiquity.
Let he who is pure taste here to see
If the ambrosial fruit is ripe.
— J. H. Voss, "The Vine Branch"

IN an essay which has now become famous, Paul de Man has suggested that early Romantic literature is largely a literature of allegory,[1] and this insight brings a new perspective to the long over-
debated yet crucial question of the difference between romantic and
classical art: If the romantic poet is one who strives for a work of
rich allegorical potential, a work whose surface and form are designed to invite the reader to a deeper exploration beneath, the classical artist is one who expends his talent on a surface which is itself so
polished that it demands the reader's attention through its very perfection of form and thus discourages deeper exploration or the search
for hidden meaning. So it is that Goethe, in a letter to Schiller,
deplores the modern, or romantic, mixture of genres and declares it
to be the duty of the classical artist to maintain a strict distinction
between the forms in which he works.[2] Each traditional form—
elegy, idyll, epic, drama—holds within itself certain expectations
which determine and even create meaning within the specific work,
and it becomes the function of the artist who uses those forms to
adhere closely to them so that the meaning may emerge clearly. The
romantic artist, on the other hand, will strive to blur one form into
another so that the meaning of the work will reside outside the
form. The work becomes, in other words, the object of allegorical
interpretation.

We might visualize this admittedly generalized differentiation by comparing a classical painting by Jacques-Louis David, the *Belisarius Receiving Alms*, to a painting by the very Romantic Caspar David Friedrich, *The Cross in the Mountains*. In the work of David, the spectator is held at arms' length as a scene is presented which is already interpreted by the soldier standing in the painting at the rear of the canvas, who sees the aged and blind general receiving alms from a woman while he rests upon a stone tablet which recalls his former victories. The spectator may enjoy the carefully constructed form of the work, may appreciate its structure and color, but he is essentially unnecessary to the meaning of the painting. In the Romantic painting of Friedrich, on the other hand, the spectator is positively invited into the picture by the cross which is turned away from him; the beholder is summoned to walk around the hill so that he may see the crucifix from the front. The juxtaposition of the cross and the rays of the sun (is it rising or setting?) create for the beholder a situation in which he is a necessary component, because it is he who must interpret the allegorical meaning so apparent in the picture.

A further example of this difference between artistic modes, and one taken from the closer realm of literature, is provided by a comparison between Goethe's *Wilhelm Meister's Apprenticeship* and Novalis's *Heinrich von Ofterdingen*. In Goethe's novel, events are related in a realistic manner; each person has his or her own specific contours, and poetry which appears in the course of the narrative is attached to a particular person in a particular place and at a specific time. We may view the characters as representatives of various social classes or intellectual outlooks, but we are seldom encouraged by the text to a reading which would endow the characters with any larger allegorical importance. The destiny we see unfold in the narrative is that of a particular young man, specific in his historical and geographical determination. In Novalis's novel, on the other hand, individual experiences blur into one another, the various persons in the novel tend to reflect one another, and the poetry which comes in the course of the story seems to come from nowhere and everywhere at once. Heinrich even learns, at the very center of the narrative, that he is only the latest in a long line of manifestations of a soul, and because Heinrich clearly represents something more than a solitary individual, all the events of the novel take on allegorical significance around him. It is characteristic that the first part of the novel (the only part completed) ends with a fairy tale of such condensed and intense allegorical potential that any hope for complete exegesis has proved futile.

Goethe himself often formulated the distinction between the two artistic modes. In describing the literary works of the ancient world in his essay on Winckelmann, Goethe writes:

> Why are the ancient poets the admiration of the intelligent and the despair of those who seek to rival them? Because the characters who are brought forth participate so fully in their own selves, in the narrow circle of their homeland, in the prescribed course of their own lives as well as in that of their fellow-citizens; because they function with all their intelligence, all their desires and energy entirely within the present. . . . For them, only what had actually taken place had any value, where for us only that which has been thought or felt seems to aspire to any value.[3]

For Goethe, speaking here as a critic, the classical poet does not seek to impose meaning on a sense of the present life, but to elevate it to an aesthetic permanence. It is against this intellectual background of classical expectations that Goethe's own classical works are written. But Goethe the artist was in fact no classicist.

Goethe's classical literary works are a body of poetry written in a spirit of anti-allegorism by a poet to whom the allegorical mode was most congenial. In much of his early lyricism, for example, Goethe shows a distinct preference for the allegorical; in "*Muhammad's Song*," the entire meaning of the poem rests on an allegorical interpretation of the river as the conquest of Islam. And later in his life, Goethe will discover in *Faust II* an enormous field for allegorical creation:

> Euphorion is not a human, but an *allegorical* being. In him is personified *Poetry*, which is not bound to any time or to any place or person.[4]

It is important to recognize that the works of Goethe's classical period (approximately 1785–1800) are surrounded at either end by works which embody the anticlassical spirit of allegory. *Wilhelm Meister's Apprenticeship*, the "classical" novel, is succeeded by an allegorical continuation of the essentially anti-allegorical primary text. The retreat to the classical forms was for Goethe a necessary strategy to achieve a kind of personal health; his most famous, and his shortest, formulation of the difference between classical and romantic art makes this clear: "Classical I call healthy and Romantic sick."[5] But, as we have seen, the retreat was fraught with a consciousness of its own impossibility. And throughout these classical works, there is ample evidence of the poet's own discomfort at his undertaking; as we have seen, "secrets" abound in these works, whether they are openly acknowledged or not, and these inevitably draw attention away from the classical surface of the work and subvert the classical intention of the work. Perhaps the greatest secret of all that lies hidden in these works is the poet's own recognition that the classical mask he has adopted is just that—a mask.

In "Alexis and Dora," an elegy written in the same year as *Hermann and Dorothea,* Goethe once again refers overtly to the secrets placed by the poet in his own work:

> So the poet often places a puzzle,
> Artfully interwoven with words before his audience.
> Everyone delights in the strange chain of picturesque images,
> But the very word is missing that would give it all meaning.
>   (26–29)

Schöne has shown convincingly that the specific solution to the "puzzle" referred to in this poem is the fact that Alexis has had an actual sexual experience with Dora just before embarking on his journey of trade.[6] Alexis, now headed away from home, thinks back on this experience and wishes desperately that he were still in his own city to protect Dora from the other men who may come to enjoy the fruits of her garden. But the poet's self-conscious allusion to his own technique of leaving puzzles for the reader has a greater significance than simply to alert the reader that something has discretely been left out of the narrative: In the midst of a classical poem, Goethe calls attention to the very anticlassical dimension of the work and suggests that beneath the classical facade the poem may possess an allegorical dimension. This intimation of allegory is the very opposite of the openness ("the beautiful openness" Schiller will call it in his foreword to *Die Braut von Messina*) of the classical work where "all his [the poet's] inner and outer relations to the world [are] recognized and presented with great intelligence."[7] Here the very element that would confer on the whole construct its meaning has been hidden from the reader, and so the reader is invited to interpretation.

Not only does "Alexis and Dora" share with the other poems we have discussed the poet's game of "hide-and-seek," but it also shares with them a preoccupation with the problematic role of the aesthetic in the resolution of life's problems. The poem ends:

But now, you Muses, enough! You strive in vain to show
How love and misery alternate in a heart that loves.
You cannot heal the wounds that Amor has struck,
But only from you, dear goddesses, can comfort come.

(155–58)

The passage is remarkable and may stand as a kind of motto over the whole of Goethe's classical endeavor: Art has neither a mimetic function—the Muses strive *in vain* to depict the reality they wish to represent—nor a curative power—the wounds are not to be healed—and it possesses neither because of its essential estrangement from life. It does, however, possess the power to soothe, and there is an irony in the fact that art alone possesses this power. Like the society in *Hermann and Dorothea*, the pain Alexis suffers is not redeemed or ameliorated by being elevated into art, but a kind of "comfort" arises from the aesthetic stasis which the form imposes onto the sufferings of reality. It must be admitted that there may also be an ironic dimension to this comfort, and here we are reminded of the introduction to *Werther:*

And you, good soul, who are filled with the same anguish as he, take comfort from his sufferings, and let this little book be your friend if through fate or your own fault you can find no one closer to your heart.[8]

If Werther's destiny is somehow to provide comfort for those whose sufferings resemble his, this is poor comfort indeed; the promise of comfort from this work of art can only be intended as ironic. Perhaps the comfort offered by the Muses in "Alexis and Dora" is just as ironic as that held forth by Werther's suicide.

In the ancient world, Goethe tells us again and again, nature and art were one: "As yet feeling and reflection were not divided, as yet the incurable fragmentation of healthy human powers had not taken place."[9] The myth of Pygmalion may stand as a symbol of this unity: the artist creates a work of such formal perfection and mimetic fidelity that divinity intercedes and gives life to the cold piece of marble. Life comes as the reward of art for the truly classical artist. Goethe refers to the myth when he relates his first experience of Rome:

Finally Pygmalion's Elisa, whom he had formed entirely according to his wishes and on whom he had lavished as much truth and being as an artist can, came to him and said, "It is I!"[10]

But for the modern artist, even an artist who consciously adopts a classical form and spirit, no such life after art is possible. All that is left to the modern poet of the ancient unity of art and life is "das entseelte Wort" ("the word without a soul"), as Schiller will phrase it in "The Gods of Greece" (second version). So, for the modern classical poet, the secret which lies at the heart of his work is that his art, far from aspiring to life, must be antithetical to life. The vision of Margarete as Medusa, turning life into stone as she is transformed into art, is the nightmare of Goethe's classicism. Medusa—life turned into stone—is the antipode to Pygmalion's marble which is already pregnant with life and eventually becomes that life; and it is Medusa, symbol of art's deadly relationship to life, that stands watch at the gates of Goethe's classical works.

In *Poetry and Truth*, Goethe recalls seeing Rousseau's play *Pygmalion* while a student in Strassburg, and he rejects the play because of its misguided attempt to resuscitate the ancient unity and to bring art and life together:

Much could be said about this, for this strange production vacillates between nature and art in the vain attempt to merge the one into the other.[11]

Goethe's criticism of Rousseau's play is founded on his firm conviction that for the modern artist, the myth of Pygmalion must remain an unattainable dream. This conviction never leaves him, and it is the constant companion to his creative spirit in his classical phase. In a world of fragmentation and self-reflection, an artist may embrace life with his art, but the embrace will be deadly.

Notes

INTRODUCTION

1. Heinrich Heine, *Sämtliche Schriften* (Munich, 1971), vol. III ("Die romantische Schule"), pp. 404–5. The sentiment has been repeated endlessly: "[Goethe] is . . . the last Greek among the Europeans. . . ." (E. M. Wilkinson and L. A. Willoughby, *Goethe: Poet and Thinker* [London, 1962], p. 9).
2. Heine, p. 395.
3. Heine, p. 399 (emphasis added).
4. Johann Peter Eckermann, *Gespräche mit Goethe in den letzten Jahren seines Lebens* (Wiesbaden, 1975), p. 275 (10 April 1829).
5. For a full discussion of the relatively few remaining documents and their relevance to the final version of the *Italian Journey*, see the commentary by Herbert von Einem in the Hamburg Edition (vol. XI, pp. 571–75) and Melitta Gerhard, "Die Redaktion der *Italienischen Reise*," in Gerhard, *Leben im Gesetz* (Bern, 1966), pp. 34–51.
6. Goethe, Weimar Edition (Wiemar, 1887– ; hereafter referred to as *WA*), Part I, vol. 30, pp. 181–82.
7. *WA*, I, vol. 30, p. 184.
8. *WA*, I, vol. 1, p. 68.
9. *WA*, III, vol. 1, p. 323.
10. *WA*, III, vol. 1, p. 323.
11. Ernst Beutler, "Die italienische Reise" in Beutler, *Wiederholte Spiegelungen* (Göttingen, 1957), p. 33.
12. *WA*, I, vol. 30, p. 185.
13. *WA*, I, vol. 30, p. 185.
14. *WA*, I, vol. 30, p. 187.

15. *WA*, IV, vol. 25, p. 118.

16. Eckermann, pp. 64–65 (27 January 1824).

17. Ernst Bertram, "Goethes Gehimneslehre," in Bertram, *Möglich-keiten: Ein Vermächtnis* (Pfüllingen, 1958), p. 36.

18. *WA*, I, vol. 1, p. 119.

19. Cf. Ronald D. Gray, *Goethe the Alchemist* (Cambridge, 1952).

20. *WA*, I, vol. 1, p. 119.

21. *WA*, I, vol. 1, p. 292.

22. *WA*, I, vol. 1, p. 292.

23. *Briefwechsel zwischen Schiller und Goethe* (Berlin, 1960), pp. 308–19 (letters of 22 June 1797–5 July 1797).

24. Eckermann, pp. 481–82 (6 June 1827).

25. Leo Bersani, *A Future for Astyanax: Character and Desire in Literature* (Boston, 1976), p. 214.

26. Bersani, p. 214.

27. *WA*, I, vol. 47, p. 104. For an excellent discussion of the implications this aesthetic held for contemporary art criticism, see Neil Flax, "Fiction Wars of Art," in *Representations* 7 (1984): 1–25.

28. Peter Szondi, *Poetik und Geschichtsphilosophie*, vol. I (*Antike und Moderne in der Ästhetik der Goethezeit*, Frankfurt am Main, 1974), p. 30.

29. Szondi, p. 48.

30. A brief but informative comparison of Weimar classicism with the classicism of France appears in Dieter Borchmeyer, *Die Weimarer Klassik* (Königstein/Ts., 1980), pp. 1–25.

31. Friedrich Nietzsche, *Menschliches, Allzumenschliches* (vol. II, part 2, section 125); in the Schlechta edition (Munich, 1966), vol. I, p. 927.

32. Beutler, p. 38.

33. Herbert Lindenberger, *Historical Drama: The Relationship of Literature and Reality* (Chicago, 1975), p. 114.

34. *WA*, I, vol. 29, p. 72 (*Dichtung und Wahrheit*, Book 17).

35. Szondi, p. 106.

36. This is the translation of David Luke in *Goethe's Roman Elegies, Translated with an Introduction and Notes* (London, 1977).

37. Beutler, p. 21.

38. *WA*, IV, vol. 21, p. 153 (letter to Reinhard, 31 December 1809).

39. *WA*, I, vol. 27, p. 110 (*Dichtung und Wahrheit*, Book 7); cf. Wilkinson and Willoughby, *Goethe: Poet and Thinker*, p. 212, for a healthy warning against taking this remark too seriously.

40. *WA*, I, vol. 15 (1), p. 7.

41. The term comes from Goethe's essay of the same name (*W A*, I, vol. 42 [2], p. 56).

42. Johann Joachim Winckelmann, *Kleine Schriften, Vorreden, Entwürfe*, ed. W. Rehm (Berlin, 1968), p. 38.

CHAPTER 1

1. J. W. Goethe, cited from the Weimar Edition (Weimar, 1887; hereafter referred to as *WA*), II, vol. 11, pp. 38–39.

2. Morse Peckham, *The Triumph of Romanticism* (South Carolina, 1970), p. 37.

3. *WA*, I, vol. 14 (line numbers from *Faust* refer to this edition and will be given in the body of the text). Translations are my own, although I am indebted in many places to the translation of C. F. MacIntyre (*Goethe's Faust, Part I: A New American Version* [New York, 1949]). My translations aspire only to accuracy, not to poetic distinction.

4. Hans Gerhard Gräf, ed., *Goethe über seine Dichtungen* (Frankfurt am Main, 1902), II, vol. 2, p. 167.

5. Gräf, I, vol. 2, pp. 787–88.

6. Albrecht Schöne, *Götterzeichen, Liebeszauber, Satanskult: Neue Einblicke in alte Goethetexte* (Munich, 1982).

7. Johann Elias Schlegel, *Canut, ein Trauerspiel* (Stuttgart, 1967), p. 22 (line 285).

8. *WA*, I, vol. 26, p. 249. The subject of the relationship between the two prologues and the rest of the *Faust* drama is discussed at length by Jane K. Brown in her *Faust: The German Tragedy* (Cornell University Press, 1986). Brown sees the prologues as integral to an understanding of the unity of *Faust*. Because of her attempt to read *Faust* as a more unified work of art, I am considerably at odds with many of her conclusions and interpretations. Nevertheless, I find her by far the most persuasive critic of the "unitarian" perspective, and I wish her excellent book had been in print earlier so I could have used it in writing my own.

9. *WA*, I, vol. 19, p. 76.

10. *WA*, I, vol. 2, pp. 83–85.

11. John Gearey, *Goethe's Faust: The Making of Part I* (Yale, 1981), p. 39.

12. Gearey, p. 38.

13. Eudo Mason, *Goethe's Faust: Its Genesis and Purport* (Berkeley, 1967), p. 291.

14. *WA*, I, vol. 19, p. 75.

15. *WA*, I, vol. 2, pp. 81–82.

16. For an analysis of Mephistopheles' outward appearances, see Stuart Atkins, *Goethe's Faust: A Literary Analysis* (Harvard, 1958), pp. 18, 43, and 73.

17. Gräf, II, vol. 2, pp. 45–46.

18. Mason, p. 184.

19. Atkins, p. 62.

20, Atkins, pp. 63–64.

21. Heinz Politzer, "Vom Baum der Erkenntnis und der Sünde der Wissenschaft," reprinted in *Aufsätze zu Goethes Faust I* (Wege der Forschung, vol. CXLV, Darmstadt, 1974), p. 602. Originally published in Politzer, *Das Schweigen der Sirenen: Studien zur deutschen und österreichischen Literatur* (Stuttgart, 1968).

22. Atkins, pp. 64–65.

23. See Introduction, p. 16.

24. Friedrich Gundolf, *Goethe* (Berlin, 1916), p. 781.

25. *WA*, I, vol. 37, p. 163.

26. *WA*, I, vol. 5(1), p. 135.

27. *WA*, I, vol. 41(1), pp. 130–31.

28. Reinhard Buchwald, *Führer durch Goethes Faustdichtung* (Stuttgart, 1964), p. 62.

CHAPTER 2

1. Mason, p. 207.
2. Politzer, pp. 589–93.
3. Atkins, p. 69.
4. This definition of realism is basic enough to be shared by medievalist and modernist, and can be found in interpretations of a Marxist as well as of a Thomist perspective. Speaking of the realism of Dante, Auerbach writes of the figures of Farinata and Cavelcante in the *Inferno:* "In their position as inhabitants of flaming tombs is expressed God's judgment upon the entire category of sinners to which they belong, upon heretics and infidels. But in their utterances, their individual character is manifest in all its force," (*Mimesis: the Representation of Reality in Western Literature,* trans. Willard Trask, Princeton [1953], p. 192). And Lukács, describing realistic literature of the modern period, says: "The literature of realism, aiming at a truthful reflection of reality, must demonstrate both the concrete and abstract potentialities of human beings in extreme situations. . . . For it is just the opposition between a man and his environment that determines the development of his personality. There is no great hero of fiction . . . whose personality is not the product of such an opposition" (*Realism in Our Time: Literature and the Class Struggle,* trans. John and Necke Mander, New York [1964], pp. 23 and 28).
5. Mason (pp. 211–12) points out the deficiencies of such a view as that so widely held by critics: "The many critics like Kuno Fischer, Scherer, Witkowski, Richert and Karl Wolff, who see in the relationship between Faust and Gretchen only idealized love, labour under a similar limitation to that which Faust ironically envies in Wagner: Du bist nur des einen Triebs bewusst;/ O lerne nie den andern kennen."
6. Schöne, pp. 177–79.
7. *WA,* IV, vol. 1, p. 207.
8. Mason, pp. 243–44.
9. Mason, p. 243.
10. Mason, p. 243.
11. Franz Kafka, *Gesammelte Werke,* ed. Max Brod, vol. 9 (New York, 1953), p. 86.
12. Johann Peter Eckermann, *Gespräche mit Goethe* (Wiesbaden, 1975), pp. 88–89. Conversation of 2 May 1824.
13. E. M. Wilkinson, "The Theological Basis of Faust's Credo," in *German Life and Letters,* vol. 10 (1957), pp. 229–39.
14. Goethe, Hamburg Edition (Hamburg, 1949), vol. 3, p. 522.
15. Ibid.
16. This assessment, put forward first by Scherer in *Aufsätze über Goethe* (Berlin, 1886), is rejected by Mason for other reasons, p. 223.
17. *WA,* I, vol. 39, p. 184.
18. *WA,* I, vol. 11, p. 52.
19. Heinrich Leopold Wagner, *Die Kindermörderin,* in *Sturm und Drang:*

Dramatische Schriften, ed. Erich Loewenthal (Heidelberg, n.d.), vol. 2, p. 547.

20. *Hamlet,* IV, v, 55–56.
21. Eckermann, p. 106. Conversation of 18 January 1825.
22. Eckermann, p. 107.
23. *WA,* I, vol. 8, p. 136.
24. Ibid.
25. *WA,* I, vol. 8, p. 169.
26. Ibid.
27. Schöne, pp. 122–49.
28. Goethe, Hamburg Edition, vol. 3, p. 525.
29. Walter Dietze, "Der 'Walpurgisnachtstraum' in Goethe's *Faust:* Entwurf, Gestaltung, Funktion," in *Aufsätze zu Goethes Faust I* (Darmstadt, 1974), p. 446; originally published in *PMLA* 84, no. 3 (May 1969).
30. Goethe, Hamburg Edition, vol. 3, p. 528, for Trunz's commentary on this strange story.
31. *Briefwechsel zwischen Schiller und Goethe* (Darmstadt, 1960), p. 369; letter no. 367.
32. *Briefwechsel,* p. 399; letter no. 392.
33. Schöne, p. 215; this important fragment appears in *WA,* I, vol. 19, pp. 296–311, in expurgated version and in full in the Artemis Edition of Goethe (Zurich, 1950), vol. 5.
34. Schöne, p. 215.
35. Schöne, p. 204.
36. Schöne, p. 151.
37. Schöne, pp. 217–30.
38. In a famous conversation with Eckermann (pp. 349–50; conversation of 21 February 1831), Goethe compares the structure of his two Walpurgisnight scenes: "The old Walpurgisnight is monarchical in that the devil there is respected everywhere as the unquestioned commander-in-chief. But the classical Walpurgisnight is thoroughly republican in that everything stands horizontally next to everything else. . . ." This remark has been used as evidence Goethe intended Satan to be included as center of the scene, but the remark is really concerned with the belief in, or the respect given to, Satan on the part of the celebrants in the scene, not with the ultimate question of Satan's actual existence.
39. Goethe, Hamburg Edition, vol. 3, p. 527.
40. MacIntyre, p. 166.
41. *WA,* I, vol. 10, p. 184.

CHAPTER 3

1. Hans Gerhard Gräf, ed., *Goethe über seine Dichtungen,* II, vol. 3, p. 202 (letter to Körner, 21 January 1802).
2. *Briefwechsel zwischen Schiller und Goethe* (Darmstadt, 1960), p. 743 (letter no. 835).
3. *Briefwechsel,* p. 746 (letter no. 838).
4. Oskar Seidlin, "Goethes *Iphigenie*—'verteufelt human'?" in Seidlin, *Von Goethe zu Thomas Mann* (Göttingen, 1963), p. 9.

5. Gräf, II, vol. 3, pp. 159–60.
6. Gräf, II, vol. 3, p. 168.
7. Gräf, II, vol. 3, p. 186.
8. Gräf, II, vol. 3, p. 184.
9. Gräf, II, vol. 3, p. 239.
10. Goethe, *Iphigenie auf Tauris*, in the Weimar Edition (*WA*), I, vol. 10. Line numbers in the text refer to this edition. The English translation is that of Charles Passage (New York, 1963), a translation which is both accurate and poetically very fine.
11. It was this very point of "yearning" which caused Goethe to wonder himself just how classical his play was: "[Schiller] proved to me that I myself, against my own will, was romantic, and that my *Iphigenie* was, because of the dominance of emotion, not at all as classical and in the ancient frame of mind as one might believe" (Eckermann, *Gespräche mit Goethe*, p. 309 [conversation of 21 March 1830]).
12. *WA*, I, vol. 28, p. 314.
13. Seidlin, p. 21.
14. Oskar Seidlin, "Goethe's *Iphigenia* and the Humane Ideal," in *Modern Language Quarterly* 10, no. 3 (1949): 311.
15. The secularization of human dependence on a transcendental realm is a recurrent theme in recent interpretations of Goethe's *Iphigenia*. Among the most important of these are Wolfdietrich Rasch, *Goethes 'Iphigenie auf Tauris' als Drama der Autonomie* (Munich, 1979); Hans Robert Jauss, "Racines und Goethes *Iphigenie*," in R. Warning, ed., *Rezeptionsästhetik: Theorie und Praxis* (Munich, 1975), pp. 353–400; Rolf Rohmer, "Classizität und Realität in Goethes Frühweimarer Dramen," in *Goethe-Jahrbuch* 93 (1976): 38–50; and Theodor Adorno, "Zum Klassizismus von Goethes *Iphigenie*," in Adorno, *Noten zur Literatur* (*Gesammelte Schriften*, vol. 11; Frankfurt am Main, 1974), pp. 495–514.
16. Cited (without reference) in Ronald Hayman, *Nietzsche: A Critical Life* (New York, 1980), p. 1.
17. Hans Wolff, *Goethes Weg zur Humanität* (Bern and Salzburg, 1951), p. 219.
18. Wolff, p. 220.
19. Gräf, II, vol. 3, p. 257.
20. Seidlin, *Von Goethe zu Thomas Mann*, pp. 12–13.
21. Daniel Wilson, *Humanität und Kreuzzugsideologie um 1780: "Türkenoper" im 18. Jahrhundert und das Rettungsmotiv in Wielands "Oberon," Lessings "Nathan" und Goethes "Iphigenie"* (New York, 1984), p. 111.
22. Wilson, p. 107.
23. Robert R. Heitner, "The Iphigenia in Tauris Theme in Drama of the Eighteenth Century," in *Comparative Literature* 16 (1964): 289–309.
24. *WA*, I, vol. 16, p. 332 ("Epimenides' Awakening").

CHAPTER 4

1. *Jahrbuch für Philologie und Paedagogik* (Leipzig, 1863), pp. 300–312; 351–71; 401–26; 451–71; 493–519.
2. *Jahrbuch für Philologie und Paedagogik* (Leipzig, 1864), pp. 180–201.
3. H. Düntzer, *Erläuterungen zu den deutschen Klassikern*, Erste

Abteilung, *Erläuterungen zu Goethes Werken: Lyrische Gedichte* (Leipzig, 1876), vol. II, p. 43.

4. *Jahrbuch für Philologie und Paedagogik* (1864), p. 185, for example.

5. *Jahrbuch für Philologie und Paedagogik* (1865), p. 401.

6. Cf. Harry G. Haile, "Prudery in the Publication History of Goethe's *Roman Elegies*," in *German Quarterly* 49 (1976): 287–94.

7. Elisabeth Eggerking, "Goethes Römische Elegien" (diss., Bonn, 1913).

8. *Jahrbuch für Philologie und Paedagogik* (1865), p. 401.

9. Cited by Heller in *Jahrbuch* (1863), p. 452.

10. *WA*, I, vol. 1, p. 253. Line numbers in the text refer to this edition.

11. *Jahrbuch für Philologie und Paedagogik* (1864), p. 453.

12. Goethe, *Zur Farbenlehre. Didaktischer Teil*, "Schlussbetrachtung über Sprache und Terminologie," section 754, *WA*, II, vol. 1, p. 304.

13. Georg Luck, "Goethes *Römische Elegien* und die augusteische Liebeselegie," in *Arcadia: Zeitschrift für vergleichende Literaturwissenschaft*, vol. II (1967), pp. 173–95.

14. Luck, p. 192.

15. Luck, p. 182.

16. *WA*, I, vol. 47, p. 81.

17. Luck, p. 194.

18. *WA*, I, vol. 47, p. 81.

19. *Jahrbuch für Philologie und Paedagogik* (1864), p. 408.

20. Cf. Haile, as note 6 above.

21. Passages from Roman Elegies X, XIV, XV, XIX, and XX are quoted from the bilingual edition by David Luke (London, 1977). At the request of the translator, these quotations incorporate a few more recent emendations which will appear in a forthcoming new edition (Goethe, *Roman Elegies* and *The Diary*, translated by David Luke with an introduction by Hans Rudolf Vaget, London: Libris, publication expected March 1988). Acknowledgment is hereby made to both publishers of this material. Other translations are my own.

22. *Jahrbuch für Philologie und Paedagogik* (1864), p. 414.

23. Düntzer, *Erläuterungen*, p. 78.

24. *Oxford Classical Dictionary* (Oxford, 1949), p. 729.

25. *Jarhbuch für Philologie und Paedagogik* (Leipzig, 1893), p. 527.

26. Meredith Lee (*Goethe's Lyrical Cycles*, Chapel Hill, 1978, p. 31) suggests that Elegy XI is intended as an introduction to Elegy XII: "The implication is clear. The space between Elegies XI and XII will not go unused. Once our attention has been diverted and we are occupied by the returning harvesters of Elegy XII, Priapus can take his place in this Pantheon. This creative potential is the essence of Rome. It is realized in the imagination of the reader."

27. Düntzer, *Erläuterungen*, p. 76.

28. Goethe, Hamburg Edition, vol. I (Hamburg 1949), p. 560.

29. See note 12 above.

30. *WA*, I, vol. 6, p. 28.

31. *WA*, I, vol. 37, p. 213.

32. *WA*, I, vol. 37, p. 210.

33. Cf. Friedrich Beissner's authoritative *Geschichte der deutschen Elegie* (Berlin, 1961), especially pp. 130–90 ("Die klassischen Elegie").

34. *WA*, I, vol 5 (1), p. 35ff.
35. Dominik Jost, *Deutsche Klassik: Goethes "Römische Elegien"* (Pullach bei München, 1974), pp. 38–39.
36. *WA*, I, vol. 53, pp. 3–7. Line numbers for these poems refer to this edition.
37. Jost, p. 184: "Philainis: Greek poetess from the island of Leukas (Homeric Ithaka?) or Samos, to whom a work on the *Figurae Veneris* is attributed."
38. Schiller, National Edition (Weimar, 1943, vol. 20, p. 465).
39. Jost, p. 55.
40. *Metamorphoses*, XI, 85–193.
41. See, chapter 1, note 4.

CHAPTER 5

1. Oskar Seidlin, "Über *Hermann und Dorothea*," in *Lebendige Form: Festschrift für Heinrich E. K. Henel* (Munich, 1970), p. 101.
2. Richard Samuel, "Goethe's *Hermann und Dorothea*," in *Selected Writings* (Assen, 1965), p. 24.
3. The full advertisement read: "Taschenbuch für 1798. Hermann und Dorothea von J. W. Göthe. Berlin bey Friedrich Vieweg dem älteren. 12°. Mit einem Calender für 1798, einem Titelkupfer von Chodowiecki, die preussische Königsfamilie darstellend, einem farbigen Modekupfer und sechs landschaftlichen Kupfer von Darmstadt nach Schubert."
4. Hans Gerhard Gräf, ed., *Goethe über seine Dichtung*, Part One, Volume One (Frankfurt am Main, 1901), p. 98.
5. Heinz Helmerking, *Hermann und Dorothea: Entstehung, Ruhm und Wesen* (Zurich, 1948), p. 15.
6. Gräf, pp. 139–40. The rest of the passage gives a good idea of the high esteem Schiller had for the poem: "Although this was only the idea of a book seller, it has created for me a particularly charming situation: it has momentarily raised the illusion that in fact our marketplaces could indeed offer us such wares, when in truth I can say without exaggeration that many a century has passed and may pass again in which such an article could not even be contemplated."
7. Gräf, p. 84.
8. Johann Peter Eckermann, *Gespräche mit Goethe* (Wiesbaden, 1975), p. 108 (18 January 1825).
9. Ibid.
10. Gräf, p. 91.
11. Gräf, pp. 188–89.
12. *WA*, vol. 42(2), p. 57 ("Wiederholte Spigelungen").
13. Gräf, p. 96.
14. Gräf, pp. 151–52.
15. Johann Heinrich Voss, *Luise: Ein ländliches Gedicht in drei Idyllen* (Tübingen, 1807).
16. *WA*, vol. 20, p. 40 (*Wahlverwandtschaften*, Part One, Chapter 3).
17. Frank G. Ryder and Benjamin Bennett, "The Irony of Goethe's *Hermann und Dorothea:* Its Form and Function," *PMLA* 90, no. 3 (May 1975):

433. This essay is to my mind a landmark of Goethe criticism; it goes further than any other critical work in casting off the worn clichés that have clung to Goethe's classical works and has begun to make these works readable in our age. I am very indebted to these two scholars for helping me to my own understanding of the work.

18. Ryder and Bennett, p. 434.
19. Ryder and Bennett, p. 436.
20. Helmerking, p. 57.
21. Gräf, pp. 90–91.
22. Seidlin, p. 115.
23. Ryder and Bennett, p. 438.
34. Ryder and Bennett, p.440.
25. Gräf, p. 175.
26. Gräf, p. 176.
27. Jane K. Brown, "Schiller und die Ironie von *Hermann und Dorothea*," in *Goethezeit: Studien zur Erkenntnis und Rezeption Goethes und seiner Zeitgenossen—Festschrift für Stuart Atkins* (Bern, 1981), p. 205.
28. Emil Staiger, *Goethe*, vol. II (Zurich, 1956), p. 252.
29. Ryder and Bennett, p. 443.
30. *WA*, vol. 19, pp. 75–76 (*Werther*, Book One, letter of 18 August).
31. Brown, p. 205.

CONCLUSION

1. Paul de Man, "The Rhetoric of Temporality," in *Blindness and Insight* (Minneapolis, 1983), pp. 187–228.
2. *Briefwechsel*, pp. 401–3 (Letter of 23 December 1797).
3. *WA*, I, vol 46, pp. 22–23.
4. Eckermann, p. 289 (20 December 1829)—the italics are Goethe's.
5. Eckermann, p. 253 (2 April 1829).
6. Schöne, pp. 55–106.
7. *WA*, I, vol. 46, p.23.
8. *WA*, I, vol. 19, p. 3.
9. *WA*, I, vol. 46, p. 23.
10. *WA*, I, vol. 30, p. 199.
11. *WA*, I, vol. 28, p. 67.

Index